THE
CRUCIAL
CENTURIES

THE CRUCIAL CENTURIES

The Mediaeval Experience

FRANCIS OAKLEY

LONDON
TERRA NOVA EDITIONS
1979

Terra Nova Editions Ltd
25, Upper Montagu St
London W1H 1RQ

PRINTED IN GREAT BRITAIN BY W & J MACKAY LIMITED, CHATHAM
ISBN 0-906490-05-7 (Cased)
ISBN 0-906490-06-5 (Limp)

To

Siobeán NíĊureán Oakley

BOOKS BY *Francis Oakley*

The Political Thought of Pierre d'Ailly
Council over Pope
The Western Church in the Later Middle Ages

WITH DANIEL O'CONNOR
Creation: The Impact of an Idea

CONTENTS

iv

SUBJECT AND CITIZEN
The Import of Medieval Politics / 103

v

REASON AND FAITH
The Direction of Medieval Intellectual Life / 137

vi

PASSION AND SOCIETY
The Texture of Medieval Sentiment / 171

EPILOGUE / 207

PREFACE TO
THE REVISED EDITION

This book is an essay in interpretation. As such it is both less and more than a textbook—less, because it lacks the austerity of generalization and fullness of coverage appropriate to that genre; more, because it seeks to pursue more publicly those fundamental issues of historical perspective that historians, by drawing unwittingly upon the common stock of assumptions belonging to their era, sometimes contrive to ignore. If I can believe my reviewers, it is a book capable of speaking to the layman no less than to the student or the professional medievalist. Certainly, in writing it, while keeping in mind the needs of students, I tried also not to lose sight of the general reader with an appetite for things historical but understandably for much else besides. While attempting, then, to convey a good deal of the requisite standard information about the medieval period, I have sought also to whet that historical appetite with less traditional fare, to stimulate, perhaps even to provoke.

I wish to record my indebtedness to the president and trustees of Williams College for a grant from the Class of 1900 Fund toward the cost of preparing the manuscript for the press. I would also like to thank my wife, Claire-Ann, and my colleagues at Williams, Dudley Bahlman, Peter Berek, and Gordon Winston, who were all kind enough to read some of the following pages and to give me the benefit of their criticism and advice. The book is dedicated to my mother, first of my teachers and best.

F. O.

Williamstown, Massachusetts
March 1979

INTRODUCTION

Of the Middle Ages medieval men and women knew nothing. When they thought at all of their own as an intermediate age, it was usually as one coterminous with the whole of human history, an age strung out between the Creation and the Last Judgment, between that first moment of inexplicable divine generosity with which it had all begun and that other dread moment of divine intrusion with which, they were told, it was all destined to end. Of the notion, so familiar to us, however, that of a middle age stretching from the decline of Rome to the rise of the movements known as Renaissance and Reformation, their minds were understandably innocent; for they failed to apprehend either their own discontinuity with the classical past or the discontinuities impending in the future. Instead, it was the humanists of the Italian Renaissance who were both the first to characterize their own age as one of glorious revival or rebirth in the arts and in letters and the first to insert a clear distinction between the era of classical Roman antiquity and those later "medieval" centuries Edward Gibbon subsequently characterized as having witnessed the triumph of "barbarism and religion."

The very idea, then, of a middle age interposed between the world of classical antiquity and the dawn of the modern world was ultimately of humanist vintage. What it lost in simplicity it gained in firmness during the Reformation era, drawing added strength from the Protestant depiction of the thousand years preceding the advent of Martin Luther as an age of moral turpitude, religious superstition, and untrammeled credulity. Even more clearly than their humanist predecessors, the reformers saw their own era as one of revival and restoration, though restoration this time not simply of the arts, of learning, and of "good letters," but also of the Christian faith to its original purity. To this profile of the course of European history the

I

seventeenth century added its own touches; in 1701 Cotton Mather, the American Puritan divine, commented that

incredible darkness was upon the Western parts of Europe two hundred years ago: learning was wholly swallowed up in barbarity. But when the Turks made their descent so far upon the Greek churches as to drive all before them, very many learned Greeks, with their manuscripts and monuments, fled into Italy and other parts of Europe. This occasioned the revival of letters there, which prepared the world for the Reformation of Religion too, and for the advances of the sciences ever since.[1]

His words deserve emphasis. If the notion of a middle age was present already in humanist and Protestant historical thinking, it was well into the seventeenth century before historians began, like Mather, to look back upon the beginning of the modern era as having occurred already in the past. It was only in the latter part of the seventeenth century, then, that the formal division or periodization of European history into ancient, medieval, and modern became current. When historians framed that division, moreover, although the cultural Renaissance and religious Reformation remained uppermost in their minds, they also took into account the political reorganization of Europe, the growth of commerce, and the geographical, technological, and scientific discoveries. Like Mather they began to assume, in fact, that in every area of human endeavor a great gulf separated them from that intermediate age, which they felt had come to an end by the beginning of the sixteenth century. In 1675, therefore, when the German pedagogue Christoph Keller began to publish a series of highly successful textbooks in general history, he organized them on the basis of a division of European history into ancient and modern periods, the two separated by a middle age. With the wide dissemination of these textbooks the new periodization may be said to have come of age.

Of the Middle Ages, then, medieval men and women did indeed know nothing. When they thought about the matter at all, they preferred to divide their histories in accordance with motifs of biblical provenance: into six ages modeled upon the six days of Creation, or, inspired by the Book of Daniel, into four world-monarchies (Dan. 2:36–40). The last of those monarchies they identified with the Roman

2

Empire, control over which they regarded as having been transferred from the Romans to the Franks, with which, therefore, they regarded themselves as being in direct continuity, and which, they believed, was destined to endure, in however attenuated a form, until the day of wrath, that awful day when the inauguration of the reign of Antichrist would signal the impending dissolution of the universe.

This last is a bizarre notion, at least to us in the twentieth century, accustomed as we are to dividing our histories in less cosmic a fashion and to dating the termination of the Roman Empire, with confident precision, to the year A.D. 476. In that year Odoacer, leader of an invading barbarian confederacy, deposed the youth who has gone down in history as the last of the Roman emperors, and who, by a sort of providential symmetry at once both improbable and ironic, bore the name Romulus Augustulus. But it was by no means so bizarre a notion to a man like the poet Dante, who as late as the fourteenth century, could make it the very foundation for his treatise on monarchy;[2] nor, one may predict, will it be so bizarre to our successors, the historians of the distant future, who from their own more ample perspective may well be better equipped than we to appreciate the length and significance of the shadow that Imperial Rome cast forward across those later centuries that we have become accustomed to calling medieval. It was only in 1453, after all, with the Turkish capture of Byzantium (Constantinople), that the Byzantine Empire—the Roman Empire of the East—came to an end. As late as the twelfth century—with a social one-upmanship worthy of memorialization by the Daughters of the American Revolution—Byzantine aristocrats had been accustomed to boasting that their ancestors had come over with Constantine and the original Roman settlers; to the very end, the citizens of Constantinople had been at pains to call themselves "Romans" (*Romaîoi*). Even in the West, where the discontinuities with the classical past were a good deal more insistent, only in 1806 was the office of Holy Roman Emperor abolished—and then by that other emperor, Napoleon Bonaparte, himself a more credible aspirant to the grandeurs of universal authority. Nor should we forget that the bishop of Rome continues to this day to call himself "supreme pontiff" (*pontifex maximus*), to claim, that is, in his capacity as pope or head of

3

the Roman Catholic church the title of one of the ancient republican offices upon which Caesar Augustus, two thousand years ago, erected his imperial position. Nor, again, should we underestimate the degree to which, in the centuries preceding the Reformation at least, the papacy could make a credible claim to have reconstituted and prolonged, in its own attenuated, religiopolitical version, the universal empire that it was the glory of Rome to have created. In a famous and much quoted passage, the seventeenth-century philosopher Thomas Hobbes described the papacy as "no other than the *ghost* of the deceased *Roman empire,* sitting crowned upon the grave thereof";[3] an observation, it must now be insisted, that was no less accurate in its fundamental perception for being derisive in its conscious intent.

All of this might well suggest that the claims medievals made for the essential continuity of their own era with that of Roman antiquity were neither as ridiculous as the Renaissance humanists once supposed nor as fanciful as we ourselves have normally taken them to be. If the same cannot be said of the whole medieval process of periodizing history into six ages or four monarchies, such theologically inspired schemata have at least one positive feature that should do much to redeem them in twentieth-century eyes, namely, their universality; for they purported to be divisions valid not just for the history of a single country or civilization, but for the history of mankind as a whole. This certainly cannot be said of the familiar periodization that has come down to us from the humanists and reformers. It is true, of course, that historians are still capable of imposing that specifically Western periodization upon the histories of other civilizations, speaking, for example, of "ancient" India or "medieval" China; but as long ago as 1869 the Russian writer Nikolai Danilevsky had attacked that practice as intellectually indefensible, and in 1917 Oswald Spengler derided it as "the *Ptolemaic system* of history," because in it "the great Cultures are made to follow orbits around *us* as the presumed centre of all world happenings," just as the old Ptolemaic astronomy had made the sun, planets, and stars revolve around the earth as the presumed still point of the turning world.[4] Spengler was expressing sentiments that were by no means foreign to other historians of his day, men who were less speculative in temperament than he, but who, in a world rapidly

4

becoming one, no longer felt comfortable with an approach to world history that instinctively molded the histories of other and vastly different civilizations to make them conform to the contours of a Western history whose reassuring familiarity in no way negated its essential provinciality.

If, then, we are to retain the conventional periodization and to speak, as in this book, of "the Middle Ages," the foregoing remarks suggest that we should do so rather self-consciously, with many a backward glance, keeping several important qualifications firmly in mind. In the first place, the periods into which the course of history is divided are not rooted immovably in the very nature of things; they are instead the creations of historians and, as such, are themselves subject to change. In the second place, the traditional division into ancient, medieval, and modern reflects the preoccupations and prejudices of Renaissance humanists and Protestant reformers. Were not the weight of academic tradition so heavy and so very hard to move, modern historians might well have chosen already to periodize their histories in a very different fashion. Even as it is, while retaining the conventional divisions, their appraisal of the medieval period is much more positive than that of its inventors, and it is now rare to see the word "medieval" used as a term of derogation. In the third place, the traditional division, unlike the theologically inspired schemata it replaced, was conceived with a view to European and not to world history. As a result, "the Middle Ages," an expression used to denote a period in history conventionally defined as stretching from about the fourth century to the end of the fifteenth, is properly used to denote a period confined to European history alone. Moreover, the very factors in the modern world that have conspired to underline that limitation also suggest the desirability of judging the significance of the medieval experience from a vantage point differing not only from that once occupied by humanists and reformers alike, but from that used by their more sympathetic nineteenth- and twentieth-century successors, too. And that observation may serve to introduce the perspective from which this book has been written, the conviction that has determined its focus, the belief that has suggested its unifying theme.

5

Not so long ago historians were prone to speak about the history of "civilization" when what they really meant was the history of "*Western* civilization." They did so without self-consciousness, secure in the belief that in the arena of world history the West possessed a manifest destiny, that the whole tide of history was sweeping irreversibly in a Western direction, that the vanished civilizations of antiquity and the seemingly moribund cultures of the non-Western world represented at best noble failures, uncompleted projects, inadequate attempts that had somehow fallen short of the goal to which all had aspired but which it had been the fate of the West alone to attain. The events of the recent past no longer permit the luxury of so distorted a perspective. While the years since the Second World War have witnessed a steady acceleration, worldwide, in the process of technological Westernization, they have also witnessed some other changes, seemingly antithetical, but no less striking for that. Though the roots of change reach back much further, these years alone have seen the demise of the great European colonial empires, the emergence of the "third world" countries, and the reawakening and reinvigorating of non-Western cultures and cultural forms that many Western observers, abysmally lacking in a sense of historical imagination, were once wont to dismiss as doomed to extinction. While at one level, then, we live in an age of increasing cultural homogenization, we live also in one of mounting cultural pluralism, an unprecedented age in which for the first time in history the world has become one and in which Western and non-Western cultures are therefore in daily and increasingly intimate contact. This being so, it becomes progressively more difficult for us as Westerners to escape the fact that many of our most cherished assumptions, beliefs, customs, attitudes, and institutions are not simply *natural* and universal, as in the past they may well have seemed to be, but are instead the product of our own peculiar history here in the West. At the same time, as the momentum of Westernization quickens, it becomes equally difficult to avoid the recognition that our history has indeed been a peculiar one, that at some point in the past our civilization took a path that led it into territory unknown to other civilizations, that it is, in effect, unique—and unique, moreover, in

6

precisely those characteristics that have enabled it to dominate and shape so much of modern world history.

On this matter, Max Weber, the great pioneer of historical sociology, was notably clear. Our characteristically Western modes of life and thought, he insisted, do not represent any natural or inevitable culmination toward which all civilizations strive or have striven. They represent instead only one very particular line of development, one possibility out of several radically different ones. "A product of modern European civilization, studying any problem of universal history, is bound to ask himself to what combination of circumstances the fact should be attributed that in Western civilization, and in Western civilization alone, cultural phenomena have appeared which (as we like to think) lie in a line of development having universal significance." [5] No question of this scope is ever easy to answer, but it is, I believe, the type of question that will confront us with increasing urgency as we move into the last quarter of the twentieth century. I believe, too, that in any attempt to answer it, an acquaintance with the history of the medieval centuries must necessarily bulk large; for those, after all, were the crucial centuries that witnessed the slow formation of a new and specifically *European* civilization in the wake of the great disaster that had overtaken the classical civilization of the Mediterranean world.

Hence the approach adopted in this book. The perspective from which it has been written is that of world history; the conviction determining its focus, that of Western cultural peculiarity or singularity; the belief suggesting its unifying theme, that it was during the medieval period—in particular, during the centuries from the eleventh onward—that the foundations were laid on which the edifice of Western cultural peculiarity was subsequently erected. This, too, is the belief that has determined the book's line of march, suggesting the propriety of pursuing a topical rather than a narrative or chronological approach and, where so many things clamor for inclusion, serving as a criterion for selection and emphasis. After an opening chapter, then, delineating the broad movement of political and ecclesiastical history and attempting to set up the necessary geographical and chronological framework, my approach is indeed topical and selective rather than

7

chronological and inclusive. Successive chapters focus on fundamental developments in religious, economic, political, intellectual, and emotional life. In the epilogue I return, briefly and by way of conclusion, to the central question concerning the roots of Western cultural singularity, which it was the distinction of Weber not only to have raised but to have done so with such insight and force.

1

SPACE AND TIME

The Shape of
Mediaeval history

The period known as the Middle Ages was shaped by many factors complex alike in their origins and interrelationships. Among those factors, however, a certain priority attaches to the influence exerted by two great institutions: the Roman Empire and the Christian church. Both aspired to universality; both, moreover, underwent dramatic changes during the course of the fourth century. With those institutions, then, and with that point in time, we shall begin.

During the first two centuries of the Christian Era, the Roman world had achieved a remarkable degree of stability and serenity. Embracing as it did the whole of the Mediterranean world and more, including within its borders not only the heartland of the Hellenic world but also the more ancient centers of civilization in the Middle East, it provided an ordered political structure within which at least the rudiments of Greco-Roman civilization could be transmitted far and wide, even as far as the centers of urban life in what we now call England, northern France, and the Rhineland, but which were then merely the outlying territories of an empire that was essentially Mediterranean. Stimulated but little by long-distance trading contacts with China and India, along the whole of its borders the empire encountered in Persia alone a rival power and mode of life that it could recognize as civilized. It was understandably easy for its inhabitants, then, to regard the empire as universal, to equate their own Greco-Roman civilization with civilization itself, and to regard its destiny as in some sense eternal. Even the dramatic breakdown of the third century, while it succeeded in shaking that belief, was not enough to destroy it. During that century, the empire, already ravaged by the onset of periodic visitations of plague, was imperiled from within by the chaos of civil war, endangered from without by barbarians attacking across the northern frontiers, and challenged by a reinvigorated Persian Empire exerting pressure in the southeast. Inviolate since 330 B.C., the city of Rome itself was now momentarily threatened by invaders, and, for the first time since 67 B.C. when Pompey had swept the eastern Mediterranean clear of pirates, the safety of shipping in those waters came into question. No less than twenty-six emperors came and went in the half-century from A.D. 235 to 284, and only one of them escaped violent death.

If the empire survived at all it did so only by undergoing a radical transformation. Survival and transformation alike were primarily the outcome of the drive, energy, and organizing skill of two great emperors, Diocletian (284–305) and Constantine (306–37). They took as precedents the emergency measures adopted during the years of chaos and confusion, systematized them, and erected them into a permanent structure of imperial government. The peculiar compromise between monarchy and oligarchy whereby Caesar Augustus three centuries earlier had succeeded in preserving many of the forms and some of the substance of ancient Roman republicanism was now abrogated. In its place was erected an absolute monarchy modeled on the forms of despotism familiar to the ancient Middle East, a centralized and burdensome bureaucratic state seeking in the name of survival itself to regiment the social and economic lives of all citizens throughout its provinces. In the interests of imperial unity, the aura of divinity that had long since gathered around the office and person of the emperor was now more consciously cultivated. From the Persian Empire Diocletian borrowed the diadem, the luxurious costume, and the elaborate court ceremonial of the Oriental god-king, and his imperial successors, though they abandoned his policy of persecuting Christians, were in no way disposed—even after they themselves embraced Christianity—to disperse the mysteries of the imperial cult or to dismantle its apparatus.

That they were able to refrain from so doing indicates something, of course, about the changes undergone by Christianity itself in the years after 313 when it was finally accorded toleration. Diocletian had seen the characteristic Christian refusal to participate in the public worship of "Rome and Augustus" not as the necessary concomitant of a

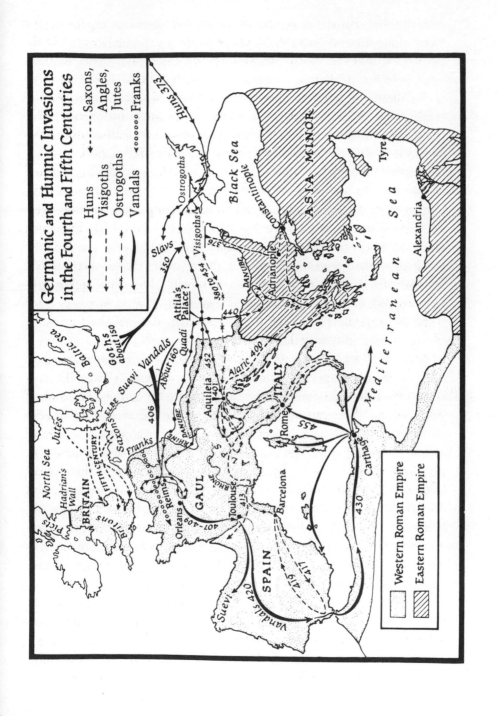

Germanic and Hunnic Invasions in the Fourth and Fifth Centuries

Huns ·——·
Visigoths –––
Ostrogoths –·–·–
Vandals ——

Saxons, ----
Angles,
Jutes
Franks ooooooo

Huns 373

Black Sea

ASIA MINOR

Constantinople

Adrianople

Ostrogoths

Visigoths 376

Mediterranean Sea

Tyre

Alexandria

DANUBE

446

Slavs

350

380 to 454

440

Attila's Palace?

Goths about 150

Vandals

Suevi

Elbe

Saxons

Quadi

452

Alaric 400

About 160

406

ITALY

Rome

455

Aquileia 401

RHINE

DANUBE

Franks

Baltic Sea

North Sea

Hadrian's Wall

BRITAIN

Jutes

FIFTH CENTURY

Britons

Picts

Scots

Reims

Orleans

407–409

GAUL

Toulouse 413

Barcelona

417

419

SPAIN

Suevi 420

Vandals 420

Carthage

430

Western Roman Empire

Eastern Roman Empire

radically monotheistic faith, but as an intolerable threat to the fragile unity of empire. He had sought, accordingly, to eliminate the danger, but without success. Where persecution had failed, however, Constantine's policy of toleration and favor succeeded all too well. By the time of his death in 337 Christianity was well on its way to being transformed from a private sect into a civic religion, one that recognized in the person of the emperor its supreme head on earth, one, indeed, that was increasingly willing to place itself at the service of the imperial ideology. To the disappointment no doubt of Constantine, whose concern for imperial unity was no less urgent than that of Diocletian, the new cult turned out to be afflicted by its own obscure internal divisions. Subsequent history showed that those doctrinal divisions were themselves intractable enough to raise formidable obstacles to the preservation or reestablishment of the imperial unity; but that fact itself signals the degree to which the destinies of church and empire had become intertwined, especially in the years after 392 when the emperor Theodosius the Great finally proscribed every form of pagan worship throughout the empire.

Theodosius was the last emperor, however, to be in any position to make quite so ecumenical a gesture; that is to say, he was the last emperor whose rule extended to every province of the old empire. After his death the practice, instituted by Diocletian, of dividing up the onerous responsibilities of government between two or more imperial colleagues ceased to be an intermittent one. His two sons divided the Roman Empire into two parts, Eastern and Western, which were largely independent of each other and whose histories increasingly diverged. If imperial unity long survived, it did so only as a beckoning fiction. By the end of the fifth century, then, though its legacy was everywhere apparent, the political structure which we know as the Roman Empire of the West had ceased to exist, and its provinces had passed under the control of the several groups of Germanic invaders—Ostrogoths, Visigoths, Vandals, Burgundians, Suevi, Anglo-Saxons, Franks—who had succeeded in breaching its frontiers. In the East, however, the empire centering on Constantinople—the "New Rome" that Constantine had built on the site of the old Greek settlement of Byzantium—survived and continued to flourish. The old Rome, then, had more than one heir, and we must hold that fact clearly before our eyes if we are to speak of the legacy of Rome.

The Heirs of Rome: Byzantium, Islam, Western Europe

IN 476, when Odoacer, the German general commanding the barbarian troops in Italy, deposed the last of the Roman emperors of the West, he preserved the proprieties by having a moribund Roman Senate inform the emperor Zeno at Constantinople that a single emperor would henceforth suffice and that a second emperor for the West was no longer necessary. Endowed in return with the imperial title of "patrician," it was in some sense as representative of the Eastern emperor that Odoacer ruled the Roman inhabitants of Italy. The same is true of his successor, Theodoric the Ostrogoth (493–526), who recognized at least in theory the ultimate sovereignty of that emperor, when he placed his image on the coins and set out to maintain the Roman system of administration in Italy and to preserve the fabric of Roman civilization.

A change in imperial policy in Constantinople, however, led to a more direct assertion of imperial authority in the West. Declaring himself to have "good hopes" that God would permit him to reconquer the lands that had once belonged to the Romans but had since been lost through "carelessness," and mustering all the resources of the provinces still subject to him, the Eastern emperor Justinian I (527–65) set out in 533 to establish direct Roman rule over the Germanic peoples settled in North Africa, Spain, France, and Italy. Over twenty years of fighting ensued. Its immediate outcome was the reestablishment of Roman rule over North Africa, the islands of the western Mediterranean, some territory in southeast Spain, and, for a short time, the whole of the Italian peninsula itself.

Its long-term results, however, were of a very different kind. Devastated by the long war of reconquest and groaning anew under a heightened burden of imperial taxation, Italy easily fell prey shortly

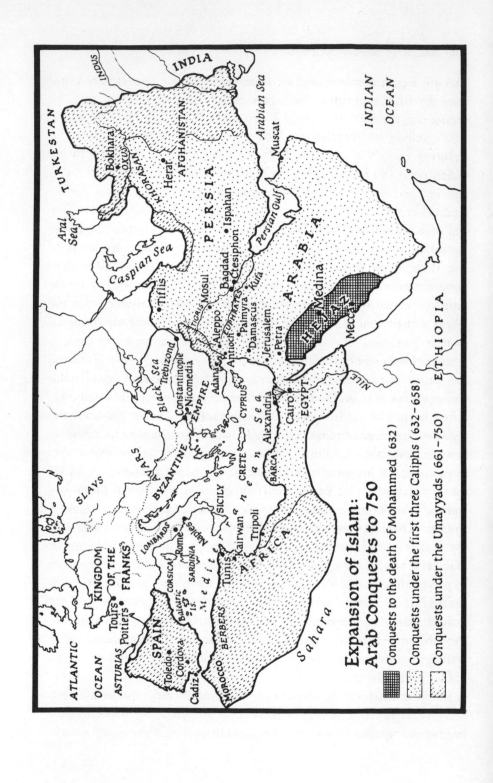

Expansion of Islam:
Arab Conquests to 750

▨ Conquests to the death of Mohammed (632)

▨ Conquests under the first three Caliphs (632–658)

▨ Conquests under the Umayyads (661–750)

after Justinian's death to another barbarian onslaught, one launched this time by the Lombards, a Germanic people who succeeded in conquering the north of Italy and a good deal of territory farther south. The resulting fragmentation of political authority turned out to be an enduring one. Not until the late nineteenth century was the entire Italian peninsula again united under a single government. Despite the ferocity and persistence of the Lombard attack, Byzantine forces retained control, it is true, of the southernmost part of the peninsula and of a few scattered holdings farther to the north, notably Naples, Genoa, Ravenna, Rome, and a strip of land connecting the two last. But despite the presence of the imperial exarch at Ravenna and persistent hopes for reconquest, Byzantine rule tended in the course of time to become a reality in the south alone, and Rome, exposed though it was to the threat of Lombard attack, had to be left increasingly to its own devices.

That this should have been the case is explicable largely in terms of the price Justinian paid in the East for his preoccupation with reconquering the West. His unrestrained commitment of men and resources to the pursuit of his Western policy meant that despite repeated campaigns and incessant diplomacy he was unable to do much more than sustain a holding action in the danger spots elsewhere in the empire. He left his successors to cope both with the Persian menace to the east and with a persistent barbarian threat to the Balkan provinces and to Constantinople itself. The latter threat was posed by the Slavs and the Avars (a people of Turkish origin), both of whom infiltrated the Balkan provinces in such numbers that not even Heraclius (610–41), one of the greatest Byzantine emperors, was able to exert anything more than intermittent control over that region. After a devastating Persian invasion, however, Heraclius did succeed in making a dramatic comeback in the southeast, defeating and killing the Persian king and destroying, once and for all, Persian imperialist ambitions.

Heraclius's great victory may not have escaped the attention of the charismatic religious leader who at that same time was uniting the fiercely independent tribes of the Arabian peninsula around his person and behind his creed of *Islam*, that is, submission to the will of God. It was the belief of his immediate followers, and of the untold millions who have since embraced Islam, that there was but one God, Allah, and that Mohammed (c. 570–632) was his prophet. The Koran, the sacred book in which the revelations of Muhammad are collected, states that "the Romans have been victorious in the nearer part of the land, but after their victory will be defeated in a few years." [1] Ironically enough, it was only to be a few years more before Byzantine and Persian alike were overcome by the followers of Muhammad, victorious Arab armies that struck out from the desert and seized rich territories in Iraq, Syria, and Palestine. These provinces fell the more easily because of widespread disaffection over the religious policies of their Persian and Byzantine rulers. The same was true of Egypt, which soon went the way of the other Byzantine possessions in the Middle East. Within a century, Arab armies—or armies under Arab leadership—had spread from Egypt across North Africa and into the Hispanic peninsula, destroying Byzantine control of the former and eliminating Visigothic power in the latter. At the same time the Arabs conquered the old heartland of the Persian Empire and were beginning to push on farther into Asia.

By the second decade of the eighth century, then, Muslim armies in the West were beginning to exert pressure in the southern region of what we now call France, in the East were moving into the Indian subcontinent, and in Asia Minor were mounting a great assault on the city of Constantinople itself. This last endeavor failed, and by the tenth century the East Roman Empire was to reach new heights of strength. Nonetheless, a new great power had clearly emerged, an Arab empire, which in the territories it had absorbed had entered into an inheritance at once both Greco-Roman and Persian and which, in the following centuries, was to give birth to the civilization known as Islamic. During the greater part of the Middle Ages, then, there were no less than three claimants to the Roman inheritance. During that time, though they were spared in part the repeated barbarian attacks that ravaged western Europe, the East Roman and Islamic empires did suffer their own vicissitudes. Having made a magnificent recovery, Byzantium slipped into the doldrums once more in the late eleventh and twelfth centuries, fell under the control of Frankish Crusaders for a time in the

Justinian's Empire, 565 A.D.

Empire in 527   Added, 527–565

thirteenth, and, having regained a harried independence, finally succumbed to the Ottoman Turks in 1453. The Islamic Empire, for its part, having lapsed first into political and religious disunity, later fell prey on its periphery to the attacks of the Western Crusaders and in its heartland, to successive waves of Turkish and Mongol invaders—people who, while they readily embraced Islam and made its militancy their own, showed much less affinity for the sophisticated and cosmopolitan civilization that had flourished in the Arabic-speaking world and had preserved so much of the Persian and Greco-Roman cultural achievement.

These vicissitudes notwithstanding, the Byzantine and Islamic empires did succeed for many centuries in preserving and developing the type of higher civilization that had flourished in the ancient Mediterranean world and had spread to its peripheries. In the early Middle Ages, at least, Byzantium and Islam rather than western Europe deserve, then, to be regarded as the true heirs of Rome. Because of this, historians have sometimes deplored the sort of western European chauvinism that induced whole generations of scholars to

19

devote their attention so exclusively to the darkling plains of France, Germany, and England, where the ignorant armies of semibarbarian noblemen and kings clashed by what was in antique, Byzantine, or Islamic terms the darkest of cultural nights. But without approving the instinct that betrayed these scholars into adopting so provincial an approach to the early medieval centuries, it is possible in retrospect to render the verdict that those who adopted it were doing the right thing, if not necessarily for the right reasons.

Without denying the classical inheritance of Byzantium or Islam, without questioning the importance of their cultural achievement, without minimizing their legacy to the modern world—the former to Russia, especially, the latter to a vast area of the globe stretching from Nigeria to Indonesia and Yugoslavia to Chad—it is still necessary to insist that neither came near to playing the extraordinary role in the arena of world history that it was to be the fate of the West alone to grasp. Unlike the West, neither came near to reshaping the course of world history to the degree that has led historians, even now when events have become global in their impact and histories universal in their aspirations, to focus their attention once more upon that most traditional of academic subjects, the history of western Europe. Whatever else the histories of Byzantium and Islam might have to tell us, they certainly suggest that we must seek the roots of the West's cultural singularity not in its classical inheritance alone, or in the Renaissance revival of that inheritance, but in what actually happened in Europe itself during the Middle Ages and even during the confusion of that early phase to which in the fourteenth century Petrarch helped attach the negative connotations summed up in the derisive title "the Dark Ages." It is to Europe itself, then, and largely to western Europe, that the rest of this chapter is devoted, the course of medieval history being divided for purposes of convenience into three subperiods.

The First Europe and Its Confines:
The Fifth to Tenth Centuries

THE immediate problem confronting the would-be historian of fifth-century Europe is that Europe did not as yet exist; that is to say, it did not exist as anything more than a geographical expression denoting the northwest prolongation of the Eurasian continent. The Roman Empire, it should not be forgotten, was a Mediterranean rather than a European power. England, the Rhineland, and even much of France were peripheral appendages of the Romanized Mediterranean world. Ireland, Scotland, Scandinavia, the Low Countries, much of what is now Germany, and the greater part of eastern Europe all lay outside its boundaries. As a result, the emergence of Europe presupposed the failure of attempts to preserve or to reconstitute the unity either of the empire as a whole or of the Roman Empire of the West; and that failure was determined during this early period by three successive waves of barbarian invasions.

The first of these was triggered in Outer Mongolia during the course of the fourth century by a confederation of warlike nomads, who, by sponsoring the displacement of neighboring peoples, generated in turn the westward movement of other nomadic tribes. Among the latter were the people who came to be known in Europe as the Huns and who succeeded either in subjugating or in terrorizing the Germanic peoples occupying the territory stretching from the Rhine and Danube frontiers of the empire eastward as far as southern Russia. The Hunnic confederacy broke up in the mid-fifth century, but not before it had generated the movement into the empire, from 375 onward, of a whole series of Germanic peoples. Though their initial objective was to seek safety from the dreaded Huns behind the imperial borders, they eventually obliterated those very borders and destroyed the unity of the Mediterranean world.

In so doing, however, they cannot be said to have substituted any unity that was specifically "European." Slavic peoples gradually moved into the regions of eastern Europe vacated by the Germans, the Scandinavian lands to the north and the Celtic lands of the far west continued to go their own ways, and a veritable mosaic of Germanic successor states replaced the several dioceses into which the Roman Empire of the West had been divided. Principal among those successor states were the Ostrogothic kingdom comprised of Italy and parts of what are now Switzerland and Austria, the Visigothic kingdom in Spain and Portugal, and the Frankish kingdom which included much of France, the Rhineland, and part of the Netherlands. No common culture as yet united these disparate kingdoms and peoples. Though Ireland was evangelized as early as the fifth century, only during the four centuries from the sixth onward did the Anglo-Saxons, continental Saxons, Franks, Frisians, Thuringians, Scandinavians, and Slavs come to embrace Christianity. The conversion early in the sixth century of Clovis, the Frankish king, meant, it is true, that all at least of the *great* Germanic successor states of Rome had become formally Christian; but even this did not necessarily serve to unite them or to win for them the loyalty of their Roman subjects. Only the Franks had accepted the Catholic form of Christianity espoused by those subjects; the others had been evangelized by missionaries adhering to Arianism, a heresy concerning the Trinitarian doctrine, and the heterodoxy of their beliefs in fact widened the gulf that divided them from their orthodox Roman subjects.

Moreover, religion aside, not even their common Germanic stock served fully to unite the invaders. Whatever their shared inheritance, they differed not least in the degree to which on entering the empire they had already embraced the rudiments of Roman culture or were already motivated by admiration for the splendors of the Roman achievement. It is understandable, then, that they should not have been moved by any sort of ambition that can properly be entitled "European," that the more Romanized among them should be concerned with the preservation of Roman civilization, and that a man like Theodoric the Ostrogoth, bearer of the imperial titles of consul, senator, and patrician, should even have toyed with the idea of reestablishing the empire of the West, though this time under the rule of a Germanic king.

Any hope that he or his successors might have succeeded in so doing was shattered, of course, by Justinian's own attempt to restore the unity of the empire as a whole, an attempt that fell short of its goals. England, France, and most of Visigothic Spain still lay beyond the confines of the reconstituted empire, and the second of the three waves of barbarian invasions did much to render abortive even the limited degree of success that his prolonged campaigns in the West did achieve. That second wave occurred shortly after Justinian's death, bringing the Avars into the Balkan provinces, turning the attention of his successors from the tribulations of the Western reconquest to the heartland of the Eastern empire and to the safety of Constantinople itself. At the same time, it brought the Lombards into Italy, shattering the political unity of the peninsula and transforming the ancient capital of Rome into a frontier town—leaving it at the very end of the long and tenuous Byzantine lines of communication, difficult to reinforce but very much open to the danger of renewed Lombard attack.

Whatever else it did, this second wave of barbarian invasions certainly ensured that any future reconstitution of the Roman Empire in the West would necessarily have to take a very different form than it had in the days of Justinian. The Arianism of the Visigoths alienated from them the loyalties of their Romanized subject population and may have played a role in their loss to the Franks of control over Aquitaine during the sixth century; but the gains involved during the next century in their conversion to the orthodox form of Catholicism and their recovery of the territory previously lost to Justinian's army of reconquest proved to be temporary. In the early eighth century, Muslim armies swept across Spain, defeated the Visigothic king, pushed the surviving Christian princes into the foothills of the Pyrenees, and conducted raids deep into France. The Visigothic kingdom ceased to exist, Spain passed into the orbit of the Islamic world, and it was left to the Franks to grasp the future leadership of the West.

That leadership they did eventually grasp, constructing a universal empire that not only embraced the greater part of Christian Europe but also expanded the boundaries of Christendom eastward into central Europe and into territory that had never been subject to Rome. Indeed, under the great king Charlemagne, Frankish rule extended over the whole of Germanic Europe, except for Scandinavia and England, as well as over the greater part of what had been Roman Europe, with the exception again of England, the southern half of the Italian peninsula, and about two-thirds of Spain; it also included some sort of suzerainty over the western reaches of the Slavic world in central Europe. Though some confusion surrounds both the event itself and the precise intentions of the participants, there was a certain appropriateness, therefore, in the decision of the pope to crown Charlemagne emperor of the Romans in 800, and in the subsequent reluctant decision of the Byzantine emperor to concede that title to him, thus admitting the reconstitution at least in legal terms of a Roman Empire of the West.

Charlemagne himself, unlike his Carolingian successors, appears to have disliked the full title, preferring to call himself simply "emperor" or "king of the Franks and Lombards." His dislike underlines the fact that whatever degree of *Romanitas* his empire did possess derived less from the Franks themselves than from their alliance with the popes or bishops of Rome and from the molding influence of the church. When they invaded the Roman Empire the Franks had been among the least Romanized of the Germanic peoples and among those most hostile to Roman power. Though, unlike others, they had embraced the Catholic form of Christianity, the alliance with the papacy that lay behind the later revival of the empire was only cemented in the eighth century. Indeed, that alliance can be said to have come into being only in the years after 751 when the pope acceded to the request of Pepin III, head of the Carolingian family and *de facto* ruler of the Franks, that Childeric III, the Merovingian who, though powerless, retained the title of king, be deposed and that he himself be given the Frankish crown. That alliance, therefore, postdated the evangelization of Germany and the reorganization and reform of the Frankish church. The Carolingian family had supported these tasks, but they owed their successful completion to the energy and leadership of the English monk Boniface, who had gone to Rome to seek authority to pursue his missionary work.

Boniface had been both aided and preceded by other devoted monks from his native land, and it is no accident that the English monks should be so active in the work of evangelization and reform on the Continent or that they should enjoy the close collaboration of the papal

24

authority. During the worst period of confusion after the fall of the Roman Empire, Christianity had taken firm root in Ireland, with church organization centered on the monasteries and church leadership in monastic hands. From Ireland monastic missionaries had made their way to England and had labored to bring Christianity to the pagan Anglo-Saxons. In that work, however, they had later been joined by additional Christian missionaries of very different provenance—monks dispatched from Italy in 596 by Pope Gregory the Great (590–604). By the early eighth century, moreover, the Roman mission had been able to impose its own mores and form of church organization on the whole Christian community in England; the Irish had withdrawn, but not before the confluence of traditions—Irish, Anglo-Saxon, and Latin—had sponsored the precocious flowering of a vigorous culture that centered on northeastern England and overflowed into continental Europe in a dramatic surge of educational and religious proselytization.

Worthy of note in all this is not only the vital surge of Anglo-Irish educational, cultural, and religious life, making its appearance on the very frontiers of the old Roman world and beyond, but also the encouragement extended by the papacy and the continuing close relationship between papal authority and the Anglo-Irish missionary endeavor on the Continent. As bishops of the city that had been not only the old imperial capital but also, it was firmly believed, the episcopal see of St. Peter and the site of the martyrdom of both Peter and Paul, the popes had long since laid claim, as successors of Peter, to a primacy of authority in the universal church. During the course of the fourth and fifth centuries, a series of forceful popes, most notably Leo I (440–61), had done their best to transform that claim from one pertaining solely to doctrinal matters into a more sweeping claim to a primacy of jurisdictional authority; but the gap between theory and practice remained immense. Those same centuries, after all, also saw the transformation of Christianity into an imperial civic religion, and, despite periodic papal challenges, the Roman emperors, summoning general councils as they had done since the time of Constantine, could make the stronger claim to be the functioning supreme leaders of the Christian world, even in spiritual matters.

This remained true even during the pontificate of so active and

25

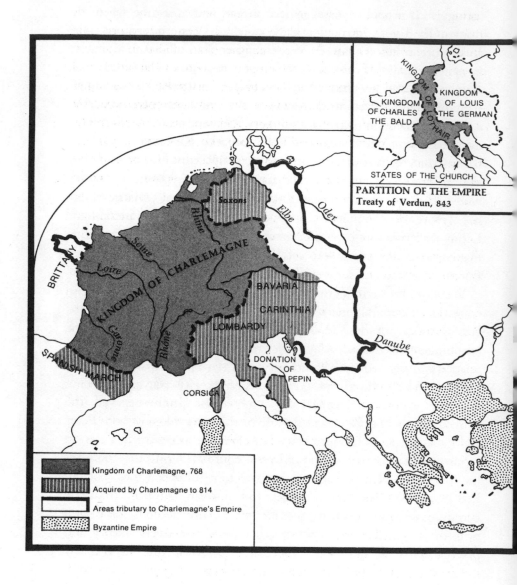

KINGDOM OF LOTHAIR

KINGDOM OF CHARLES THE BALD

KINGDOM OF LOUIS THE GERMAN

STATES OF THE CHURCH

PARTITION OF THE EMPIRE
Treaty of Verdun, 843

BRITTANY

Saxons

Rhine

Seine

Loire

Elbe

Oder

KINGDOM OF CHARLEMAGNE

BAVARIA

CARINTHIA

Garonne

Rhône

LOMBARDY

SPANISH MARCH

Danube

DONATION OF PEPIN

CORSICA

Kingdom of Charlemagne, 768

Acquired by Charlemagne to 814

Areas tributary to Charlemagne's Empire

Byzantine Empire

distinguished a pope as Gregory the Great, and at a time when the frailty of the Byzantine hold on the conquered Western territories was already becoming evident. As the leading civilian official surviving at Rome, Gregory had had to take it upon himself in the absence of effective imperial government to negotiate with the Lombards and to supervise the civil administration of the city, marshaling the resources of the Roman church by reorganizing its landholdings throughout Italy and Sicily in a desperate attempt to feed the Romans, to pay the soldiers, and to buy off the invaders; but imperial influence at Rome survived even the Lombard invasions and the actual demise of imperial protection. As befitted a former civil servant, Gregory's loyalty to the empire was almost instinctive. His pontificate marks no definite break in the pattern of subservience that had usually characterized the relationship of the popes with the Byzantine emperors, and, as late as 663, the emperor could visit Rome and be accorded all the honors pertaining to its lawful ruler.

To the inhabitants of the provinces still subject to Byzantine rule, then, Gregory and his papal successors for a century and more remained leading dignitaries in what was still an imperial church. To the barbarians of the West, however, they represented something different and more grandiose. They enjoyed a prestige that, while undoubtedly enhanced by the association of their authority with the work of evangelization and church reform in England, Germany, the Low Countries, and France, was grounded in something more powerful—the fact that to the new peoples of the West the bishops of Rome represented in unique combination both the lost glamour of imperial Rome and the mysteries of Petrine apostolicity. In the mid-eighth century, then, when the rise of Islam had dealt shattering blows to the empire of the East, when the Byzantine emperors themselves had fomented a schismatic quarrel in the church by prohibiting as idolatrous the devotional use of icons and pictures, and when the Lombards had renewed their drive against the surviving Byzantine territories in Italy, the popes finally turned their backs on the East and sought the protection of the Carolingian rulers of the Franks. In so doing they may have hoped to crown the existing moral leadership of the church in the Western countries with the papal headship of a new and universal Christian society. Just as papal authority guaranteed in 751 the legitimacy of the Carolingian title to the Frankish throne and conferred the title of *patricius Romanorum* on the Frankish king, so, too, papal authority revived the empire of the West in 800 and conferred the office of emperor upon the greatest of the Carolingian kings. By taking those steps the popes revealed their willingness to embark upon the exercise of some sort of supreme political authority, which, if it belonged to anybody, belonged rightfully to their erstwhile masters, the emperors of Byzantium.

Nonetheless, the outcome of the papal alliance with the Frankish monarchy was perhaps not quite what the popes had hoped for. In the first place, by undercutting even the fiction of a universal political unity, it promoted the growing division between the Eastern and Western churches, to which diverging customs were already contributing and which the schism that began in 1054 was destined to make permanent. In the second place, though the so-called Donation of Constantine[2] furnished the popes with a persuasive if spurious title to the central Italian territory known in later centuries as the Papal States (and to a great deal more), it was in fact Frankish armies that in this same period forced the transfer of those nominally Byzantine territories from Lombard into papal hands. With the advent of Charlemagne (771–814), who in 774 seized the Lombard crown for himself and who exercised authority in matters ecclesiastical and civil with a truly Byzantine impartiality, it soon became clear that the papacy, by linking its fortunes with the Carolingians and committing itself to the exercise of temporal power in Italy, had not necessarily won the freedom of action its position within the Eastern Roman Empire had previously denied it. True, the period of Carolingian dominance was short and for a few brief years in the latter half of the ninth century dynamic popes like Nicholas I (858–67) and John VIII (872–82) were able not only to affirm the primacy of honor due to the papacy but also to reassert with considerable force, in the teeth of Byzantine opposition, its claim to a primacy of jurisdiction. They were able to do so, however, only because the revived universal empire of the Carolingians was already on the way to total disintegration. With the cessation in the 870s of real imperial government in Italy, the bishopric of Rome, like lesser

28

bishoprics elsewhere in Europe, far from attaining liberty of action, was delivered into the rapacious hands of the local nobility.

Dynastic dissension within accounts in part for the precipitate decline in Carolingian fortunes. The major cause, however, was the arrival of the third and last great wave of barbarian invasions. Viking sea raiders streamed out of Scandinavia from the early ninth century on into the tenth, attacking every European country from Spain in the southwest to what is now Russia in the northeast but concentrating their most devastating attacks on the British Isles and France. At the end of the ninth century and for sixty years more, a nomadic people called the Magyars came out of Asia and raided southern Germany, northern Italy, and as far afield as eastern France. At the same time, though they can hardly be called barbarians, Muslim sea raiders from Africa, having won the upper hand over Byzantine sea power in the Mediterranean, conducted piratical raids along most of the northern coastline and caused great turmoil in Italy and southern France.

The outcome of all this was the collapse of the reconstituted empire of the West and of all large-scale political structures, the concomitant fragmentation of political authority and allegiances, and a marked retraction in the borders of Latin Christendom. By the early tenth century, Sardinia, Corsica, Sicily, and even parts of the Italian mainland had shared the fate of Spain and had been annexed to the Islamic world. By about the same date, Normandy, a large part of the British Isles, and the heartland of old Russia had been conquered and drawn into the orbit of a Scandinavian world that was eventually to stretch westward as far as Greenland and the North American coast and that became in time the focus of a brilliant and independent Nordic culture. In the territories that remained, however, ravaged and divided though they were, the years of Carolingian hegemony and partnership with church and papacy had not been entirely in vain. Already in Charlemagne's day ecclesiastical writers had begun to equate the term *Europe* with the territories over which he ruled or exercised suzerainty and to regard both as coterminous with the world of Latin Christianity. Latin, Christian, and Germanic elements had merged to create a new cultural unity that may without qualification be called "European." The bonds that held it together were admittedly fragile ones. By the late ninth century all hope of realizing its political unity was lost. Its boundaries were contracting and its fate hung in the balance; but it survived. By the late tenth century it had ceased to be on the defensive. By the end of the Middle Ages it had expanded to include practically all the countries—Russia excepted—that today we call "European."

Medieval Europe at Its Height: The Eleventh to Thirteenth Centuries

IN Germany the Carolingian dynasty came to an end in 911; in France, it lasted until 987. Even before the first of those two dates the Carolingian kings had been reduced to a condition bordering on political impotence, their powers usurped by quasi-tribal leaders in the east and by counts and dukes in the west. Also before 911, however, two forces were already working to restore public order in Europe, to revive prosperity and political strength, and to make European expansionism possible. The first of these was the continuing process of evangelization, which by the early eleventh century had brought Norway, Sweden, Denmark, and Hungary into the orbit of Latin Christendom and had helped curb the unruliness of Viking and Magyar alike. The second was the emergence of that more effective mode of military, social, and political organization known as feudalism.

Because it involved the parceling out of public authority into private hands and the fragmentation of royal central government into a host of localized units, the emergence of feudalism can easily be regarded as a retrograde step. It also involved, however, the passing of political authority into the hands of those local magnates best able to support the skilled, heavily armored cavalrymen who had proved to be the most effective soldiers of the day and to marshal sufficient numbers of them in the localities that were most directly endangered but that the distant royal armies had proved powerless to defend. Moreover, in the right hands and under the right circumstances, the new institutions of feudalism could be manipulated and developed to promote the

30

emergence even of strong centralized governments. This became evident already in the eleventh and twelfth centuries with the appearance of the powerful states that the Norman dukes were able to create first in Normandy and then, after the conquest of 1066, in England and that Norman noblemen, having wrested southern Italy and Sicily from Muslim and Byzantine rule, went on to create in those lands.

Nonetheless, as it spread, the initial impact of feudalism everywhere was to fragment political authority and to undermine the possibility of maintaining strong central monarchies. This process was first and most notably evident in the Rhineland and northern France, the very heartland of the Carolingian Empire. It is understandable, then, that the most powerful of the regional monarchies that replaced that empire should have emerged farther to the east in Germany, the least civilized part of the old Frankish realm, where feudal institutions developed more slowly and where both kings and subjects proved to be more robust in defending themselves and their territories. By 1056, German kings first of the Saxon and then of the Salian dynasties had imposed crushing defeats on Viking and Magyar alike, had begun at the expense of the Slavs the long process of extending Germany's frontiers eastward into the lands beyond the Elbe, had acquired Burgundy, had established a degree of intermittent political control over northern Italy, and had assumed the title of emperor of the Romans.

The revived empire was the most powerful state in Europe; but it could make a less credible claim to universality than the empire of Charlemagne, and there were marked fluctuations in the ways in which successive German emperors conceived of their imperial title, as well as in the degree to which they regarded themselves as successors to the ancient Roman emperors. At the same time, however, there was a great deal at once both Roman and Carolingian about the way in which they conceived of their relationship with the Christian church. Equating the church with Christian society at large and aligning both—at least by fiction—with the Christian empire, neither they nor their ecclesiastical advisers saw anything odd about the intimate intermingling of the religious and political that characterized their successive regimes as it had those of Charlemagne and Justinian before

31

them. Nor, by virtue of having been anointed with the holy oil during the coronation rite, did they see anything odd in believing themselves to be possessed of quasi-priestly powers, in calling themselves "vicars of Christ," or in regarding themselves as responsible more than anyone else for the guidance and order of the churches within their dominions.

In this way of thinking the German emperors differed little from the kings of France and the Anglo-Saxon kings of England. The difference lay rather in the strength of the power the emperors wielded. It lay also in the degree to which that power depended on the willingness of higher ecclesiastics to serve as imperial administrators; on the ability of the emperors, by controlling their appointment, to ensure the loyalty of those administrators; and on continuing imperial access to the military and financial resources of the bishoprics and monasteries. The difference lay, further, in the claim to universal leadership implicit in the imperial title and in the fact that, within its boundaries, the empire included the seat of those other sometime claimants to the legacy of Roman universality, the bishops of Rome. And it was not the similarity but the difference that eventually proved to be critical for the future political development of Europe and for the subsequent shape of medieval history.

The years of turmoil and confusion inaugurated by the last wave of barbarian invasions had seen the disintegration not only of political organizational structures but also of ecclesiastical. They had seen the extension of lay control over every level of ecclesiastical office and personnel: the local parish churches and their priests, the monasteries and their abbots, the bishoprics and archbishoprics and their incumbents, not excluding, indeed, the bishopric of Rome itself. Those years had also seen an unprecedented growth of clerical corruption manifested most obviously in the twin abuses of simony (the buying and selling of church offices and functions) and clerical marriage—long prohibited in the Latin church and carrying with it the attendant danger of hereditary succession to ecclesiastical offices being established as a norm. Both corruptions reflected the extent to which, during the period of invasion and chaos, family and political interests had triumphed over the church's spiritual goals and stifled its original sense of prophetic mission.

During the course of the tenth and early eleventh centuries, corruption was countered by two streams of reform, the one clerical, the other royal. The first of these embraced twin movements centering particularly on Lorraine and Burgundy (where the famous monastery of Cluny was its focus) and had as its objectives the elimination of simony, the establishment of the rule of clerical celibacy, and the general restoration of church order. The second shared similarly conservative aims, and the two streams converged in 1049 when the emperor Henry III (1037–56), who had earlier deposed three rival claimants to the papacy and installed his own candidates, intervened again to appoint Leo IX (1049–54). Himself a representative of the Lorraine movement, Leo set out to provide the reforming forces with unified guidance and control, abandoning the preoccupation with local Italian politics characteristic of his immediate predecessors and appearing in person at a whole series of synods in France and Germany to investigate, to judge, and to legislate.

Enjoying as he did the enthusiastic support of Henry III, Leo did not contest the degree of control that that ruler, even more than the kings of England and France, continued to exercise over the churches within his domains. There is nothing noteworthy about this; the religious character of kingship and the custom of royal control over the higher church offices were by then as deeply rooted in social custom and ecclesiastical tradition as was the peculiar institution of slavery in the Southern states of the Union before the Civil War. What *is* noteworthy, however, and historic too, is the fact that some of the pope's supporters were now beginning to question that custom and to attack that tradition. Some were beginning to proclaim, with truly revolutionary audacity, that the days of "King-priests and Emperor-pontiffs" were past, and many of them felt that the clergy must be freed from all lay domination if ever the church was really to be reformed.

It was only in the years after 1056, however, that the papacy moved to embrace the more radical approach to reform. After Henry III's death, a royal minority had left the Roman church without imperial protection, giving the local Roman nobility the opportunity to try to regain control over the making of popes and forcing the papacy to seek security in an alliance with the new Norman rulers of southern Italy and Sicily. The outcome was the disastrous clash between papacy and empire that broke out in 1075 when the young German king, Henry IV (1056–1106), who had reclaimed most of the power wielded by his father but had openly revived the practice of simony, too, was confronted by an old and unbending pope, Gregory VII (1073–85), who—with a single-mindedness and intensity of purpose that would have done credit to a New England abolitionist of the nineteenth century—had brushed aside the pleas of the moderates and gradualists among church reformers with the fateful words, "The Lord hath not said: 'I am tradition,' but 'I am the truth.'"

The ensuing struggle was only the beginning of several centuries of intermittent strife between the papacy and the German Empire, strife that reached its peak in the mid-thirteenth century but that was still able to generate a pallid harmonic even in the fourteenth century, when popes as well as emperors had lost much of their former prestige and power. Over the course of these centuries there were shifts in the precise points at issue, as also in the principles the two sides evoked and the strategy and tactics they pursued. At the heart of the conflict as it developed lay the fact that the emperors and popes both saw themselves as rightful custodians of the ideal of universal leadership in Christian society that was the legacy of Rome to the Christian world and that an increasing acquaintance with Roman law both fostered and intensified. At its heart lay also the concomitant claim, advanced by both, to control the ancient capital of Rome and the territory in central Italy in which it was located, a claim that the papacy could not abandon without also losing its independence of action, but one that became increasingly important to the emperors as the bases of their power in Germany were progressively eroded by the rise of a feudal nobility impatient of any sort of monarchical control.

By the end of the thirteenth century, the papacy appeared to have triumphed over its opponents. After a bitter and compromising struggle it had destroyed in Italy an imperial authority that had already been marginalized in Germany. Though the empire survived, it did so as a loose confederacy of increasingly autonomous principalities, fiefdoms, and towns in which the effective power of the emperor

34

depended less upon his possession of the imperial office than upon the private dynastic territories belonging to him as yet another (and not necessarily the strongest) of the German feudal magnates. The fate of Germany, as also of Italy, was thenceforth and until the nineteenth century to be one of political fragmentation, and it was the popes who now emerged as the authentic heirs to the legacy of Roman universalism. Having long since moved to adopt the title of "supreme pontiff" (borne by the ancient Roman emperors) and having already begun to monopolize that of "vicar of Christ" (borne earlier by bishops, kings, and emperors alike), they also adopted many of the trappings of imperial splendor and not a few of the prerogatives of imperial office. By equating the pope with the emperor, and the cardinals—his chief advisers—with the Roman Senate, ecclesiastical lawyers were able to place the revived Roman law at the service of the papal jurisdiction, extending its reach and refining the modalities of its exercise, but at the expense, it should be realized, of transforming its nature. What was involved was a thoroughgoing politicization of ecclesiastical affairs and a substitution for papal leadership *in* the church of papal monarchy *over* the church—not only over the church defined in its narrow sense as the hierarchical organization of clergy but also in the broader sense denoting the whole of Christian society, few segments of which were left untouched by the increasingly vigorous exercise of papal authority.

It is true that the realities of papal power in no way matched the theoretical claims to supreme authority over temporal rulers and in temporal affairs that the popes and their propagandists did not hesitate to advance. Nor were even the most aggressively political of their actions necessarily based on anything so abstract or general as that theocratic claim. During this period, nonetheless, in the absence of any rival political authority that could claim to be truly universal, the popes did succeed, to an impressive degree, in exercising a universal leadership in Christian Europe. Already in the late eleventh century, having first encouraged the Christian princes of Spain in the early days of their struggle to reconquer the peninsula from the Muslims, the popes had gone on to place themselves in the vanguard of the forces for European expansionism. They had sponsored the Crusading movement that established first a Christian foothold in Palestine and Syria and then, later on, a Latin empire at Constantinople. That empire proved to be more ephemeral than the embittered schism between the worlds of Latin Catholicism and Greek Orthodoxy that its brutal establishment helped perpetuate, but papal leadership or encouragement of other developments European-wide in their scope produced more lasting results. Notable among them was the emergence in the late twelfth and thirteenth centuries of the new institutions of higher learning that came to be called "universities," granting degrees recognized as valid throughout the Latin world and becoming the focus of a great intellectual flowering. Notable, too, were the activities of the Dominicans and Franciscans, the new orders of itinerant monks or "friars" who staffed the inquisitorial machinery that the papacy set up to combat the rise of religious heterodoxy and who, in a more benign vein, conducted missionary work as far afield as the court of the great Khan at Peking and did so much, closer to home, to bring the Christian message to the new unchurched poor, the growing town populations for whom the existing parish structures had failed to provide.

When the needs of the early church had demanded it, it had been the emperor Constantine who in 325 summoned the Ecumenical Council of Nicaea, presided over its deliberations, and approved and promulgated its decrees. It is of more than symbolic importance that when the needs of the medieval church demanded it, it was Innocent III (1198–1216), by common consent the most distinguished of medieval popes, who in 1215 summoned and played the dominant role in the Fourth Lateran Council, the greatest of medieval ecumenical councils. More than any recognizably "political" entity it was the papacy then, that in the centuries subsequent to the Carolingian era, inherited and embodied the old Roman ideal of universal empire, exploited its legacy, and perpetuated its memory.

The Time of Troubles:
The Fourteenth and Fifteenth Centuries

DURING the fourteenth and fifteenth centuries, men continued to
honor that universalist ideal—and none more eloquently than the poet
Dante. The political realities of the day, however, conspired to make it
clear, and increasingly so, that it was to be the destiny of that ideal to
remain incapable of political realization. When the German emperors
could no longer convincingly claim to be the bearers of the universalist
hope, it was in no small part because they had encountered in the popes
implacable adversaries who were at the same time more convincing
claimants to that role; but, then, it was to be the fate in turn of the
medieval papacy to meet its own downfall, at least as a power with
universalist pretensions, through the working of forces antipathetic to
the ideal of universalism itself.

The Norman conquest of England in 1066 had led to the creation of
a powerful and governmentally sophisticated Anglo-Norman state,
which, by the late twelfth century, had acquired domains stretching
from the borders of Scotland right down to the Pyrenees and which
had already embarked upon the conquest of Wales and Ireland. The
powerful French monarchy that emerged somewhat later did so, in no
small degree, by capitalizing on the weaknesses of the English kings
during the first half of the thirteenth century and absorbing the greater
part of the English royal holdings on the Continent; by the end of the
century, only a small coastal region in what is now Gascony remained
in English hands. Both of these monarchies had sought to exercise the
type of control over the churches within their territories that the
radical Gregorian reformers had attempted to eradicate in Germany
and Italy; but because of the initial papal preoccupation with the
pretensions of the German emperors and because the English and
French kings had wedded their ambitions more successfully to their
resources, they could permit themselves the sort of compromise on
control of ecclesiastical appointments that an emperor like Henry IV
simply could not afford to entertain. As a result, neither became
involved in the type of violent and protracted conflict with the papacy

that did so much to destroy the very foundations of a viable German empire.

By the late thirteenth century, however, their power, prestige, and pretensions had risen to such a degree that they posed a threat not only to one another, but also to the smooth operation of the whole machinery of jurisdictional and fiscal control that the papacy had constructed during the previous two centuries. The working of that machinery had long since become a stimulus to anticlerical complaints, the more so when men began to question the degree to which papal policy was responsive to truly spiritual needs. Such doubts multiplied when the popes proved willing to debase the spiritual weapons at their disposal by launching crusades first against the German emperor Frederick II (1212–50) and then against the king of Aragon, who had assumed the rulership of Sicily that papal decree had previously placed in French hands. If the success of the former crusade did much to disillusion Europeans in general with the quality of papal leadership, the failure of the latter did even more to disillusion the French in particular. It was the French, for centuries the faithful allies of Rome, who were to launch the attack that many historians have regarded as signaling the downfall of the medieval papacy.

The election of Boniface VIII (1294–1303) brought to the papal throne a formidably stubborn old man committed to a high notion of papal authority and to a vigorous implementation of the jurisdictional and fiscal rights that flowed therefrom. It was a case of the wrong man in a crucial role at quite the wrong time. The ambitions of the French and English kings had precipitated the outbreak of war between their countries, and neither king, harried by the costs of war, was willing to tolerate Boniface's untimely assertions that in the absence of papal permission he lacked the right to tax the clergy in his kingdom. In the prevailing climate of opinion threats of excommunication proved to be of no avail. The prestige of the papacy had fallen too low to permit the successful deployment of such traditional spiritual weaponry—so low, indeed, that in 1303 it was possible for a band of mercenaries in French pay and under French leadership to surprise Boniface at his residence in Anagni, publicly humiliate him, and take him into captivity. He was quickly released but died almost immediately at Rome, and the

38

aftermath of the "outrage of Anagni" was what contemporaries were soon to portray as a new "Babylonian captivity"—the desertion of Rome by a whole series of subsequent popes and their long residence (1309–77) at Avignon, on the very borders of the French kingdom itself.

The Avignonese papacy was neither as morally corrupt nor quite as responsive to French pressure as contemporaries assumed it to be or as later propagandists were to claim; but, during a period of intermittent Anglo-French war, it was overwhelmingly French in complexion, and this, along with the general evils attendant upon its intensified fiscal and administrative centralization, sponsored the growth of doubts about the credibility of its claims and imposed severe strains upon the unity of the church at large. Those strains mounted and the doubts multiplied when a disputed papal election led in 1378 to the establishment of two competing lines of claimants to the papal office, one at Rome and one at Avignon, the European kingdoms, principalities, and powers aligning themselves with one or the other in accordance with their political predilections and with the configurations already traditional in the arena of European diplomacy.

The ensuing "Great Schism of the West" sponsored a good deal of confusion in the church at large. It also spawned in the central organs of the rival papal administrations (and especially the Roman), an unprecedented degree of corruption, not fully to be moderated until the onset of the Protestant Reformation lent a heightened urgency to the efforts of those Catholic churchmen already in the early sixteenth century struggling to implement reforms at Rome itself. By embracing the program of the ecclesiastical constitutionalists known as Conciliarists and by claiming for itself, therefore, an authority superior under certain circumstances to that of the pope himself, the Council of Constance (1414-18) succeeded, if not in reforming the church, at least in ending the schism. It deposed the rival claimants to the papal office and brought about the election of Martin V (1417-31), a man whom all factions could recognize as the true pope. By pursuing a policy of firmness and diplomatic skill, Martin V and his immediate successors were able to ward off the constitutionalist threat that conciliarism posed to the absolute nature of their power. They were destined, however, to rule over a church that had undergone what was, in effect, a constitutional revolution of a different type and to hold an office that had lost in practice what it had become increasingly willing to concede even in theory—namely, any serious claim to a role of truly universal leadership.

One of the most persistent features of ecclesiastical life from the early fourteenth century onward had been the extension once more of royal or princely control over the local churches. In ways subtle and not so subtle the work of the Gregorian reformers was being undone, and rulers were moved increasingly to assert their sovereign jurisdiction over all groups and institutions—clergy and churches included—within the territorial boundaries of their states. By the early fifteenth century the kings of France and England, in particular, had become adept at the art of marshaling national antipapal feeling in order to bring pressure on the papacy to concede them a handsome share of the taxes levied on their national churches and of the benefices or ecclesiastical positions belonging thereto. Given the difficulties that the Avignonese popes and the popes of the schism had had to face, they had had little choice but to yield to such diplomatic blackmail, even though by so doing they had committed the church piecemeal to a revolution that would ultimately leave to their successors nothing more than a theoretically supreme authority, the substance of power having passed in fact into the hands of kings, princes, and rulers of city-states like Venice. The concordats that Martin V concluded in 1418 with the English and with other national groupings marked a decisive moment in the history of this development. The infamous concordat of 1516, which effectively delivered the French church into the hands of the monarchy, marked its peak. Its corollary, even before the Protestant Reformation, was the effective transformation of the international Catholic church into a series of national or territorial churches and of the fifteenth-century popes into sophisticated Italian princes–sometimes of dubious personal morality, always preoccupied with the restoration and preservation of their Italian principality and the consolidation in their own hands of despotic power over it, conducting as equals their diplomatic relations with the secular princes of Europe and increasingly prone to the type of dynastic ambition current among those princes. It was a fitting adaptation, in truth, to a European world that responded no longer to the lure of the old universalist ideal but was moved instead by the urgencies of dynastic aggrandizement and quasi-nationalistic sentiment.

Historians have frequently chosen to take this transformation of the church and the accompanying decline of papal fortunes as symptomatic of a more profound crisis in the very soul of medieval civilization itself. It is easy enough to understand why they should have been tempted to do so. The outbreak in 1296 of the war between France and England, which had led so rapidly to the disastrous confrontation with Boniface VIII, had marked the end of a comparatively peaceful era and the beginning of the prolonged struggle between the two major European powers, which, punctuated with intermittent truces and periods of peace, was to drag on well into the fifteenth century. While it lasted it caused a great deal of devastation in France and sponsored in that country a recrudescence of the aristocratic feuds and rival private armies characteristic of the anarchic early phase of feudalism. A similar growth of what has been called "bastard feudalism" occurred in England during the dynastic conflicts between the Yorkist and Lancastrian claimants to the throne which broke out in 1450 after the end of the war with France and which have gone down in history as the "Wars of the Roses." The fourteenth and fifteenth centuries marked, then, at best a pause in the development of the English and French states and at worst a positive setback. Certainly, they witnessed the breakdown of public order and the growth of violence to a degree that would have been unimaginable in the late thirteenth century.

To the social dislocations caused by invasion and civil war must also be added the tribulations consequent to the ending in the early fourteenth century of the great economic boom that had gathered force in the tenth century, accelerated in the eleventh and twelfth centuries, and reached its peak in the thirteenth. Even before the advent of the Black Death (1348–50), population expansion had ceased, serious and widespread famines had reappeared, and the European economy had begun to slide into a financial crisis and a depression that was to last until the latter part of the fifteenth century and even, in some sectors, into the sixteenth. The economic situation, along with much else that was troubling fourteenth-century Europe, was much exacerbated by the appalling disaster of the Black Death, the first great outbreak of plague since the mid-eighth century and one so massive that in three short years it was to sweep away what is usually estimated as about one-third of Europe's population; it dislocated the lives of the survivors, created a labor shortage, spawned a good deal of religious fanaticism and social unrest, and, along with its repeated secondary outbreaks, understandably sponsored the profound pessimism that is one of the distinguishing features of the later Middle Ages.

If one took that pessimism and the disasters that helped account for it, noted that both were preceded already in the thirteenth century by the loss of the last Christian foothold in Palestine, the halting of the Christian reconquest of Spain, the cessation of the German expansion into eastern Europe, and the invasion of Hungary and Poland by the Mongol horde, and if, in addition, one interpreted the marked shift in the movement of theological and philosophical thinking that occurred in the early fourteenth century as reflecting a catastrophic loss of confidence in the power and reach of human reason, it would be easy enough to portray these later medieval centuries as constituting for Europe a period of civilizational decline, of geographical and political contraction, of social, economic, and cultural retardation. To do so, however, would be to ignore the unmistakable signs of vitality that punctuated the disasters of the period and to pay too high a price for historiographic symmetry. Not all historians, it should be observed, are willing to dismiss the new philosophy of the fourteenth and fifteenth centuries as decadent scholasticism, and those who do so are themselves the least likely to ignore the fact that these are also the centuries that gave birth to the great cultural and artistic flowering known as the Italian Renaissance. These were the centuries, too, that saw the final destruction of Muslim power in Spain, the discovery of the Canary Islands, and the beginning of the great voyages of exploration that were to open up new worlds to Europe, setting its feet on the path that led it ultimately to transform the whole face of the globe.

That is another story, however, and the dawn of what has been called "the heroic age" of European expansion marks an appropriate point at which to terminate this brief sketch of the course of medieval history. It marks, moreover, a fitting moment to recall the question raised already in the Introduction, to ponder what exactly it was in the medieval experience that can help explain the extraordinary energy, vitality, and power that European civilization was to manifest in the modern period as it overflowed its original confines, spreading into so many distant parts of the world and leaving none unaffected by its passage. Of course, once such a question is raised, the factors that clamor for attention are both multiple and complex; and if the foregoing sketch has emphasized the centrality of the role played by the Christian church, it should be realized that in so doing it has not so much suggested a solution as raised a problem. For there is nothing, after all, so very obvious about that role. Brooding about the great catastrophe that overtook the Greco-Roman civilization of antiquity and remarking on the truly extraordinary powers of recovery that medieval Europe was to betray, the English historian Hugh Trevor-Roper has observed that by our retrospective efforts at explanation we contrive always to make the course of history seem "automatic, natural, inevitable." "The trouble about history," he grumbles, "is that we take it too much for granted." [3] Certainly, one of the things about the course of medieval history that we do take altogether too much for granted is the crucial role played by the Christian church in the molding of the medieval experience—not only the *type* of role it played, but also the very fact that it played so crucial a role at all.

ii

CHURCH AND SECT

The Role of Mediaeval Christianity

Over the centuries the amount of disagreement about the nature of the primitive Christian church has been simply enormous. Already in the Middle Ages, with a degree of confidence to which their more historically minded successors can no longer aspire, heretics, hierarchs, reformers, and reactionaries alike sought to reinforce their respective positions by appealing to the conditions they believed to have prevailed in the era of Christian beginnings. In the wake of the Reformation, Protestant controversialists and Catholic apologists did likewise, surrendering without resistance to the narcissism that so often overtakes men when they address themselves to the distant past, peering anxiously into the mists that gathered increasingly around that era of beginnings and discerning therein, with a glad if often overhasty recognition, the looming outlines of their own respectively cherished but frequently conflicting ideals. A scarcely diminished urgency has characterized the efforts of more recent investigators: the liberal Protestants of the nineteenth century, their neo-orthodox critics of the twentieth, and the paleo- or neo-Catholics of more recent years, for whom the nature of the earliest ecclesiastical structures has become a matter of revitalized concern and increasingly contentious debate.

In this particularly difficult area of historical inquiry, in which a superfluity of competing convictions conspires to exacerbate the problems already posed by a shortage of hard data, the possibility of anything approaching complete agreement is exceedingly remote. Some fundamentals, however, lie clearly beyond the reach of dissent. Nobody today, certainly, would regard the form that the church took in the Middle Ages as identical with the one it had taken in its earliest centuries, and few would regard the role it played in medieval society as in any sense a *necessary* development of the role it had played in the ancient world. In this connection, there are few better points of departure than the sociological typology that Ernst Troeltsch, sociologist, historian, and theologian, elaborated over sixty years ago in his great book *The Social Teaching of the Christian Churches*. Although the historical account in which it is embedded has been criticized at more than one of its phases, that typology continues to maintain its usefulness, and it will serve as the organizing principle for this discussion of medieval Christianity.

Friend and admirer of Max Weber, Troeltsch believed that Christianity, insofar as it was itself a social phenomenon, was open to investigation in accordance with the modes of analysis proper to historical sociology. As a result of pursuing precisely such an investigation, Troeltsch concluded that in the course of its historical career Christianity had found expression not in one type of socio-religious organization alone but rather in three. These he called the church, the sect, and mysticism, and it is with the two first that the following account is concerned.

By the church, Troeltsch meant the type of socioreligious organization that reaches out to comprehend and to Christianize society as a whole and that contrives to do so by manifesting a willingness to compromise with the mores it finds embedded already in society, foregoing, therefore, the imposition upon its members of any moral code or standard for admission that the masses would find too exacting to meet or too rigorous to sustain. As a corollary, it foregoes also any rigid insistence upon the individual sanctity of its members and focuses attention instead upon its own institutional holiness, locus as it is of the regenerative working of the Holy Spirit. The emphasis, then, is on both the sacramental and the objective. The efficacy of the sacramental channels of supernatural grace depends upon the personal moral worthiness neither of minister nor of recipient, and infant baptism, therefore, is readily accepted as an appropriate mode of entry into the society.

While the church thus strives to include the masses, the sect resigns itself to excluding them. Its emphasis lies less upon the exploitation of the sacramental channels of grace than upon the rigors of moral

48

striving. Setting as its goal the preservation of the exacting moral ideal proclaimed by Jesus in the Sermon on the Mount, it is of necessity a voluntary society that eschews talk of institutional sanctity, stressing instead the subjective holiness of its individual members and seeking to protect the purity of their moral commitment by imposing very strict criteria for admission into the fellowship of believers and for continuing membership thereof.

In order to underline the significance of the contrast involved here, it may be helpful to refer by way of rough analogy to the partially comparable contrast that exists in our own contemporary political life between the national party and the radical fringe "movement." The former aspires to establish a sufficiently broad basis of electoral support to be entrusted with the government of the country and the opportunity, therefore, to implement its program. In order to attain that goal, it is willing to forego an uncompromising ideological purity, to open its membership to all, and to couch its appeal in terms acceptable to the mass of voters. The latter, on the other hand, prefers to harangue the voters rather than genuinely to solicit their support. It demands of its supporters the type of life commitment to which the many may periodically aspire but which only the few can long sustain. Highly selective in its admission criteria, it can normally hope to do no more than bear witness to its ideals; but that is itself a major goal. The remote possibility of being entrusted with governmental authority it rates much lower than the vindication of its own ideological purity, and it can hope to combine the two only as the result of a revolutionary seizure of power. If that path is rejected or seen as lying in the distant future, it is sometimes driven to seek the purer maintenance of its ideals in isolated utopias, communities persisting on the margins of society and awaiting, perhaps with impatient longing, the future dawning of the millennium.

Analogies, however, although helpful, can also be misleading, and this one is no exception. When Troeltsch uses the terms *church* and *sect* he is referring not to concrete entities existing in the real world but to conceptual constructs of the sort that Weber called "ideal types"— *types*, because they comprehend neither the totality of the characteristics possessed by religious societies at all the points in their respective

49

histories, nor even the totality of the traits that all such societies have in common, but rather stress the characteristics or traits most typical of a particular sort of religious society; *ideal,* because such constructs rarely or never find, in all their purity, a counterpart in the actual course of history. Hence, for Troeltsch, church and sect reflect persistent tendencies in Christianity, tendencies that, while fluctuating periodically in their respective prominence, remain interwoven in the actual course of historical events. Both types, he argues, are rooted in the message of the New Testament itself; both "are a logical result of the Gospel, and only conjointly do they exhaust the whole range of its sociological influence." Nonetheless, the church-type alone has "the power to stir the masses in any real and lasting way"; and if, admittedly, "the main stream of Christian development" has flowed "along the channel prepared by the Church-type," [1] never has it been confined more fully within that channel than it was in the medieval West, where, in the hierarchical Latin church presided over by its papal theocrats, the church-type was most purely realized and most coherently developed.

If one keeps Troeltsch's intriguing distinction in mind when one examines the role that the Christian church played in shaping the medieval experience, it becomes clear that one must first ask why that church played so crucial a role at all. In other words, why was it that medieval Christianity came to exhibit so very fully the characteristics associated with Troeltsch's church-type? There was, after all, nothing inevitable about that development. The sectarian element was very strongly represented in the early church. Its subsequent marginalization in the medieval church, where it survived largely in the form of monasticism,[2] clearly calls for an explanation. And in any such explanation, the main stress should be placed on two factors: first, the transformation undergone by the church in the wake of Constantine's grant of toleration; second, the particular cast assumed by Latin Christianity as a result of the heated debates of the fifth and sixth centuries concerning sin, grace, the economy of salvation, and the role of the church therein.

50

The Early Church and the
"Constantinian Revolution"

WHATEVER the degree of "Catholicity" one ascribes to primitive Christianity and however much one insists that the tendency to develop a religious society having the characteristics of the church-type was already present in the teaching of the New Testament, the very situation of the earliest Christian communities militated against any rapid development of that tendency. Composed as they were of those who had undergone the experience of personal conversion, the contrast between their own way of life and that of society at large did much to bolster the distinctive group identity that helped sustain them, and there was little to tempt them to relax the rigor of their religious and moral commitment. Moreover, flourishing first among the alienated and oppressed segments of the Roman world, living their lives, as it were, on the margins of classical civilization, preoccupied with the imminence of the kingdom of God that Jesus had preached, anxious to avoid involvement in warfare, urged to eschew litigation, and resistant to the temptation of political office, there was little to encourage them to imagine the desirability, let alone explore the possibility, of reaching out to attempt a Christianizing transformation of Roman society as a whole—so little, indeed, that they appear at first to have resisted the temptation even to understand their own organizational structures in terms applicable also to secular organisms. Thus it is becoming a commonplace today to acknowledge that when the New Testament authors described ecclesiastical offices or ministries they studiously avoided the seemingly obvious words available to them in the Greek vocabulary of politics and chose instead to develop a new term: *diakonia,* "service." Whereas the other words available to them expressed a political relationship, that of governor to governed, and injected a note of authority and power, this word did not. Instead, bringing with it connotations of self-abasement and used by the New Testament authors to denote service to one's fellow men, it was a conception of governmental office as ministerial, as grounded in love

51

for others, a conception that contrasted sharply with secular notions of office as grounded in power and in law.

As the Christian communities grew in number, size, and importance, however, it is understandable that there should also have developed a tendency to assimilate the biblical notion of office to the less demanding, more familiar, and administratively manageable *political* pattern of thought. Moreover, as their membership came more and more to be composed of "cradle" Christians, those who had not themselves undergone the transforming experience of conversion, it is understandable that there should have been a relaxation in the severity of the moral standards that could realistically be imposed upon the faithful as a whole. At the same time, there was an increasing disposition to regard the more rigorous exhortations of the Gospel as counsels of perfection, ascetic prescriptions to which one could realistically expect only a small minority of spiritual athletes to adhere. Even before Constantine extended toleration to Christianity in 313, then, it is clear that there had been a palpable lowering in the barriers separating the church from the world; but that should not lead one to underestimate the impact upon the church of the "Constantinian revolution," or, indeed, the widening of that impact in the West by the subsequent disintegration of Roman imperial power.

If the rate of conversion to Christianity had quickened during the course of the third century, the savage persecutions launched by the emperors Decius (249–51) and Diocletian (284–305)—along with the massive waves of apostasy they generated—still served to remind would-be converts of the seriousness of the step they were taking and the price of alienation from the expectations of society at large that was attached to it. In the years after Constantine's own conversion, however, the rewards attached to embracing Christianity and the drawbacks attendant upon any quixotic loyalty to ancestral paganism mounted dramatically. The fourth century witnessed, therefore, a massive influx of self-servers into the church. The concomitant lowering in the quality of Christian religious and moral life became the object of contemporary criticism, and that fact is set in relief by the quickening under lay rather than clerical leadership of a countervailing and clearly sectarian impulse, one that found particular expression in

52

the organization of monastic communities composed of Christians who pledged themselves voluntarily to poverty, celibacy, and the pursuit of a rigorously ascetic life.

Again, although bishops in the third century had already been acting as legislators, administrators, and arbitrators in the churches under their supervision, they had been doing so as leaders of private societies whose membership was no less voluntary than is that of such comparable social organizations in the modern world as colleges, trade unions, or fraternities. The churches, then, were organizations that directly concerned only one segment of human activity, and the decisions of their leaders possessed binding force solely in the degree to which they were able to touch the consciences of the faithful. No more than the leadership in any modern private social organization could they claim to wield any public, coercive power. By the fifth century, however, as Christianity was transformed from the proscribed religion of a suspect minority into the official religion of the empire—taking the place, therefore, of the civic cult of pagan antiquity—ecclesiastical authority, supported increasingly by the public force of the imperial administration, was becoming political and coercive in nature. It was also beginning, especially in the Western provinces, to reach out into areas that today we would regard as pertaining to the state: assuming the burden of public functions particularly in the realms of what we would call health, education, and welfare. These developments persisted during the centuries that followed, and, as overt paganism was suppressed, membership of the church and membership of the state gradually became coterminous. The church ceased to be a voluntary, private organization comparable to other social organizations and became instead a compulsory, all-inclusive, and coercive society comparable to what we call the state and in its totality well-nigh indistinguishable from it.

As a result, by the time of the emperor Charlemagne in the early ninth century, there had emerged in the West a single public society—church, empire, Christian commonwealth, call it what you will—a universal commonwealth that was neither voluntary nor private. To that commonwealth all Europeans, even after the collapse of the Carolingian Empire, felt they belonged. And the idea of a

53

universal Christian commonwealth coterminous with Christendom, sustained in theory by memories of ancient Rome and guaranteed in practice by the universal and international character of the ecclesiastical structure itself, lingered on long after the appearance of the national monarchies until, with the advent of the Protestant Reformation, the unity of that ecclesiastical structure was itself finally destroyed.

Of course, long before the emergence of Charlemagne's empire, the Roman Empire of the East had itself been transformed into a comparable Christian commonwealth. Moreover, in the East, to a greater degree even than in the West, the emperor functioned as the effective head of that commonwealth, wielding power over layman and cleric alike and exercising authority over a range of religious matters that we today would regard as lying beyond the purview of any state. Nothing stands as clearer evidence of the degree to which the "Constantinian revolution" had transformed the church both in its governance and in its self-understanding; for if it had been a commonplace throughout the ancient world to see what we would call the "political" as encompassing all dimensions of life, including the moral and religious, it was a commonplace that the New Testament authors had sharply challenged. In particular, their monotheism permitted them to have no truck with the widespread ancient notion that kings were themselves manifestations of the divine or mediators between their peoples and the divine. At the beginning of the Christian Era that ancient notion had found influential expression in the Hellenistic philosophy of kingship to which the Roman emperors were falling heir and which was reflected in such characteristic royal titles as "shepherd," "savior," "mediator," "benefactor." Some scholars have seen in the application of such royal titles to Christ an emphasis upon the fact that Christ alone was savior and mediator with the divine Father and a concomitant deprecation of the prevailing royal cult. In the Gospel according to St. John and St. John's first Epistle there is implied an open opposition between the kingdom of God and the established powers of this world, and that opposition moves into the foreground when, in the name of the kingdom of God, the Apocalypse of John denounces as satanic the blasphemously divinized emperors of Rome.

Nonetheless, there is in the New Testament one element that, while not in itself of explicitly political import, did serve to ease the way for those sophisticated Christians of Hellenic background who in the second and third centuries were already daring to look forward to a more positive relationship between Roman Empire and Christian church. That element was the frequency with which Luke had correlated the Gospel story with the history of the empire at large, noting in particular the coincidence of the birth of Christ, proclaimer of the new order of redemption, with the reign of the first emperor, Caesar Augustus, savior and renovator of the Roman world.[3] Eusebius of Caesarea (c. 260–c. 340), court bishop and biographer of the emperor Constantine (and not necessarily the most uncritical of his clerical adulators), regarded this last correlation as nothing less than providential, linking it with the Hellenistic belief in the interrelationship of universal monarchy and monotheism, political unity and the unity of the cosmos. Thus it was possible for him to construct a picture of the course of history in which Augustus's imposition of imperial order was nothing less than the fulfillment of Old Testament prophecies concerning the dawn of the Messianic peace, and Constantine's inauguration of Christian empire was affiliated with the redemptive mission of Christ and seen almost as its completion. Eusebius overlooked no opportunity, therefore, to stress the sacred nature of Constantine's imperial position, as well as his personal proximity to God. The emperor was "like some general bishop constituted by God," one for whom it was entirely proper to involve himself deeply in the governance of the church.[4] He was a priestly figure, therefore— indeed, perhaps something more, for in one passage of the *Oration . . . in Praise of the Emperor Constantine* that attributed to Constantine a victory that in a parallel passage elsewhere was attributed to Christ, Eusebius presented the emperor as a quasi-messianic figure, "the Servant of God" who had finally vanquished the "numberless" forces of evil.[5]

If such views proved popular among the Christian clergy of the later empire, they did so in part because of the unprecedented nature of the circumstances that gave them birth. New Testament political teaching had concerned, after all, a situation in which Christians confronted pagan rulers, whereas now, by what could surely be nothing other than a wondrous dispensation of divine providence, they enjoyed the favor of Christian emperors. It is really not too surprising, then, that most of them were willing to accept those emperors' own estimates of what their place should be in the economy of salvation, nor is it surprising that those emperors should feel no need to dissociate their own position in religious matters from that occupied by their predecessors, the emperor-gods of Rome or the priest-kings of antiquity. Constantine had not even been baptized when in 325 he summoned and presided over the ecumenical Council of Nicaea, and he and several of his successors continued to bear the pagan religious title of "supreme pontiff" (*pontifex maximus*). Even when they discreetly abandoned that title, the emperors continued to use of themselves "the old pagan vocabulary of divinity" and to regard themselves as possessing authority, even supreme authority, in religious matters—especially those relating to church property, discipline, and appointments but frequently also in matters of doctrine.

Insofar as it succeeded in transforming Christianity into something approximating a civic cult, then, the "Constantinian revolution" provided a major impulse to the abandonment of sectarian aloofness from the world and to the emergence of a church-type religious society. Presupposing as it did a complex amalgamation of Christian and pagan elements and the demolition of the major barrier dividing Christian social attitudes from those of the world at large, it stands as the single most significant precondition for the emergence of the type of Christian sacral society that was later to flourish alike in the Eastern empire and in the Carolingian Empire of the West. But already in the Carolingian era there were differences between Eastern and Western religiopolitical attitudes that cannot be accounted for simply by the destruction of the Roman governmental apparatus in the West or by differences in their respective levels of political sophistication. In the East, Eusebius's Christianized version of the Hellenistic philosophy of kingship had taken firm root, so much so, indeed, that it was to retain its vitality and popularity right through to the extinction of the Byzantine Empire in the fifteenth century and, via the intermediary of the Orthodox church, to contribute something also to the emergence in the modern era of a distinctively Russian political consciousness. In the West, however, the clerical hierarchy already cherished aspirations to a degree of independence and political influence undreamed of by its Eastern Orthodox counterpart. This has to be accounted for not simply by the degree to which the Western bishops, as the surviving representatives of the imperial tradition, had had such influence thrust upon them during the period of invasions. Attention must also be paid to the doctrinal developments of the fourth, fifth, and sixth centuries that did so much to give Latin Catholicism its particular cast and to enhance, in the territories that fell within its orbit, the dignity and importance attached to the members of the sacerdotal hierarchy.

St. Augustine and the Doctrinal Foundations of Sacerdotalism

THE ease with which Eusebius had been able to portray Constantine as a quasi-messianic figure, one closely associated with the eternal Christ not only in the work of government but also in that of salvation, reflects the unsettled state of Christian theologizing about the nature of the Trinity in general and of the Second Person of the Trinity in particular. It also reflects the difficulty with which educated Christians, their thinking shaped by assumptions and categories rooted in the Greek philosophical tradition, succeeded in coming to terms with the doctrine of the Incarnation—the belief that God the Son, Second Person of the Trinity, had become man. There are good reasons for this. Whatever the similarities between early Christianity and the other salvational mystery cults of the day, and however much ideas of Hellenistic provenance appear in the New Testament, Christian belief also contained fundamental novelties that imposed a considerable burden on the comprehension of anyone whose mind set had been shaped by the Greek philosophical tradition.

When such a person embraced Christianity, he would have no difficulty in accepting the idea that there was but one God. To that conclusion the philosophical tradition had persistently tended and it

57

was a commonplace for the intellectually sophisticated to see in the unity and order of an eternal cosmos the reflection or indwelling of a single divine principle. That the divine principle, however, should be identified as Yahweh, the God of Abraham, Isaac, and Jacob, a personal God of power and might who was not to be identified with the cosmic order but upon the free decision of whose will that order and indeed the universe itself was radically contingent—this was a notion far harder to domesticate within the hallowed categories of the philosophic tradition, as was the related belief that the universe was not eternal but had been created out of nothing by God. Similarly, that one should feel the need to distinguish a supreme ordering rationality or *Logos* and to see it as an intermediary between God and the world was understandable enough and again something of a commonplace; but to assert, as did the prologue to the Gospel according to St. John, that in the person of Jesus Christ the *Logos* or Word "became flesh and dwelt among us"—in other words, that the *Logos,* instead of finding a multiple manifestation or an enduring expression in the order of the cosmos, found a unique incarnation once and for all in a single human being and at a particular moment in history—this was a total novelty and one very difficult for any Greek to assimilate.

It is understandable, then, that it took so much time and effort for Christian intellectuals to come to terms with these issues and to assimilate in categories accessible to the philosophically trained mind exactly what they believed about the attributes of God, about the creation of the universe, about the relationship of Father, Son, and Holy Spirit, and about the human and divine natures of Christ. The process was well under way by the lifetime of Eusebius, but it was not to be completed for another two centuries or more, and then largely through the efforts of Eastern rather than Western theologians. Greek theologians of the Eastern churches were characteristically driven by their own educational heritage to scratch the philosophic itch and to worry at the speculative problems that such Christian doctrines raised, but the thinkers of the Western Latin church were characteristically inclined to think in legal terms. Philosophical and speculative thinking had much less of an appeal for them; their own concerns focused much more obsessively upon matters more susceptible to formulation in legalistic terms: upon the moral life and societal organization, upon practical obstacles in the way of moral living and the means by which those difficulties might be overcome, upon such matters, therefore, as sin and grace, salvation and the church. It was in these areas that they made their principal contribution to the development of Christian theology, and it was from the particular nature of that contribution that so much of what was to be distinctive about Latin Christianity was ultimately to derive.

True to their philosophic heritage, with its conviction of the importance of true knowledge and its confidence in the saving power of reason, Eastern theologians were prone to see man's sinfulness as rooted in his ignorance, to understand redemption, accordingly, as a process of enlightenment, and the role of Christ, incarnate *Logos*, therefore, as one of bestowing upon man the illumination he sorely needed if he was to be saved from the darkness of error. Already in the third century, however, in the thinking of the North African theologian Tertullian (d. c. 230), one can detect the beginnings of what was to become a marked divergence between the thinking of the Eastern and Western churches on the subject of man's sinfulness and his hopes for redemption. Behind that divergence lay a very Roman tendency to think of God primarily as sovereign lawgiver, to apprehend his relation to man very much in juridical terms, and to conceive of sin, accordingly, as an act of willful rebellion. Behind that divergence, too, lay an assessment of man's moral capacities far gloomier than that current among the theologians of the Eastern church, a pessimism that led to an emphasis on the importance of Adam's sin and fall from grace that those theologians could match neither in its intensity nor in its persistence.

At the same time, a comparable though not quite so marked divergence was occurring between the Eastern and Western understanding of the nature of the church itself, with Western thinkers—notably Cyprian, Bishop of Carthage (d. 258)—moving away from mystical conceptions, adopting a more juridical approach, and emphasizing the importance of submission to the ecclesiastical authorities as a criterion of church membership. Both of these distinctively Western theological tendencies came together in the thinking of St. Augustine

59

of Hippo (354–430), the North African theologian who was one of the very greatest of the church fathers and the principal architect of the type of Christian theology espoused in the West by the Latin Catholic church.

More than is the case with most theologies, Augustine's was rooted in the turbulent conditions of his own life: his sense of sin and moral helplessness, the long intellectual pilgrimage undertaken before his conversion first to the Neoplatonic philosophy and then to Christianity, the trials and tribulations encountered as bishop of Hippo, the religious and theological controversies in which he was involved both as pastor of his flock and as the leading Christian intellectual of his day. Of those controversies, two were of particular importance for the development of his thinking concerning the relationship of man to God, of grace to salvation, and of the role played by the church in both. The first was his struggle against the new threat posed in the early fifth century by the followers of Pelagius (c. 354–c. 418); the second, his long-drawn-out battle with the old danger posed so acutely in his own diocese by the schismatic sect known as the Donatists.

Pelagius was a British or Irish monk who had become a fashionable teacher in Rome during the early years of the fifth century and who, along with his pupil Coelestius, had spent some time in North Africa around the year 410. By temperament a moralist, he had apparently been shocked by the low standard of moral conduct he had observed at Rome and by the increasing prevalence of what he regarded as a demoralizingly pessimistic view of what could realistically be expected of human nature. The belief that man did not have it within his natural powers to avoid sin struck him as derogating from the very power and goodness of the God who had created human nature—hence his rejection of Tertullian's teaching that as descendants of Adam the souls of all men had inherited the damaging effects of that progenitor's Original Sin, his disdain for the idea that as a result of the Fall the human will had any intrinsic bias towards sinfulness, and his minimization of the role of divine grace in the process of salvation. It is not so much by God's favor as by their own merit that men progress in holiness. Indeed, it may be possible for man in the freedom of his will and by his own natural powers to avoid sin, and, by a strenuous and persistent effort of the will, to attain perfection. As Coelestius is said to have put it, "If I ought, I can."

Such views were anathema to Augustine. Because of the moral and spiritual struggles of his own earlier life—struggles whose anguish and intensity he conveys so movingly in the *Confessions*—he himself was in no way prone to doubt the reality of Original Sin or the searing impact of Adam's Fall upon the souls of his descendants. As a result of that unhappy event, human nature itself was scarred so deeply and corrupted so fearfully that it had become enslaved to sin, to ignorance, and to death. The ability to refrain from sin and to attain the good—an ability that had been Adam's natural prerogative in the state of innocence—was now lost, to be recovered only by the merciful infusion of God's grace. While this does not mean that man has forfeited his free will, too, in his fallen state the inevitable use to which he puts that free will is to do wrong.

Given Augustine's firm adherence to so pessimistic an appraisal of the human condition, there is nothing surprising about the hostility with which he reacted to the teaching of Pelagius. It was the challenge of that teaching, indeed, that spurred him on to state his own doctrine in its harshest and most uncompromising form. Left wholly to himself, he argued, man can do absolutely nothing to achieve his own salvation. Without divine help he can no more turn to God than he can turn away if God, by an irresistible grace, chooses to turn to him. He is shipwrecked on the sin of Adam, drifting helplessly into sin, at the mercy of the turbulent seas of his own fallen and depraved nature, incapable even of hoisting a sail or charting a course for land. From such a desperate plight he can be delivered only if God, of his infinite and incomprehensible mercy, reaches out, raises him up, and draws him to himself; hence, of course, Augustine's further commitment to the doctrine of predestination. It is up to God to determine which men will be the recipients of that mercy and which will not. This, Augustine believed, he has done from all eternity, basing his dread decision not upon any foreknowledge of the lives men contrive to lead but upon a secret and inscrutable justice that transcends the categories of any merely human equity.

Pushed to its logical conclusion, of course, it would have been the effect of this position to deprive the sacramental ministrations of the visible hierarchical church of any importance at all in the economy of salvation. If salvation was entirely dependent upon the free choice of an inscrutable God, not even the most assiduous exploitation of the sacramental channels of grace could do anything to promote the chances of a single individual. In this Augustine's position shares a common potential with the Pelagianism to which it was diametrically opposed. If pushed to its logical conclusion, Pelagius's fundamentally optimistic appraisal of man's moral capacities, while it need not have eliminated the sacramental channels of grace, would certainly have tended to render their significance marginal, as well as the sacerdotal ministrations upon which they depended; but then neither Augustine nor Pelagius did push these positions to their logical conclusions. And in Augustine's case, that fact is underlined by the doctrinal stance he adopted in his struggle against the Donatists.

The point at issue in that struggle was nothing less critical than the nature of the Christian church itself. In the absence of a comparable confrontation, the theologians of the Eastern church were never nudged into systematizing their understanding of the church. As a result, the ecclesiological thinking of the Eastern Orthodox churches has persistently moved on a more mystical or "spiritual" level than has that of any of the Western churches. The birthplace of Donatism was the North African province where, by Augustine's lifetime, it had split the Christian community into bitterly opposed orthodox and schismatic churches. Its point of departure had been the persecution of Diocletian, under whose pressure some of the clergy had apostatized. After that persecution, a group of zealots including Donatus, the bishop from whom they were later to derive their name, had challenged in particular the authority of Caecilian, bishop of Carthage (on the grounds that he had been ordained by one who had repudiated his faith and lapsed thereby into mortal sin), had questioned in general the validity of sacraments administered by clergy of immoral or unworthy lives, and had adopted the position that the church had forfeited its claim to be holy if it tolerated within its ranks members guilty of the cardinal sin of apostasy or clergy morally unworthy of their high office.

In its implications this was clearly no merely academic dispute but one that raised in very acute form the whole question of the relationship of the church to the world. For the Donatists, inclusiveness was not to be bought at the price of compromise with the morals of ordinary men, universality was a less important criterion for identifying the true church than was holiness, and that holiness was to be judged solely in terms of the moral rigor with which its individual members conducted their lives. The church, therefore, was for them to be a body of the elect, its members, clerical as well as lay, restricted to the ranks of the righteous—it was, in Troeltsch's terms, to be a *sect.* This being so, the Donatists were eventually willing to make the startling claim that their own church, limited though it was to the North African province and schismatic at that, alone could claim to be the one true Catholic church.

When Augustine became bishop in 396, the Donatist movement had reached its peak. It was particularly strong in his own diocese of Hippo and he was to struggle against it for the rest of his life; but the theoretical position he adopted in opposition to it is not an easy one to reconcile with his teaching on grace. The confrontation with Pelagianism led him to state his belief in predestination in a particularly uncompromising form, thus identifying the true church not with any visible fellowship of men but with the invisible body of the elect of which the membership is known only to God. In his confrontation with the Donatists, on the other hand, he stressed the visible, institutional church, present in this world as a hierarchically organized society possessed of the authority to preach the Gospel and administer the sacraments—nothing other, in fact, than the historical Catholic church, the only true Catholic church, holy as well as universal, because through it alone, and irrespective of the worthiness of its ministers, can the Holy Spirit be received. Outside that church, therefore, there could be no salvation. If, strictly speaking, its membership is more inclusive than that of the "essential" or "invisible" church, which is composed exclusively of those truly committed to Christ, it is not God's will that we, like the Donatists, should presume to do what he himself will not undertake to do before the Last Judgment—namely, to separate the wheat from the chaff, the saints from the sinners.

Thus, while in the context of his writings on grace and salvation Augustine was led to define the church as the invisible body of the elect, foreknown to God alone, in the context of his writings against the Donatists he was led to identify the visible church, with its saints and sinners, hierarchy and sacraments, as the true Catholic church and the sole ark of salvation. The medieval church did not attempt to reconcile these two positions. Whereas the teaching on the church that Augustine elaborated in opposition to Donatism was destined to become the prevailing orthodoxy, his views on grace and predestination were admitted only with modifications that served (though they were not necessarily intended so to serve) to bring them into line with that teaching on the church.

The official condemnation of Pelagianism issued by the General Council of Ephesus in 431 did not mean the endorsement of the whole of Augustine's anti-Pelagian teaching. Semi-Pelagian views were reiterated, indeed, on more than one occasion during the course of the fifth century, a fact indicative of the degree to which churchmen were finding it hard to domesticate Augustine's harsh teachings on predestination and irresistible grace within the confines of the Catholic tradition. If semi-Pelagian views were never wholly to disappear, however, it was the semi-Augustinian position adopted by the Council of Orange in 529 and endorsed by Pope Boniface II (530–32) that established the norm of medieval orthodoxy in these matters. Endorsed was Augustine's emphasis on the enduring and devastating impact of Adam's Original Sin on the religious and moral capacities of all his descendants. Endorsed, too, was the assertion that without the prior gift of divine grace man can do nothing to please God, for even the desire to believe is the result of the merciful workings of the Holy Spirit; but the idea that God has predestined some men to evil was roundly condemned and there was no mention of irresistible grace. It clearly lay within man's power, then, to say no to God, and, only a little less clearly, it was suggested that man retained some power to cooperate freely with God's grace and by such cooperation to do at least something to further his own salvation. The council so treated the subject of grace as to stress its sacramental nature and to link its mediation, in particular, with the reception of baptism. "We also believe this . . . that after grace has been received through baptism all the baptized, with the aid and cooperation of Christ, have the power and the duty to perform all things that pertain to the soul's salvation, if they will labour faithfully." [6]

What emerges, then, is a modified version of Augustine's teaching on grace that coheres well with the doctrine of the church he had elaborated during his struggle against the Donatists. It is a version that, while affirming man's inability to engineer his own salvation, attributes to him the power—and burdens him, therefore, with the responsibility —of cooperating with the workings of divine grace. This version, while affirming the necessity of that grace, goes a long way toward confining its dispensation to those channels of grace called sacraments, which were the possession of the Catholic church alone and which to be efficacious had in most cases to be administered by one of that small ordained minority within the church that constituted its priesthood. It was this version of Augustinianism, packaged and popularized in the West by the influential writings of Pope Gregory the Great (590–604) and underpinning the power and prestige of the sacerdotal hierarchy, that was to play so great a role in the history of the medieval world.

The Church and the World

"CONSTANTINIAN REVOLUTION," then, and the acceptance of a modified Augustinian theology—without doubt there were myriad other factors involved, but these go further than any others toward explaining the marginalization during the greater part of the Middle Ages of the sectarian impulse so evident in early Christianity and the emergence instead of the form of religious society that Troeltsch called "church-type" Christianity and which he believed to have been exemplified most purely in medieval Christendom. What was made possible thereby was something that no aloof, exclusive, sectarian form of Christianity could have attempted, nor, indeed, would have wished to attempt: nothing less than the reaching out to embrace the half-pagan barbarian West, to remold it in the Christian image, and finally to transform it into a new quasi-sacral society, the medieval civilization that reached its peak in the thirteenth century and that we tend to regard as quintessentially Christian.

Over the centuries, as many or more have lamented the decline of that civilization as have applauded its demise. Certainly, few today would wish in any way to minimize the splendor of its achievement. In matters economic as well as artistic, political as well as intellectual, technological as well as literary or musical, the range and stature of that achievement is not to be gainsaid. What can be questioned, however, is the degree to which it can be claimed to embody fully any truly Christian ethos. For every piece of territory won, after all, a price was exacted. For every opportunity to exert influence on society at large, some moral or religious ground had to be conceded. For every move away from the closed world of sectarian exclusiveness, the Christian church had to open itself to the distorting influences of the society it aspired to comprehend and reshape. According to Troeltsch it was church-type Christianity alone that had "the power to stir the masses in any real and lasting way"; but to do so it had itself to respond to the hopes and fears of popular belief and the urgencies of popular need. It had, in short, to compromise its principles; but to what degree, and how compromising a compromise?

From the vantage points either of the pre-Constantinian church or of the Christian churches in the modern world, it is tempting to reply that the church was indeed too much at home in medieval society, that it had adjusted its own ideals to those embodied in that society to a degree that was altogether too compromising. Evidence to that effect, after all, abounds. Even the monasteries, themselves the products of a sectarian reaction to the dilution of Christian fervor in the Constantinian and immediately post-Constantinian era, did not escape the fate common to the church at large. From the seventh to the tenth centuries, the Celtic and Benedictine monasteries played a very noble role in the evangelization of western Europe and in the maintenance of learning, but the world was very much with them and they ceased, by and large, to be communities that fostered any sort of deeply personal religion. At worst, they were subjected to wanton exploitation at the hands of lay

66

abbots. At best, they became communities that existed to serve the familial and spiritual needs of their aristocratic founders and benefactors, providing a suitably honorable career for landless young sons and unmarriageable daughters and, by their ceaseless round of communal devotions, discharging, as substitutes, the penitential burdens those sponsors found too onerous to sustain themselves. The great monastic reforms that swept across Europe during the eleventh, twelfth, and thirteenth centuries, producing such new orders as the Carthusians and Cistercians, the Franciscans and Dominicans, did much to restore the original sectarian vigor of the monastic impulse; but few monasteries were capable of sustaining that vigor in any truly enduring fashion. Renewal was followed almost inevitably by compromise and decline, and it is perhaps symptomatic of the final confused state of medieval monasticism that Martin Luther, himself in many ways the product of a rigorist reform within his own order of Augustinian Eremites, was first moved to challenge the corrupt religious practices of his day by his outrage at the bland willingness of a Dominican friar to attribute to indulgences, in an unorthodox but widely tolerated fashion, what amounted to a magical efficacy.

Yet so much that was pure in medieval Christianity, so much that was rigorous and uncompromising, was the contribution of monastic leaders—from Gregory I to the great abbots of Cluny, from St. Bernard of Clairvaux to St. Francis of Assisi and St. Dominic. In the church at large the degree of accommodation to the beliefs and practices of society was much more striking. On the missionary front, the practice of substituting Christian feasts for seasonal pagan celebrations, churches for pagan shrines, and the cult of some Christian saint for that of a local spirit or deity may well have been regarded as shrewd tactics,[7] but the price paid was for centuries a larger one than we usually tend to suspect. The African Christians of Augustine's day regarded it as a devout practice "to take meal-cakes and bread and wine to the shrines of the saints in their memorial days," and his mother, Monica, abandoned the practice only when they went to Milan where Bishop Ambrose, recognizing it for what it was—a survival in barely Christianized guise of the ancient cult of the dead—had forbidden it.[8] Certainly, in the years after the barbarian invasions, it is doubtful

67

whether bishops even of Ambrose's stature, confronted by less sophisticated flocks, would even have attempted to impose so ambitious a prohibition. Popular Christianity already embodied too many quasi-pagan practices. It was to continue to do so for centuries, as is testified by the intensity of the medieval cult of relics. Modern sociological investigations, indeed, have raised serious doubts about the degree to which some of the more remote rural areas in Catholic western Europe can ever be said to have been Christianized at all. As one might expect of a society that was overwhelmingly agrarian, the old nature religion, with its sense of the indwelling of the divine in the natural world, its rites for the promotion of fertility, and its nostrums for the prevention of natural disasters, proved to be very robust indeed. Half-understood remnants of such beliefs and practices, after all, survived in European legend and folklore right down into the nineteenth century, and some of the more speculative students of the early modern witchcraft craze have argued (admittedly, without great success) that those who were accused by their Christian prosecutors of participating in the obscenities of Satan worship were adherents, instead, of surviving versions of the old nature religion and were reenacting what were, in fact, fertility rites of pre-Christian provenance.

In ancient times—and in the Celtic and Germanic worlds as well as the Mediterranean—kings had played a prominent role in the various forms of nature religion, held responsible by virtue of their sacral status or even of their own divinity for the rotation of the seasons, the fertility of the land, and the general prosperity of their subjects. Such ideas, too, long survived the conversion of the European peoples to Christianity. As late as 1527, King Gustaf Wasa could complain bitterly at a meeting of the representative assembly that "the Swedish peasants of Dalarna blamed him if bad weather prevailed, as if he were a god and not a man." [9] The tenacious belief in the healing power of the royal touch—a claim officially asserted on behalf of the French and English monarchs right down to the eighteenth century—would have been inconceivable apart from the survival into the Middle Ages of pre-Christian notions about the sacred status of kings. It would have been inconceivable, too, apart from the willingness of the leading

68

clergy to domesticate such notions within the boundaries of ecclesiastical approval, even if to do so meant stretching the framework of Christian belief itself. For the late Roman and Byzantine churches, Eusebius's influential imperial theology was the pivotal manifestation of that willingness. For western Europe, it was the papal recognition in 751 of the Carolingian claim to the Frankish throne and the subsequent spread of the rite of royal unction (anointing with holy oil). This rite, adapted to Christian purposes especially for baptism and the ordination of priests, had played an important role in ancient Near Eastern and Hebrew ceremonials and in ancient practice had been used to effect the transfer of a person from the realm of the profane to that of the sacred. In the West it became part of the elaborate liturgical ceremonies that the clergy constructed around the coronation of kings, and it was considered to be a sacrament comparable to the consecration of bishops, one that conferred a sacral status on the king and incorporated him in some sense within the body of the clergy. It is hardly surprising, then, that Charlemagne was portrayed by his propagandists as a new Moses, a new David, a new Solomon, one who had every right to govern in religious as well as secular matters, and one whom the assembled clerics of his kingdom had properly acclaimed in 794 as "king and priest."

There can be few more dramatic examples than this of the type of compromising accommodation that the Christian church was forced to make when it undertook a civilizing mission and reached out to comprehend and reshape a whole society—the less so in that the Gregorian reformers of the eleventh century themselves came to the conclusion that the price being paid was too high and launched their frontal attack on the whole tradition of "pontifical kingship." That accommodation was so successfully made and that tradition so firmly established, however, that the papacy, which itself had led the onslaught, succumbed in the twelfth and thirteenth centuries to many of its allures. The popes of the High Middle Ages emerged very much as sacral monarchs, the true medieval successors of the Roman emperors, claiming many of the attributes of those emperors and using some of their titles, surrounded by their ceremonial, wearing their regalia, and ruling a highly politicized church via a centralizing bureaucracy and in accordance with a law modeled on that of Rome.

The degree to which the medieval church had compromised its principles is evident, moreover, in matters not only ideological but also moral and practical. The turbulent martial energies of a warrior nobility were wedded to the oddly un-Christian ideal of holy war and consecrated by the constant preaching of Crusades. The popular anti-Semitism, which the Crusading movement helped stimulate in Europe and which some of the higher clergy fought to restrain, was in some degree legitimated by Innocent III's ruling in 1215 that Jews should wear distinctive clothing. The financial needs of rulers were acknowledged at the expense of the local churches by the ultimate willingness of the popes to share with kings the spoils of ecclesiastical appointments and (though in this they had less choice) the proceeds of papal taxation.

Nor are these judgments simply retrospective. The ecclesiastical reforms that dominated the history of the late eleventh century sponsored a revival of the Donatist vision of a church of the pure, the essentially sectarian vision of a church composed exclusively of the committed and the saintly set against the manifest evils and corruption of the world. The ultimate failure of those reforms to attain their goal actually extended that vision and led to the emergence of an underground current of opposition to official ecclesiastical pretensions. The religious calm of the later medieval centuries, therefore, was repeatedly shattered by the appearance of sectarian movements—sometimes simply antiestablishmentarian, frequently, however, antisacerdotal and heretical, claiming to assert a truly Christian witness in face of the massive corruptions of an official hierarchical church, which, it was said, in embracing the world so eagerly, had betrayed the ideals of its master and prostituted itself to Antichrist. The call for a return to apostolic simplicity, issued in the late twelfth century by Peter Waldo of Lyon and repeated during the following centuries by those followers of his who became known to the authorities as the "Waldensian heretics," represents this type of movement at its purest. The doomed struggle during the fourteenth century of the "Spiritual" or radical wing of the Franciscans to recall the more relaxed majority of the order back to the purity of their founder's commitment to apostolic poverty represents it at its most poignant.

One could go on. The amount of criticism heaped upon the church during these later medieval centuries was enormous. By no means all of it, however, emanated from those who, by embracing doctrines now denounced as heretical, had placed themselves beyond the pale of the official church. From the early fourteenth century onward, programs for reforming the church "in head and members" became so common as to constitute almost a distinct genre in the ecclesiastical literature. There was little that the Protestant propagandists of the sixteenth century would subsequently say about ecclesiastical corruption that they could not have found (if, indeed, they had not themselves actually found it) in those earlier reforming programs—many of them, it should be noted, the work of men highly placed in the ranks of the clerical hierarchy. And that fact tells us something very important about the degree to which the church-type Christianity of the Middle Ages did succeed in imposing its ideals upon the civilization of the era; for whatever its barbarisms, its corruptions, its malformations, whatever its evasions and dishonesties, in the medieval church men and women still contrived, it would seem, to encounter the Gospel. Few aspects of their lives went entirely untouched by that encounter, and few areas in their society were not, at one level or another, reshaped by it. If, in a history of the medieval church, it would be entirely proper to focus on the distortions in belief and corruptions in practice that the church suffered because of its aspirations to universality and its openness to society, any attempt to comprehend the significance of the medieval experience in the development of Western civilization must turn attention instead to the changes that Christianity wrought in the lives and thinking of medieval people—and at so heavy a price.

More than once in the chapters that follow, it will be argued that the roots of so much that is singular about modern Western civilization lie in those changes, in the new forms created by compromises between the pre-Christian order and ideas and practices of Christian provenance. Those compromises, it is true, were doubtless the occasion of much of the restlessness that characterized medieval civilization and of much of the instability that was to occasion its decline. Had a more purely sectarian form of Christianity prevailed, leaving the greater part of society untouched, or had a more purely Christian order somehow been established, the reasons for much of that instability would have been lacking; but, then, before we slide into nostalgia for a past that never was, perhaps we should ask ourselves to what degree the very dynamism and vitality of Western civilization was the outcome of that critical, if deplorable, instability. Nowhere, perhaps, is that question more forcefully posed than by the history of medieval economic life.

MAKING AND DOING

The Nature of Mediaeval
Economic Life

For the last five thousand years or so, perhaps longer, the greater part of mankind has supported itself by farming the land or by herding domesticated livestock. This first became true when the bulk of men in the rain-watered lands as well as in the irrigated river valleys had turned from a life of hunting and gathering to one sustained by planned food production. It may well cease to be so in our own century, for our age is already distinguished from those that have gone before by the size of the minority that does not find its livelihood in agricultural work, the speed with which that minority has been growing, and the means by which most of those who comprise it support themselves—namely, by engaging in commercial, industrial, or related urbanized occupations. Before the First World War, only the countries in the west European heartland of the industrial revolution had seen the bulk of their populations abandon agriculture for essentially urban modes of occupation. By the Second World War, however, that shift had become a commonplace not only in the highly industrialized countries of western Europe but also in Japan, the United States, the USSR, and elsewhere. Since the war, moreover, efforts in the developing or underdeveloped countries to sponsor modernization and, with it, the industrialization and technological complexity that lies at its core, have accelerated the growth of urbanized minorities in the midst of populations that are still predominantly agrarian.

No one today is likely to gainsay the importance of this change. Implying as it does "a mutation in the economic and social life of mankind comparable in magnitude with the Neolithic transition from predation to agriculture and animal husbandry," [1] its truly historic significance is evident; so, too, is that of its underlying cause: the

75

industrial revolution that began in England in the eighteenth century; that spread in a somewhat uneven fashion during the nineteenth century to continental Europe, North America, Japan, and some countries beyond; and the continuing progress of which across the face of the globe it has been the concern of governments and development economists alike to promote and guide. Indeed, the very difficulties that economic planners have encountered in their efforts to sponsor modernization and industrialization in underdeveloped countries have conspired to focus attention on the conditions—political, social, and intellectual—that made possible the original success of those processes in Europe. The 1960s, after all, were to have constituted the "decade of development." By a combination of sophisticated planning, generous extension of credits or infusions of aid, and skillful manipulation of the means of production and exchange, it was hoped that numerous countries throughout the underdeveloped world might be nudged across the "sound barrier of capital accumulation" that separates dynamic from static economies. The "decade of development" is now over, but as the richer countries continue to become richer and the poor (despite impressive growth) relatively poorer, its results have not been such as to encourage optimism—all the more reason, then, to wonder how it was that western Europe in the eighteenth and nineteenth centuries succeeded in making spontaneously what appears to have been the same transition, and how it did so without the benefit of coherent planning, the stimulus of economic aid, or the encouragement provided by the example of a successful predecessor.

One would have to be very bold indeed to claim sufficiency for any explanation of a historical development at once so vast and intricate as the industrial revolution; but among the numerous partial explanations commonly advanced, one stands out as clearly fundamental. It concerns the contrast in technological maturity and economic wealth between the Europe of the period immediately preceding the industrial revolution and the preindustrial regions of the world today. Defining the industrial revolution as "the first historical instance of the breakthrough from an agrarian, handicraft economy to one dominated by industry and machine manufacture," David S. Landes has described its "heart" as an interrelated succession of technological changes. The material changes took place in three areas: (1) there was a substitution of mechanical devices for human skill; (2) inanimate power—in particular, steam—took the place of human and animal strength; (3) there was a marked improvement in the getting and working of raw materials, especially in what are now known as the metallurgical and chemical industries. Concomitant with these changes in equipment and process went new forms of industrial organization.

He has also argued that long before the industrial revolution western Europe had made "substantial . . . progress" in the direction of the critical technological changes described, that its economy (in part as a result) had long since passed the subsistence level, that over the centuries it had succeeded, therefore, in accumulating a considerable body of capital, that it was, in fact, "already rich . . . by comparison with other parts of the world of that day and with the pre-industrial world of today." [2]

Whatever the attraction, then, of historical parallelisms, it is not quite proper to regard western Europe on the eve of the industrial revolution as an underdeveloped region in quite the same sense as the preindustrial nations of our own day. If income per capita may be taken as an adequate indicator, a better comparison would lie with the semi-industrialized states of the Latin American world. Thus, in terms of real buying power, the English income per capita in 1750 seems to have been about the same as it is today in Brazil but between three and four times what it is in India. Moreover, the really very high level that western European income per capita had reached by the mid-eighteenth century represents the culmination of a gradual but very considerable rise—perhaps even a tripling—over the course of the preceding thousand years.[3] In any attempt, then, to explain why it fell to western Europe to be the first to make the critical breakthrough to full-scale industrialization and the self-sustaining and cumulative technological growth that appears to be its inevitable concomitant, it becomes necessary to inquire into the deeper roots of European economic vitality and, as a result, to address ourselves to the nature of medieval economic life. At once we confront a puzzle; for the Middle Ages ended, as they had begun, in deep economic depression.

Economic Contraction in the
Early Middle Ages

[It is] a world every day better known, better cultivated, and more civilized than before. Everywhere roads are traced, every district is known, every country opened to commerce. Smiling fields have invaded the forests; flocks and herds have routed the wild beasts; the very sands are sown; the rocks are planted; the marshes drained. There are now as many cities as there were once solitary cottages. Reefs and shoals have lost their terrors. Wherever there is a trace of life there are houses and human habitations, well-ordered governments and civilized life.[4]

The words are those of Tertullian, the great North African theologian. They refer to the conditions of life in the Roman Empire toward the end of the second century of the Christian Era—toward the end, that is, of almost two centuries of peace and order during which the Roman world reached the peak of its economic development. They support Edward Gibbon's claim that "notwithstanding the propensity of mankind to exalt the past and depreciate the present, the tranquil and prosperous state of the empire was warmly felt and honestly confessed by the provincials as well as Romans." [5]

The contrast, it must be confessed, with conditions in western Europe some seven centuries later could scarcely have been more complete. By that time peace had long since ceased to be even a distant memory, prosperity had become an impossible dream, and the collapse of public order occasioned by the third wave of barbarian invasions had accelerated an already long-established drift into economic self-sufficiency. Commerce and craft industry had not totally disappeared; they may even have expanded somewhat along the shores of the Baltic and the North Sea, where some rudimentary towns had appeared. They also survived, though at a vastly reduced rate, in Italy and along the shores of the western Mediterranean where, even after the disintegration of the Western empire, the continuity of city life and urban occupations was never entirely broken. Everywhere, however, even in those regions distinguished by the survival of remnants of commercial and industrial activity, agrarian pursuits dominated to a degree that would have been hard to predict in Tertullian's lifetime. Everywhere, moreover, such pursuits were geared less to the production of the food surpluses needed to sustain substantial numbers of people engaged in nonagricultural occupations than simply to survival. Nor was survival easily won. The population decline that the influx of barbarians did not succeed in reversing was balanced by a decline in the level of agricultural technique. It was balanced, too, by the impossibility of exploiting land efficiently when political conditions were such that every small district, whatever the problems of its terrain, had to strive for self-sufficiency in its food supply. In the absence of such other cheap carbohydrates as rice and potatoes, bread was the staple diet; and that meant assigning the greater part of the cultivable land to the raising of grain, however improbable the conditions of the climate and however poor the quality of the soil.

It is not surprising, then, that contemporary sources stress the depressed conditions of the age, or that available figures on the yield of cereals confirm that story, and do so, as Robert S. Lopez has pointed out, "with a terrible eloquence."

Under the late Roman Republic and early Empire, the average yield on the Italian peninsula was four times the seed, with peak harvests above ten times the seed in the better soils of Sicily and Tuscany; much later, in thirteenth-century England, a three-fold yield was regarded as unprofitable unless prices were unusually inflated; but in the Carolingian period . . . , the largest harvests on record were just above twice the seed, the lowest areas fell below one and a half times the seed. This means that at least one half of the cultivated area served merely to produce seed. No doubt hunting, fishing, dairy-products, and vegetables grown in well-manured backyards supplemented the diet; but it is no wonder that in a society where bread was so scarce and uncertain the term "keeper of loaves," *hlaford*, came to mean, in Anglo-Saxon, "master" or *lord*.[6]

No less eloquent are the grave finds from the period that have yielded skeletons whose deformed bones witness to the inroads of diseases of malnutrition of the type still found today in parts of the underdeveloped world—a type of indicator lacking in most of the grave finds that can be dated with any degree of confidence to the Roman era. Under the economic and political conditions of the day, the margin of safety against the destruction wrought by natural calamity or public disorder, however local, must clearly have been a very narrow one. Under such conditions, it seems, famine was not necessarily any less fatal in effect for being localized in extent.

Because the contrast in economic conditions between the first and second centuries on the one hand and the eighth and ninth on the other appears in so dramatic a light, historians were once prone to seek the explanation in some catastrophic transformation wrought by the rapid political changes of those centuries. Both the first wave of barbarian invasions culminating in the collapse of the Western Roman Empire and then the later Muslim conquest of so much of the Mediterranean world were cast in the role of culprit. After decades of controversy, however, the inclination is now, without denying the importance of either of those events, to stress the continuous and gradual nature of economic decline and to push its beginnings well back into the Roman period—as far back, indeed, as the golden age that Tertullian described with such enthusiasm. Certainly, already in the second century, as the Roman world achieved greater uniformity and provincials learned to make themselves the industrial products previously imported from Italy or elsewhere, there is observable a decline in interprovincial trade and a tendency toward regional economic self-sufficiency. The crippling taxation, fiscal confusion, famine, and general economic dislocation occasioned by the military anarchy of the third century pushed the process a good deal further, as did the periodic visitations of plague that began in 180 and continued until the mid-sixth century. The draconian measures of social and political regimentation to which Diocletian and Constantine resorted in their attempts to stave off disaster did little to slow down the process and much to sap still further the waning vitality of the cities. With the cities in full decay, especially in the West, commerce declined still further, and that decline continued throughout the fourth and fifth centuries.

Nor did agriculture lack its own quota of tribulation. The type of intensive dry farming originally pursued with such sophistication in the light soils of Greece and Italy proved ill suited to the wetter climate and richer but heavier soils of northern and western Europe. Even in

80

Greece and Italy overcropping and deforestation had led by the fourth century to widespread soil exhaustion, to the erosion of upland slopes, and to the creation of malarial swamps in some of the lowlands. Moreover, the gradual impoverishment of the small independent farmer, already underway in Italy in the second century B.C., had reached such proportions by the time of Constantine that the bulk of the farming population, freemen as well as slaves, were now concentrated in the *villae* or huge estates of the great landowners. These great estates, which had their own artisans as well as farm laborers, their tenants cultivating land for themselves as well as their dependent laborers working the land at the behest of the owner, increasingly aspired to self-sufficiency, thereby accelerating the decline of commerce. Despite the fact that they were managed with profit in mind, whereas the medieval manor of the ninth and tenth centuries was forced to concentrate on survival, they are recognizable as in many ways its forebears.

The economic depression so evident in the early Middle Ages, then, was long in the making—so long, indeed, that it is tempting to dismiss the Roman economy as itself a sick economy. But to do so would be to slip into a serious error of perspective. That economy appears, after all, to have been the most successful one the Mediterranean and Middle Eastern world had known, and the wealth and power of Byzantium during the early Middle Ages bear witness to the enduring strengths of the Roman economic system at least in the more urbanized eastern provinces of the empire. Whatever its strengths, however, it is necessary to be conscious also of its limitations if one is to appreciate the true significance of the medieval economic achievement later on.

There was nothing exceptional about those limitations—nothing, at least, if we keep antique attitudes and conditions in mind. Given the availability of slave labor it is perhaps understandable that there was so little exploitation of mechanical power in industry even when, as in the case of the water mill, the necessary machinery had been devised and had proved its efficiency. Given the intensive garden-type cultivation prevailing in the Mediterranean world and the lack of large amounts of readily available pasture land, it is understandable, too, that animal power was underexploited in Roman agriculture. In any case, it is unwise to take for granted the efficiency with which, for example, men had learned to utilize horsepower, both for transportation and for agricultural work, by the end of the nineteenth century. It was not until about 900 B.C., after all, that riding on horseback had become at all common; a thousand years later, the Romans were still riding without benefit of stirrups and their horses were cantering even in rocky terrain without the protection afforded by that humane (but later) invention, the nailed, metal horseshoe. Like their more ancient predecessors, moreover, the Romans harnessed horses in so inefficient a fashion as to preclude their use for plowing and severely to limit their value for road haulage. Rather than the modern rigid horse collar, which permits the horse to breathe freely even when exerting its full weight, they used a type of yoke harness that worked well enough for oxen but was ill suited to horses—so ill suited, indeed, that modern experiments have demonstrated the ability of a team of horses equipped with the collar harness to pull between four and five times the weight it can pull when equipped with the old yoke harness. This, coupled with the fact that for road haulage the Romans relied mainly on two-wheeled vehicles, helps explain the startling fact that bulky products, when they could not be moved by water, more than doubled their price for every hundred miles hauled overland.

It has been argued, moreover, that whatever their cost and however frequent the incidence of localized dearth at the time of their construction, the width and some of the gradients of the Roman roads reveal them to have been designed to serve military goals rather than to promote the cheaper haulage of goods. That fact witnesses eloquently to the condescension with which the Romans, like the Greeks before them, viewed commerce. Trade was simply not a fit occupation for anyone who aspired to be a gentleman. It was specifically prohibited to members of the senatorial class, and the objective of those enriched by it was frequently to cover their tracks by purchasing land and putting their money into agriculture.

Given these limitations, then, which were coupled with inadequate financing and primitive credit arrangements, it is not surprising that the Roman economy, however successful it may have been in comparison with its ancient predecessors, was not a growth economy.

Its goal was stability, and, for all the magnificence of Roman public life, stability at a level not so very far above subsistence. In this, again, it was not exceptional but represented something close to the ancient norm in economic matters. What was exceptional, instead, was the comparative dynamism of the medieval economy from the eleventh to the fourteenth centuries—so exceptional, indeed, after the severe economic contraction of the era of invasions, that historians have not hesitated to speak about "the agricultural revolution" of the early Middle Ages and "the commercial revolution" of the High Middle Ages. They have done so in all sobriety and without hyperbole, and there need be no hesitation about following their example.

Agricultural Revolution and Population Boom

DEVELOPMENT economists disagree about many things, not least about the role of agriculture in the drive toward modernization, toward industrial revolution, toward the achievement of sustained economic growth. By no means all would agree with W. W. Rostow's claim that "revolutionary changes in agricultural productivity are an essential condition for successful [economic] take-off";[7] but the importance of at least the eighteenth-century agricultural revolution to England's prototypical industrial revolution can scarcely be gainsaid. Similarly, though medieval Europe never broke through to the type of sustained economic growth that has characterized modern industrialized countries, the centrality of its own agricultural revolution to the unprecedented measure of growth that characterized its economic life is certain. In its absence, the reversal in the long-established downward demographic trend that had already occurred in the tenth century could not have led to the sustained population increase that persisted right up to the fourteenth century. An increase in the number of mouths to be fed calls necessarily for an increase in the supply of food; but an enlargement of the available labor force does not necessarily mean a proportionate enlargement of the food supply. In any event, during the tenth, eleventh, and twelfth centuries, there was more than a proportionate increase in the food supply. Agricultural productivity went up; so, too, did the nutritional value of the food produced. The food surpluses necessary to sustain a more vital town life and to support a larger and more significant segment of the population in the nonagrarian occupations of industry and commerce were created. If the history of this obscure but critical change could ever be fully written, it would be in large part a repetitive chronicle of a thousand and one small, highly localized but cumulatively vital experiments, adaptations, and adjustments in the traditional routines of rural life. At the risk of the type of massive simplification in which, by a sort of professional masochism, historians find it at once both necessary and painful to indulge, two major developments may be selected as crucial to the whole process. The first is the occupation and agricultural exploitation during these centuries of a vast amount of new land; the second, the marked improvement in agricultural techniques that manifested itself during the same period.

The first of these developments involved both external and internal colonization. To the east it meant the organized settlement of German migrants in the Slavic lands beyond the Elbe; to the far west, the Scandinavian settlement of Iceland and of part of Greenland. To the north it meant the draining of coastal marshes and the recovery of cultivable land from the sea; to the south, the reclamation in Italy of lands once farmed but since lost to second-growth timber or degraded into swamps. In the heartland of northwestern Europe it meant encroachment upon the untouched forest that surrounded existing settlements and the extension of agriculture into virgin land, much of it extremely fertile. This process of colonization was itself enough greatly to increase agricultural production; but much of it would have been forbiddingly difficult and production accordingly lower had it not gone hand in hand with improved techniques of cultivation.

Whereas the older techniques of Roman agronomy were adequate for the challenge presented by the dry, light soils of the Mediterranean world, many of the most promising and fertile regions of north and northwestern Europe were alluvial lowlands where the soils were rich and heavy and presented to the would-be cultivator a challenge of an entirely different order. Because of this, during the pre-Roman and

84

Roman periods, agriculture in the north had been confined to the lighter upland soils where the natural drainage was better. Improvements in techniques during the early Middle Ages, however, gradually made it easier to extend the cultivated area to include much of the richer land. They made it possible also to cultivate more land with less labor, to increase the yield on the land cultivated, and, through diversification of crops, to improve the level of nutrition enjoyed by the general population.

The improvements in question involved changes in the animals and tools employed in agricultural work, changes in the rotation of crops, and changes in the nature of the crops grown. These innovations were multiple and their adoption was gradual and subject to national, regional, and even local variation. It is, accordingly, well-nigh impossible to chart in detail the whole complex process of change. Three fundamental innovations, however, having made their appearance somewhat earlier, were adopted widely across northern and northwestern Europe during the period running from the ninth to the thirteenth centuries.

The first of these was the replacement of the older scratch plow, which was effective enough in the lighter and drier soils of the Mediterranean world (where, indeed, it continued to be used), by the heavy-wheeled plow equipped with plowshare, colter, and moldboard, designed not merely to burrow through the soil but to cut into and under the turf and turn it over. A powerful tool, it not only saved labor by eliminating the second cross-plowing of the field—needed when the old scratch plow was used—but also reduced immensely the difficulty of expanding cultivation into the heavier and richer soils to which that older plow had not been well suited. Its drawback was the increased amount of animal power required to pull it through the earth. Given the general scarcity of fodder, medievals found it very hard to maintain livestock through the winter and plow teams of eight oxen were expensive to support. It has been speculated that the use of the new plow accelerated the clustering of the peasantry into the cooperative village communities we associate with the manorial system, communities that were organized for collective survival, characteristically replacing the individually demarcated square fields with huge and

85

unfenced open fields, sharing in common pasture lands and woods, and pooling their plow teams for communal use.

The second major innovation was the gradual introduction of plow teams made up of horses, more rapid than teams of oxen and capable, under proper conditions, of greater endurance. This innovation became possible with the introduction and adoption of three pieces of equipment unknown to the Romans: the nailed horseshoe, the rigid horse collar, and the tandem harness, all of which enabled a plow team of horses to exert its full strength and to prove its greater efficiency. Some idea of that greater efficiency may be conveyed by the findings of modern agronomists who have calculated that for a day's work a horse is only two-thirds as expensive as an ox.

Of course, in making such calculations, those agronomists have had in mind breeds of horses probably more powerful than those available in the early Middle Ages. Moreover, they have not had in mind the greater difficulty that medieval farmers encountered in trying to feed any type of horse properly. Oxen feed on grass; horses do best if oats are included in their diet. Oats had been a weed to Virgil, and, as was the case with rye (which had also entered Europe as a weed mixed with wheat), its cultivation was not developed until the introduction of the last of the three major innovations during the Middle Ages: the more or less gradual replacement in northern Europe of the two- by the three-field system of crop rotation. Under the two-field system, the arable land was typically divided into halves with one half in any given year planted in autumn with winter wheat and the other half left fallow, though plowed at least once to keep down weeds. Under the three-field system, the same land would be divided into thirds, with one third planted in autumn with winter wheat (or rye), the second third planted the next spring with oats or legumes, and the remaining third left fallow, though again plowed at least once to keep down weeds. Where the nature of the soil and climate permitted the adoption of this latter system, less land had to lie fallow and more could be given over to crops in any given year without risk of degrading the soil. Without any additional plowing, then, there was a significant increase in the quantity of food produced. In the second place, the diversification of crops that the system involved permitted raising the oats needed to feed horses properly. In the third place, that same diversification, which increased the amounts of vegetable protein available, cannot but have improved the level of nutrition enjoyed by the population—hence also, or so it must be presumed, the level of its energy, its resistance to illness, and its general vitality.[8]

These three innovations in agricultural techniques, though fundamental, were by no means the only ones that occurred during the medieval centuries. It was only in the Middle Ages that large amounts of iron came to be employed in the fashioning of agricultural tools, and its use made them not only more durable but also more efficient. Again, along with the increasing use of horsepower went also an increasing use of the toothed harrow, which, to be effective in breaking up clods of earth, had to be pulled across the ground quite rapidly. Moreover, from the fourth century onward, the use of the hinged flail began to spread, and great claims have been made for the degree to which it served to enhance productivity.[9] Finally, the startling multiplication first of water mills and then of windmills magnified still further the drive to save human labor and to replace it by animal or mechanical sources of power that is so striking a feature of the medieval agricultural revolution; without it the food surpluses necessary to sustain the growing population involved in urbanized activities could not have been achieved. Those surpluses were achieved, however; industry and commerce did grow, and the exploitation of water and wind power had an economic importance that reached far beyond the agricultural sector.

The Commercial Revolution of the
High Middle Ages

THROUGHOUT western Europe, the increase in agricultural productivity, the creation of food surpluses, and the rise in population was accompanied by a marked quickening of urban life. Old urban centers began to grow; new ones were established. Artisans who had previously functioned in the comparative isolation of the manors now began to cluster in the towns and to address themselves to the needs of much larger groups of customers. Everywhere there began to emerge or reemerge the division of function between urban manufacturers and rural food producers that seems so much a matter of common sense today. Everywhere, too, the exploitation of water or wind power for industrial as well as agricultural purposes became increasingly common. Thus there were mills used for operating the hammers of forges or the bellows of blast furnaces, mills designed for crushing ore, mills for sawing, for tanning, for fulling cloth, and so on.

Nowhere, however, not even in Flanders or northern Italy—the regions that constituted the industrial heartland of medieval Europe—did the rate of mechanization or production even approximate that attained later on during the industrial revolution. However vital when compared with that achieved by Rome, industrial activity in general remained nonetheless at the craft level. It was undercapitalized, undermechanized, organized in small units, concerned more with the security and predictability of its returns than with the lure of dramatic profit, content with the prospect of modest and very gradual growth, geared to stability, and closely regulated to secure that end. A few industries broke out of that pattern, notably the wool industries of Flanders, Italy, and England and the silk industry of Italy. They did so by the sheer amounts they produced, the comparatively huge numbers of workers they employed, and the extent to which they achieved specialization and division of labor in their manufacturing processes. They did so, too, by virtue of the fact that they developed into capitalist industries, the ownership of the materials remaining in the hands of the employers, the workers transformed into a wage-earning and frequently discontented proletariat. Thus a contemporary chronicler, himself a cloth merchant, wrote that the Florentine wool industry was capable of producing at least seventy thousand pieces of cloth in a single year and of employing no fewer than thirty thousand people, approximately one-third of the whole Florentine population.

These are striking figures indeed. They help explain why the medieval textile industry has attracted so much attention from historians; but they should not encourage us to think in terms of modern factory production or of the type of mechanization characteristic of the industrial revolution. The work was done instead in a multitude of independent workshops. It had been accelerated, it is true, by the introduction of pedal looms and spinning wheels, but water power was used only for the fulling process. Such figures, then, should not serve to deflect our attention from the sector of the economy that did indeed undergo revolutionary change between the tenth and fourteenth centuries; for without that change, the unquestionable successes of the Flemish and Italian cloth industries would have been altogether inconceivable.

The sector in question is that of commerce. Given the subsequent development of the European economy in the modern era, that fact should occasion no surprise. "One of the ways—the commonest way perhaps—by which an economy can develop from a pre-industrial into an industrial economy is to exploit the opportunities open to it from international trade." [10] Far from forming an exception to that generalization, medieval (and early modern) Europe constitutes its prototypical confirmation, and a very striking one at that. No one today would claim that long-distance trade had entirely collapsed by the ninth century, but all would agree that compared with the trade of the Roman era it had been reduced to a trickle. All would agree, too, that by the thirteenth century such trade had far surpassed that of Rome, even in its heyday, and that it had surpassed that trade not only in its bulk but also in its complexity and organization, which had reached a degree of sophistication never before attained—a truly remarkable success story of which it is possible to convey in brief only the broadest of outlines.

If the achievement of agricultural surpluses and the beginnings of population growth were the main prerequisites for the recovery of urban life and the revival of commerce, the principal determinants of the shape that medieval commerce was to take were the growth in population and importance of north and northwest Europe and the vigor and enterprise shown by several of the Italian seaports in seizing the initiative in the Mediterranean.

The Italian seaport towns had never abandoned their trading contacts with Byzantium—nor, directly or indirectly, with Muslim Africa and the Levant. During the ninth, tenth, and eleventh centuries, first Venice and Amalfi, and then Genoa and Pisa, were able to intensify their trade with Byzantium and to establish their combined naval supremacy in the Mediterranean. Even before 1095, when the first Crusade was preached, these four towns had succeeded in gaining commercial privileges in both Byzantine and African coastal towns; but it is clear that successive Crusades enabled them to extend those privileges, to increase their profits, and to enlarge their contacts with the rich societies of the Near East.

At the same time, the mounting population of north and northwest Europe provided a market for southern and Oriental goods larger in scope than anything that had existed during the Roman era. The Flemish seaports were the end points of trade routes leading to England, Scandinavia, and north Germany, and the early development of the textile industry in Flanders itself (the first region to produce reasonably priced, fine woolen cloth) also stimulated the development of commerce with districts unaffected by the contemporaneous revival of trade in the Mediterranean. As a result, then, Flanders became a commercial and industrial center of sufficient importance to attract the attention of the Italian merchants. Travel by sea being at the start unduly hazardous, the overland routes were most frequented, and during the twelfth and thirteenth centuries the point of contact most favored by northern and southern merchants came to be the great fairs strategically located in Champagne. There, under the protection of the counts of Champagne, Blois, and Chartres, merchants from the north came to dispose of the furs, hides, and raw wool produced by their own region, and Italian merchants, to sell the exotic goods they had imported from the East, most notably silks and luxury items as well as the spices needed to preserve food. In the late thirteenth and early fourteenth centuries, when the Venetians and Genoese succeeded in opening up a seaborne trade route from Italy to England and the Netherlands, the fairs of Champagne went into decline, and the great international fairs of Bruges and (later on) Antwerp replaced them as the principal meeting points for the Italian merchants and the traders of the north—not only Flemings but increasingly German, English, and French.

Despite such internal displacements, the main lines of international trade continued to run between the two great focal points of Italy and northwest Europe throughout the Middle Ages. From each of those focal points subsidiary lines were extended to points near and far—the Italians penetrated into the Black Sea after the Latin conquest of Byzantium in 1204, and, later on in the century with the rise of the Mongol Empire, reached even as far as Peking itself. The achievements of their northern counterparts, if less dramatic, were not wholly dissimilar. By the late thirteenth century, in the absence of a strong imperial authority capable of keeping the princes under control, groups of north German towns were forming leagues for mutual protection and for the extension of their commercial interests. During the fourteenth century, a particularly effective grouping known as the Hanseatic League emerged under the leadership of Lübeck, and for a time it wielded a degree of power that many a king might have envied. Establishing depots at points as far distant as Novgorod to the east and London or Bruges to the west, it brought to fruition the process by which the German merchants had displaced the Scandinavians as the long-distance traders of the northern seas, and during the late fourteenth and fifteenth centuries it secured an effective monopoly of trade in northern products. The items in which it traded—largely raw materials such as timber, wool, hides and furs, and foodstuffs such as grain, fish, and honey—were a good deal less romantic than the luxury goods that, though not constituting the whole of the Mediterranean trade, gave it its particular character. While not the source of vast fortunes, the bulk trade was more representative of the totality of medieval commercial activity, and it should not be forgotten that the items involved had made their way to the larger collection centers and thence to the main thoroughfares of international trade via the more modest efforts of a host of local merchants.

It was one of the great strengths of international commerce in the Middle Ages that it was not merely a big-time trade in luxury goods, however profitable, but was articulated effectively with an increasingly complex infrastructure of localized commercial endeavor and presupposed extensive collaboration with a host of small-time local merchants. By the same token, few areas did not directly or indirectly feel the impact of international trade, with its encouragement of regional specialization in industry and even in agriculture and its progressive disruption of the older ideal of local self-sufficiency. It was an even greater strength of medieval international trade that it first succeeded in calling forth and then, in its full extension and eventual complexity, later presupposed business arrangements, banking operations, and accounting procedures of a degree of flexibility and sophistication hitherto unknown.

Among the factors inhibiting the development of commerce in the Roman era, the prohibitive cost of overland transportation, the undercapitalization of mercantile enterprise, and the sparse and primitive nature of credit arrangements had been prominent. In the first of these areas, the Middle Ages saw real but not particularly dramatic advances. Better harnessing and improvements in the design of carts did reduce overland haulage costs. Neither these improvements, however, nor the improvements in shipping design that began to make their impact in the fourteenth and fifteenth centuries can be compared in either novelty or importance with the great leap forward that occurred in financial operations during the twelfth and thirteenth centuries. That advance was all the more striking in that it had to be made in the teeth of the church's attempted prohibition as usurious of practically every type of loan made at interest; but, then, those teeth were blunted somewhat by the pressing financial needs of the papacy itself which could ill afford to examine too closely the procedures of the bankers whose services it needed to shuttle funds from one part of Europe to another, to help it anticipate its revenues, and to extend it credit from time to time when it had to cope with mounting deficits. In any case, in their efforts to conceal the taking of direct interest, bankers and merchants alike resorted to a whole array of complicated stratagems, and even for the most zealous of investigators the detection of the usurious amid the maze of contractual arrangements could not always have been an easy task.

The innovations made in the world of finance can be grouped under three headings. The first of these includes the broad range of contractual arrangements that had been developed by the thirteenth century and were in use throughout the Mediterranean world though not necessarily in the northern trade. The majority of these contracts, unknown or only hazily anticipated in antiquity, appear to have been medieval inventions, and they made possible not only a rational sharing of risk but also the concentration of capital in the large amounts needed to fuel the ambitious commercial operations that Italian merchants were mounting with increasing frequency in the long-distance trade. Of these new contractual forms, the *commenda* was probably the most important and did much to promote the rapid expansion of the maritime trade. By its terms a wealthy home-based lender undertook the financial risk of putting up the capital for a single, round-trip trading voyage and received, for his pains, the bulk of the profits. In return, the borrower managed the whole enterprise, providing the necessary expertise and undertaking the physical risks of the voyage, receiving for his pains the rest of the profits.

The second group of innovations comprehends the whole complex of banking operations and credit organization that emerged as an offshoot of commerce as merchants built up a surplus of capital and began to put it to work; without those innovations the Mediterranean trade could hardly have attained the flexibility and vitality that distinguished it in the late thirteenth and early fourteenth centuries. By the thirteenth century, it was possible to transfer increasingly large sums of money across Europe by means of letters of exchange and without undertaking the risk of moving actual coinage. During the same century it also became possible, at least in the Mediterranean world, to cut down the risks involved in the maritime trade by purchasing insurance. By the end of the century, many Italian merchants had entered the business of commercial banking and a few were specializing in it, maintaining agents in the principal cities of Europe, receiving deposits at one place and paying out at another when their depositors asked them to do so, acting as financial agents for papal and royal governments alike, amassing enviable amounts of capital, making available the large-scale credit that big commercial operations needed, and, though at much higher risk, advancing the huge, high-interest loans upon which the realization of royal ambitions increasingly depended.[11]

The mounting complexity of the financial arrangements involved in commerce and banking demanded, of course, a comparable sophistication in the type of accounting procedures followed if fiscal chaos was to be avoided. The advances in this area constitute the third group of innovations in business methods owed to the Middle Ages in general and to the Italian merchants in particular. It was the Italians, who, in their efforts to keep abreast of their increasingly complex and variegated business endeavors, developed first the practice of systematic bookkeeping and then, during the fourteenth century, the double-entry system which balances credits against debits, enables the businessman to estimate his profits and losses on a given enterprise with great precision, and remains the foundation of modern accounting procedures.

No medieval would have taken these innovations in financial operations and business techniques for granted—least of all the northern trader to whom, even in the later Middle Ages, maritime insurance and double-entry bookkeeping were apparently unknown. Nor would their Greek or Roman predecessors whose own procedures seem, in comparison, to have been very crude. Indeed, it is these innovations, no less than the startling bulk and impressive reach of commerce or the preponderant role it came to play in the economy as a whole, that permit historians, without hyperbole, to speak of the commercial revolution of the High Middle Ages and to risk comparing it in importance with the industrial revolution of the eighteenth century.

The Dynamism of the Medieval Economy

BY the mid-fourteenth century the commercial revolution had run its course. In the latter part of the thirteenth century the population boom had petered out under conditions that would seem to indicate that Europe was already beginning to press "against the technological upper limit of its food supplies." [12] Bad weather and poor crops in 1314 and 1315 led to European-wide famine during the years 1315–17. Smaller regional famines punctuated the history of the next half-century and it may be that an actual population decline had set in during the two or

94

three decades before the disastrous years 1348–50, when the Black Death swept across Europe, reducing the population by as much as a third. The same period also saw the beginning of a series of long-drawn-out wars in Europe and a concomitant slackening of the steady growth in agriculture, commerce, and industry that had characterized the three preceding centuries. As a result, Europe slid into an economic depression that was in some sectors to last into the sixteenth century. During this period of depression the volume of goods produced in agriculture and industry and exchanged in commercial transactions appears overall to have stabilized and probably to have declined. In the absence of precise and comprehensive statistics there has naturally been much disagreement about the range, impact, and duration of this depression, as also about the degree of seriousness to be accorded to it. As time goes on, however, fewer historians are inclined to deny that such a depression did occur or that it was, indeed, a serious one.

The significance one chooses to ascribe to this depression depends very much upon the focus of one's interests. In the context of this discussion, its principal significance lies in the fact that it constituted *no more* than a depression—no more, that is, than a temporary setback in the process of sustained growth that the European economy had enjoyed from the tenth century onward and, beginning again in the sixteenth century, was to culminate in the industrial revolution. Serious though it was, it did not constitute the sort of catastrophe that had destroyed the economy of the Roman world; and that it did not do so is perhaps the strongest of all testimonies to the vitality the medieval economy had shown and the strength it had attained during centuries preceding.

It remains, then, to inquire briefly into the reasons for that vitality and strength—no easy task, of course, given the daunting multiplicity of factors involved, the intricacy of their mutual relationships, the long span of time during which they were at work. Nonetheless, just as it is comparison with other times and places that makes manifest the extraordinary nature of medieval economic life and suggests the very need to explain it, so, too, is it comparison with other times and places that conspires to suggest the centrality of two factors of such fundamental importance that, while they should in no way be taken to furnish sufficient explanations, can with some confidence be claimed to constitute necessary conditions. The first relates primarily though not exclusively to commerce; the second, primarily though not exclusively to agriculture and industry.

The Middle Ages dreamed of universal empire but produced the nation-state. Carolingians, Ottonians, Salians, Hohenstaufen, the great popes of the High Middle Ages—all aspired, in their different ways and on different foundations, to reconstitute some form of universal empire that could assuage the persistent nostalgia of their age for the grandeur that had been Rome's. Despite massive attempts to realize those aspirations they failed to do so. Much of the glamour and drama of medieval political history hinges upon those attempts; much of its tragedy and waste attends their failure. There is a striking contrast between the peace and order that the citizens of the Roman world had enjoyed in the great days of the empire and the turbulence and disorder that was so often the lot of their medieval successors. The fragmentation of Europe into a congeries of independent or quasi-independent political entities and the ultimate failure of the Christian church to maintain any viable supranational supervision goes a long way toward explaining that turbulence and disorder, as well as the restlessness and instability characteristic of medieval society. These are conditions, no doubt, to be deplored, but conditions, also, that go no little way toward explaining the fact that medieval people did succeed in sponsoring and sustaining a commercial revolution, whereas their predecessors or contemporaries in the much more stable universal empires of Rome and China did not succeed in doing anything of the sort.

There is nothing paradoxical about this. Political disunity and disorder do not necessarily foster economic enterprise; on the contrary, they may well impede it. They do, however, open up freedom for maneuver, however risky, in a way that imperial unity and a successful universal order do not. In the interstices of a fragmented political world, private enterprise found the favorable soil and the room to grow in the medieval West that were denied to it in the great empires of the ancient world and of the Orient, achieving, as a result, "a social and political vitality without precedent or counterpart." [13] This is evident

96

in many phases of medieval commercial and industrial activity, but nowhere more clearly than in the success with which the Italian merchants were able to seize the commercial initiative at a time when the demographic tide was turning, agricultural surpluses were being achieved, and opportunities for economic expansion were once more opening up. For the Italian towns rose to commercial prominence under very peculiar political circumstances. Located on the fluctuating borderline between Byzantine and Frankish spheres of influence and detached from their rural hinterland, they enjoyed a good deal of freedom, not only from control by larger political entities, but also from the influence of landed wealth. As a result, they were unusually sensitive to the needs and ambitions of their merchants and were even willing to back with their own naval power the bold commercial initiatives those merchants took in the Mediterranean world.

Those first initiatives were crucial to the development of the whole commercial revolution, and the independence of action their authors enjoyed in taking them was, of course, exceptional; but the other autonomous or quasi-autonomous cities of Italy, Germany, and elsewhere in Europe and those towns that managed to achieve a special juridical status within the more cohesive European states all strove to guarantee at least some measure of freedom of action to their commercial and industrial entrepreneurs. The ultimate failure of church and aristocracy alike to impose upon medieval society at large an economic ethos shaped by the conditions of rural life testifies to the success of their efforts. Landed aristocrats in the Middle Ages, after all, were no less contemptuous of merchants and commercial activity than their Roman predecessors or their contemporary Chinese counterparts. Nor did medieval churchmen spare any effort in their attempts to inculcate the agrarian-inspired economic ethic they found in the classical authors, with its prohibition of usury, its advocacy of price regulation in the interest of the common well-being, and its hostility to the capitalist goal of maximizing profits. In the end, however, they failed. If the subsequent history of Europe attests eloquently to that failure, its previous history explains it; for already by the eleventh and twelfth centuries, Europe had become politically too pluralistic, too fragmented, too disorderly, either to sponsor or to admit the successful imposition upon all groups within it of a single standard of economic behavior.

On this very point, the contrast with China during the same era is instructive. In its cultivation of bureaucratic centralization, the pride of place it gave to agriculture, the harmony of outlook between its landholding aristocracy and its officialdom, and the degree to which it pursued the goal of stability rather than growth, Chinese society and the Chinese economy under the Han dynasty (202 B.C.–A.D. 220) had much in common with that of Rome. Unlike the Roman Empire of the West, however, China proved resilient enough to survive its own three centuries of barbarian invasion, internal division, and public disorder. Imperial unity was established in A.D. 589, and, during the successive Sui, T'ang, and Sung dynasties, while the imperial power waxed and waned, considerable economic growth took place. This growth culminated in a marked development both of internal and of coastal trade under the favorable conditions of Mongol domination (1280–1368). As a result, with the imperial sponsorship of a series of great naval expeditions under the first emperors of the Ming period (1368–1644), China was able to establish itself as the dominant naval power in the Indian Ocean. Between 1405 and 1433, indeed, the spectacular expeditions led by the admiral Cheng-Ho saw hundreds of ships bearing thousands of men penetrate into the Indian Ocean, some of them sailing as far as the Persian Gulf and the coast of Africa. The commercial possibilities were immense and China might well have been about to launch its own commercial revolution; but, in a startling reversal, the emperor ordered a halt to the expeditions, forbade Chinese subjects to leave the country, and put an end to the building of the large ships required for the overseas trade. By the end of the century even the official records relating to Cheng-Ho's activities had been destroyed, and soon the very memory of his expeditions was well-nigh lost.

Unlike medieval Europe, then, China underwent no commercial revolution. Instead, its economy stabilized and agricultural interests remained predominant into the modern era. But unlike Europe, too, China was united in a universal empire under a more or less effective central authority possessed of power and prestige sufficient even to

98

enable it to stifle overseas trade. That it was able to do such a thing reflects the further fact that unlike Europe, again, Chinese society continued to be dominated by a landowning gentry who shared with the imperial bureaucracy a common devotion to the Confucian ideal that saw trade as inferior and merchants as little more than social parasites. The power of that ideal remained unshaken by the favor the Mongols had shown to commerce. Under Mongol rule trade had been left very often in foreign hands or in the hands of Chinese who had something about them that was foreign—men who were Muslims or eunuchs or, like Cheng-Ho himself, both. Such men and the activities with which they were concerned attracted nothing but the scorn of the Confucian bureaucracy, the continuing bearers of China's destiny, and it appears to have been at the insistence of the latter that the emperor finally called a halt to the overseas expeditions and committed China to a policy of isolationism.[14]

In relating this episode we have been at pains to stress the contrast it reveals between China and Europe. If in so doing we were to overlook the similarities between them, we would mistake the precise nature of that contrast; for the fundamental difference lay in taste and choice rather than in ability and resources. The extraordinary scope, range, and success of Cheng-Ho's expeditions make it abundantly clear that China in no way lacked the resources and ability to embark upon an ambitious policy of expanding maritime commerce. They make it clear, too, that it already possessed the technology required for such an enterprise, not only in the realm of shipping design but also in that of navigational aids. The magnetic compass, for example, was mentioned in Chinese sources as early as the twelfth century. The real contrast with medieval Europe, then, resides in the fact that in China it lay within the power of a single ecumenical authority to decide to use those resources in a different way, to direct that ability toward different ends, and, in conformity with the prevailing ideology, to control the uses to which that technology was put—just as, for that matter, the imperial authority was also able to control for its own ends the exploitation of such other technological advances as the invention of printing (eighth century) and of gunpowder (c. twelfth century). Necessity may indeed be the mother of invention, but it is well to remember that "it is ideas which make necessity conscious." [15] Ideas, attitudes, choices—these play a fundamental role in sponsoring or inhibiting technological advance and a still more fundamental one in determining in what ways and to what degree an existing technology is exploited. Here, again, the contrast between China and Europe is a striking one, and it may serve to introduce the second of the two preconditions necessary to the dynamism of medieval economic life: namely, the extraordinary, sustained drive, evident both in agriculture and industry, to harness the forces of nature, to substitute for human effort natural or mechanical power, to develop and exploit a labor-saving technology.

The fundamental importance of the Western drive to achieve such a technology has frequently been attested and we have already seen the centrality of the contribution it made to the early medieval agricultural revolution and to the development of medieval industrial life. How extraordinary it was has less often been remarked—though already in the fifteenth century a distinguished Byzantine visitor to Italy expressed his own astonishment at its fruits. What made it extraordinary was less the capacity to invent than the readiness to learn from others, the willingness to imitate, the ability to take over tools or techniques discovered in other parts of the world, to raise them to a higher level of efficiency, to exploit them for different ends and with a far greater degree of intensity. Thus, to take one example, although the water mill was known to the Romans and, apparently, to the Chinese, and although they used it to grind grain, neither they, nor, it would seem, the peoples of the Byzantine or Islamic worlds, saw fit to put it to any of the multiple industrial uses that became commonplace in western Europe. Something similar can also be said about the windmill, a medieval invention known elsewhere but for centuries intensively and extensively exploited in Europe alone.

The outcome of this extraordinary technological drive was very striking: "By the latter part of the fifteenth century, Europe was equipped not only with sources of power far more diversified than those known to any previous culture, but with an arsenal of technical means for grasping, guiding and utilizing such energies which was immeasurably more varied and skilful than any people of the past had possessed, or than was known to any contemporary society of the Old World or the New." [16] How to account for it all, however, is somewhat less obvious and a good deal more open to dispute. Once again the factors involved are multiple and their interactions complex; but Lynn White, Jr., has made a persuasive case for emphasizing the molding influence of Christian attitudes toward the world of nature and the status of man.[17] By teaching God's uniqueness, omnipotence, and transcendence, Christianity shattered the archaic sense of the divine as a continuum running through the worlds of nature and of man and binding the two together. By preaching a God who was related to the world of nature not as soul to body but as creator to a creation radically contingent upon his will, it sponsored a thorough-going desacralization of the natural world, emptying it of spirit and destroying the very basis for any religion of nature. By leaving nature thus "disenchanted," it removed what had been in the ancient world, and continued to be in the Orient, a formidable spiritual obstacle to its rational exploitation for human ends.

At the same time, by teaching that the natural world was explicitly created to serve man's proper purposes, that man himself was created in the image and likeness of God, that no individual, however lowly, fully deserved to be denied the essential dignity that as a child of God was rightfully his, it seems likely that medieval Christianity acted also as a spur to promote the active search for ways and means by which animal power or the forces of nature might be harnessed and used to relieve men of the inhuman drudgery that the ancient world had accepted as being part of the very nature of things. And to say this is to say also that at least at one of its levels the medieval drive to develop and exploit a labor-saving technology was fundamentally humane in its goals and religious in its presuppositions.

Thus, the attempt to seek the wellsprings of medieval economic vitality has in part led back once more to the question of the impact of Christianity on the medieval world, in this case, to the failure of the medieval church to reestablish a viable universal authority capable of imposing upon the whole of Europe its own economic ethos and to its success in promoting and disseminating its own novel vision of nature, of man, and of the proper relationship between the two. Failure, it should be noted, as well as success—the pattern is not a simple one. Nor will we find it any less complex when we address ourselves to the intricacies of the medieval political outlook.

iv

SUBJECT AND CITIZEN

The Import of Mediaeval
Politics

"[T]he Kinge, . . . yea, though he be an infidele, representeth as it were the image of God upon earthe." Thus wrote Stephen Gardiner, bishop of Winchester, in 1535. "The state of Monarchy is the supremest thing upon earth; for kings are not only God's lieutenants upon earth and sit upon God's throne, but even by God himself they are called gods." Thus spoke King James I of England in a speech delivered at Parliament in 1610.

God has the Kings anointed by his prophets with the holy unction in like manner as he has bishops and altars anointed. But even without the external application in thus being anointed, they are by their very office the representatives of the divine majesty deputed by Providence for the execution of His purposes. . . . The power of God makes itself felt in a moment from one extremity of the earth to another. Royal power works at the same time throughout all the realm. It holds all the realm in position, as God holds the earth. Should God withdraw his hand, the earth would fall to pieces; should the King's authority cease in the realm, all would be in confusion.

Thus Jacques Bossuet, bishop of Meaux, wrote around 1670 for his pupil, the son of the French king Louis XIV.[1]

King and God, authority and grace, throne and altar—if one were to take the sixteenth and seventeenth centuries as point of departure and to listen exclusively to the royal ideologists, it would be very easy to conclude that *the* political vision the Middle Ages bequeathed to the modern world was that religious understanding of kingship which, promoted assiduously by the Christian clergy and placed at the service of the royal absolutism that was the fashionable ideology of the day, has since come to be known as the divine right theory of kingship. On the other hand, taking the same point of departure but listening exclusively to the constitutionalists or advocates of resistance to tyranny, it would be just as easy to conclude that the medieval political legacy was fundamentally constitutionalist, fundamentally concerned, that is, with the imposition of limits, both legal and institutional, on the exercise in government of monarchical or executive power; fundamentally concerned, too, with the development or preservation of those institutional forms whereby the monarch might be obliged to seek some form of popular consent to the principal policies to which he chose to commit his government.

Of course, neither conclusion would be at all satisfactory. Anyone tempted to question the reality of the constitutionalist legacy handed down from the Middle Ages to early modern Europe would have to ignore the testimony not only of such historically minded constitutionalists of the sixteenth and seventeenth centuries as François Hotman in France or Sir Edward Coke in England but also of so distinguished a proponent of divine right kingship as Sir Robert Filmer (d. 1653), who, in a famous passage, complained that the idea of government as based upon the consent of the people dated back to the "time that school divinity [medieval scholastic theology] began to flourish." [2] At the same time, however fashionable divine right theory may have been in the sixteenth and seventeenth centuries and however "modern" it may have seemed at the time, its more novel and distinguishing characteristics would have been inconceivable apart from the monarchical pretensions of the high medieval papacy and the late medieval reaction against them, while its less novel aspects had their roots in a still more distant past.

Both the triumphal royalist ideologizing and the more fustian constitutionalist claims of the early modern period bore the clear imprint, then, of the medieval experience. Of the two it is the latter that still retains the power today to compel something more than a historian's sympathetic understanding. Of the two, it is again the latter that can claim to represent the creative contribution of the Middle Ages to the Western political ethos. Of the two, finally, it is the latter that can be seen to lie at the very heart of Western cultural singularity in one of its most striking aspects. For if royal absolutism, along with its pretensions to a religious sanction, was drawn down to utter ruin at the end of the eighteenth century, with the collapse of the *ancien régime* and the upheavals of the modern era of revolution, its fate should in no way be taken for granted. On the contrary, when viewed in the context of world history it is not the esotericism of the royalist ideology that stands out as peculiar and calls for explanation but rather the familiar contours of Western constitutionalism.[3] On this matter, historians have much to learn from the apocalyptic rigors of twentieth-century political life. The failure in so many of the ex-colonial nations of newly minted constitutionalist forms and the earlier flowering in the very heartland of Europe of totalitarian despotisms of the most squalid kind should serve to remind us that in the long course of history, constitutionalist regimes of any type have been very much the exception rather than the rule and that in most of the large and complex societies that men have constructed one or another form of despotism has been the norm. In particular, it should serve to remind us, too, that the specific type of constitutionalist regime that the establishment of representative machinery has made possible in many of the large territorial states of the world today is something of a novelty on the world historical scene—a Western novelty at that, one with only the most shadowy anticipation in some of the small city-states of classical antiquity and very much, therefore, the product of the medieval political experience.

In comparison, representing as they do something much closer to the norm of civilized political life, even the most pretentious of monarchical claims smack very much of the commonplace. Nonetheless, it was with such a commonplace that the Middle Ages not only ended but also began. It is with monarchy, therefore, that we, too, shall begin. More than once in the preceding chapters we have had occasion to speak of sacral kingship, its encounter with the Christian church, and the transforming impact upon both institutions of that encounter. It is now time to put the pieces together and to view them in a fuller context.

Kingship and the Gods

RECOGNIZING that too insistent a sense of symmetry can seriously impede accurate historical analysis, one may resist the temptation to correlate the decline in the modern world of the institution of kingship with the rise of industry and technology and the ending of the age-old predominance of agricultural pursuits. Nonetheless, a good case can be made for correlating its rise to prominence with the growing dominance of an agrarian mode of life about three thousand years ago.

The primitive mentality, anthropologists never tire of reminding us, was thoroughly monistic. "The mainspring of the acts, thoughts, and feelings of early man was the conviction that the divine was immanent in nature, and nature intimately connected with society." [4] The sharp distinction that modern Westerners are accustomed to make between nature and supernature, between nature, society, and man, between animate and inanimate, were almost wholly lacking. Nature was alive; it was "full of gods"; it expressed, both in its benign cyclical rhythms and in its intimidating and catastrophic upheavals, the movements and indwelling of the divine. It is hardly surprising, then, that man himself should have been conceived less as an individual standing ultimately alone than as an integral part of society, deriving therefrom his identity and whatever value he possessed and responding in his daily life to the exigencies of its collective rhythms. Nor is it surprising that society itself should be conceived as "imbedded in nature," as entangled intimately in the processes of the natural world: the fertility of the land, the balance of the weather, the rotation of the seasons. It is hardly surprising, again, that its primary function should be something that exceeded the powers of any ordinary man: namely, the preservation of the natural order by a complex system of ritual and tabu, the prevention of natural catastrophe, the "harmonious integration" of man with nature. Nature being but a "manifestation of the divine," the primary function of society (the family, the tribe, and ultimately what we would call the state), the first object of its anxious, daily solicitude, should be what we, again, would call the religious.

Such was the context in which the institution of kingship first arose,

108

so that, Henri Frankfort has said, if we refer to it as "a political institution, we assume a point of view which would have been incomprehensible to the ancients. . . . Whatever was significant was embedded in the life of the cosmos, and it was precisely the king's function to maintain the harmony of that integration." [5]

The ancient kings, then, were regarded as sacred figures—always priestly, frequently divine—and divine kingship, with all that it involved, has been described well as "the archetypal pattern of the archaic culture which underlies all the most ancient civilizations of the world." [6] Evidence for its existence is broadcast across the globe in regions as far distant from one another as China and West Africa, Scandinavia and Polynesia, India and Peru, Ireland and the Nilotic Sudan. It is spread across an extraordinary span of time, pointing back to those prehistoric chiefs and medicine men whose power over the phenomena of nature had enlarged their dominion, reaching forward to the modern sacred monarchs of Polynesia, Africa, Central and South America, Asia.

Nowhere has the continuity of this archaic pattern been more readily evident than in China, where, even until 1912 and through all changes of dynasty, it remained the sacred duty of the Chinese emperor, himself the "Son of Heaven," to harmonize or coordinate the orders of heaven, nature, and society by the scrupulous performance of a cycle of traditional ritual acts, and where Mao Tse-tung, for that matter, recently attributed the strength of the "cult of personality" to the habits formed during three thousand years of emperor worship.[7] And nowhere were the lineaments of that pattern more strikingly evident than in ancient Egypt, where the pharaoh was regarded quite literally as a god incarnate, whose task it was to ensure the cyclical rhythm of the seasons, to guarantee the fertility of the land, and to secure the prevention of any disharmony between the supernatural forces and human society.

Egypt, it is true, was an extreme case, but similar prerogatives were claimed to a greater or lesser degree by the other sacred monarchs of the ancient Middle East. The belief in the divinity of the ruler was, via the Hellenistic empire of Alexander the Great and its successor states, to exert a profound influence over the political thinking of the late classical world, and it was able to do so because it came not as an alien heterodoxy but as the return to an orthodoxy whose ideological underpinnings had never been fully dismantled. If the Greeks of the earlier era of city-states had long since left their own institutions of sacral monarchy behind them, their political theory and practice acknowledged no real distinction between the political and the religious. Politics included religion. The loyalty men owed to their city was equally a loyalty to their city's gods, and (despite the novel and dissenting position occasionally expressed by Plato and Aristotle) that loyalty was in general conceived to be an ultimate loyalty from which there could be no appeal to any higher norm.

The same was true of the Roman state, both republic and empire, and in this context it should be noted that the ultimate insistence on the divinity of the emperors and the obligation to perform public worship to "Rome and Augustus" is not to be dismissed anachronistically as "merely political," and possessed of no religious significance. Emperor worship, particularly in the Eastern provinces, was quite capable of reflecting a genuine piety—though, of course, a piety of the antique civic mode. Its spread throughout the empire owed less to governmental enforcement than to popular sentiment. If it was, indeed, a political act, it was not political in our narrow modern sense of that word, but in the old, broad, inclusive sense that bears the clear imprint of the archaic social vision.

In terms, then, of its antiquity, its ubiquity, its extraordinary staying power, divine or sacral monarchy with all that it entails can lay a strong claim to being the most common form of "political" institution known to those men who have lived in civilized societies. In particular, the blending of the political with the religious that it presupposes undoubtedly reflects man's customary mode of apprehending social realities. This being the case, of course, the familiar distinction between religion and politics, the degree of freedom from governmental control claimed thereby for a whole segment in the life of the individual citizen, the essentially secular nature of Western political societies, and the complex constitutional devices functioning to prevent their becoming anything more than secular political entities—all of these characteristics, so much a matter of common sense to us today, stand out instead as developments peculiar to modern Western civilization, explicable only in terms of the unique history of that civilization. For the emergence of those novelties one period in European history may be singled out as crucial and one factor as fundamental: the period, the medieval centuries stretching from the late eleventh onward; the factor, the distorting impact upon archaic or Hellenic modes of thought of the peculiar conception of the divine nature that is basic to Judaic and Christian belief.

Involved in that belief was a restriction of the meaning of the divine in a manner no less incomprehensible to the ancients than is the archaic pattern of thought to us. If we ourselves find that pattern to be well-nigh incomprehensible today we would do well to remember that we do so precisely because our very idea of what it is to be divine has been radically reshaped by centuries of Judeo-Christian thinking with its obdurate insistence on the unity, omnipotence, and transcendence of God, centuries during which the meanings ascribed to such words as *god, divine, religious,* and so on have, by primitive or archaic standards, been narrowed down to a degree bordering on the eccentric. Moreover, in shattering the archaic sense of the divine, as a continuum running through the worlds of nature and of man, Judeo-Christian beliefs undercut also (and therefore) the very metaphysical underpinnings for the archaic pattern of sacral kingship.

It would be unwise to exaggerate the degree to which the Hebrews were able to break away from that archaic pattern. The Old Testament itself indicates, after all, the extent of the impact upon Hebrew thinking of the Baalist fertility cults or of the Babylonian religion, with its presupposition of the immanence in the natural world of the divine and its concomitant espousal of sacral kingship. Certainly, despite some amount of intricate scholarly wrangling, there seems to be no real ground for denying that Hebrew kings, both in pre- and post-Exilic times, exercised, like other Middle Eastern kings, functions of a priestly nature. Even if one were willing to be anachronistic, one would find difficulty in distinguishing "church" and "state" as distinct corporate entities at any point in the histories of any of the successive Hebrew regimes. If the archaic pattern of attributing divine characteristics to earthly kings was excluded, it should be remembered that it was excluded in the name of the overriding sovereignty of God, and it would be improper to read the modern distinction between the religious and the political into a society in which Yahweh alone was recognized as the true king, a society that looked forward to the day when his kingdom would be established on earth and cherished as its governmental ideal, therefore, what the Jewish historian Josephus was later on to call "theocracy."

Nonetheless, the truly striking fact is not the extent to which Canaanite or Babylonian materials were incorporated into the Old Testament but the extent to which they were demythologized, transmuted under the influence of a more exclusive conception of the divine into something rich and strange. Again in comparison with other Middle Eastern monarchies, the truly remarkable thing about the Hebrew monarchy is not so much the degree to which it retained a religious aura, but rather the degree to which it was a *secular* institution. Even in the very early period there is little evidence of divine honors being accorded to Hebrew monarchies, and none in the later. "Of no King of Israel could it be said as of a Pharaoh of Egypt that he was the cause of natural phenomena." [8]

With the coming of Christianity, moreover, the process of desacralization was pushed to its completion and the "state" finally reduced to the position of a merely secular entity. The kingdom of God (for the Hebrews an as yet unrealized ideal, no doubt, but nevertheless a "this worldly" conception) was now declared to be a kingdom "not of this world." As a result, the Hebrew denial of anything more than a conditional allegiance to the present powers that be ceased to be a merely temporary restriction destined for removal when God's kingdom was finally to be established on earth, and became in Christian hands a permanent, universal, and dramatic limitation on the allegiance men can owe to any earthly society. Even the most affirmative strand of New Testament thinking never went so far as to endorse the classical view of the state as existing to make men good. Instead, it conceived of its function in a startlingly negative fashion as a consequence of Adam's Fall, as a "punishment and remedy for sin." The famous New Testament injunctions to "obey God rather than man" (Acts 5:29) or to "render to Caesar the things that are Caesar's and to God the things that are God's" (Mark 12:17) were themselves fraught with revolutionary implications.

These implications were not to be drawn effectively for centuries. The archaic pattern of sacral kingship—firmly rooted in the Roman world and familiar also to the invading Germanic peoples—proved to be very tenacious. The extraordinary accommodations of the fourth century enabled it to survive in barely Christianized guise, not only in the Roman Empire of Byzantium (whose political ideology Czarist Russia revived) but also in western Europe where it was not until the latter part of the eleventh century that it came under serious challenge at the hands of the Gregorian reformers. While the investiture conflict effectively undercut the priestly status of the German emperors, the sacral aura surrounding the French and English monarchs was never fully dispelled. Moreover, though a Gregorian propagandist could boldly assert that Emperor Henry IV was "neither monk nor clerk; just a layman, nothing more," [9] there was at the time no complementary disposition to insist that the pope was himself, in turn, nothing more than a cleric. As a result, the popes of the High Middle Ages themselves emerged as something more than priestly figures, as the true successors of the Roman emperors, as sacral monarchs claiming supreme authority in matters temporal as well as spiritual. It was by way of reaction to such papal claims, especially in the wake of the Protestant Reformation, that the lingering memories of early medieval sacral monarchy were reinvigorated; and when that happened, those memories were linked with the newer notion that royal power could not be annulled if it had been handed down by hereditary succession and primogeniture in the legitimate dynasty and shaped into the early modern ideology that historians have become accustomed to call the divine right theory of kingship.

To say that, of course, is to say also that however Christian or medieval a legacy to the early modern world it may seem to have been, divine right theory was ultimately pagan in its presuppositions and ancient in its provenance. That it was able to take on a Christian coloration should not blind us to the fact that it sprang from a view of the world, the nature of God, and the destiny of man profoundly at odds with that inculcated by Christianity. Nor should its survival into the sixteenth and seventeenth centuries delude us into thinking that medievals themselves had totally failed to perceive that incompatibility. In this respect, whatever the theocratic aspirations of the later medieval popes, the onslaught launched by the Gregorian reformers against the "pontifical kingship" of the German emperors had constituted a major turning point. It had marked the onset of several centuries of intermittent but widespread tension between the ecclesiastical and temporal authorities in western Europe—tension not simply between competing ideals, but between rival governmental structures, secular and ecclesiastical, both of which contrived to limit each other's effective power.

To the distinction between religious and secular introduced in the New Testament, therefore, was now added an institutional dualism, which, from the eleventh century onward, served increasingly to give that distinction teeth. There was something quite novel about the state of affairs thus engendered. "[T]here is really nothing unusual," Brian Tierney has said, "in one ruler aspiring to exercise supreme spiritual and temporal power. That . . . is a normal pattern of human government." What was unusual about the Middle Ages "was not that certain emperors and popes aspired to a theocratic role but that such ambitions were never wholly fulfilled." [10] No doubt the governmental dualism that sponsored this novel state of affairs was also the cause of an immense amount of wasteful and destructive conflict; but it was conflict that marked, nonetheless, the birth pangs of something new in the history of mankind: a society in which the state was stripped of its age-old religious aura and in which its overriding claims on the loyalties of men were balanced and curtailed by a rival authority, a society distinguished, therefore, by an established institutional dualism and racked by the internal instability resulting therefrom. Earlier in this book, stressing the breakdown of effective political universalism in Europe, we argued that it was in the interstices of a fragmented political world that private economic enterprise found room in the Middle Ages to grow. To that it must now be added that it was between the hammer and the anvil of conflicting authorities, religious and secular, that Western political freedoms were forged. Medieval constitutionalism was the product of many mutually supportive factors, by no means all of them religious; but whatever the strength of those factors, without the Christian insertion of the critical distinction between the religious and political spheres and without the instability engendered as a result by the clash of rival authorities, it is extremely unlikely that the Middle Ages would have bequeathed to the modern world any legacy at all of limited constitutional government.

The Feudal Contribution

IF the sacral monarchs of the pre-Gregorian era, unlike the divine right kings of the sixteenth and seventeenth centuries, were unable even to aspire to absolute rulership, it was less because of theoretical restrictions on their authority (though such existed) than because of the lack of adequate communications and administrative structures and because, within their kingdoms, they had to face, in their own dukes, counts, and lesser nobility, rival possessors of real and extensive governmental powers. Without the last wave of barbarian invasions and the disintegration of the Carolingian Empire such a state of affairs would probably not have arisen. Without the emergence of feudalism it would certainly never have been established as firmly as it was or left so deep and permanent an imprint upon Western legal thinking and political institutions. What the disintegration of empire meant is clear enough: in matters economic, a further retreat into local self-sufficiency and a concomitant acceleration in the shrinkage of anything approximating a money economy; in matters political, an increasing inability on the part of the central government to have its authority recognized throughout its realms and to extend the benefit of its protection to all its subjects; in matters social, the growth of public disorder, the catastrophic loss of any sense of security and the increasing degree to which the mass of small men were at the mercy of the more powerful. What the emergence of feudalism meant, however, is a good deal less clear, primarily because of the problematic status of the term itself.

Medieval kings have often been portrayed as waging unrelenting war against the forces of feudalism, but were we able to ask them what exactly that feudalism was, they would be unable to answer the question. Like the rest of the "isms" the word itself is of postmedieval origin; like some of the other "isms," again, it has been used in more than one way. Of these, the least helpful (if not, necessarily, the least common) has been its usage as a broad-gauged term of derogation, to be applied to any sociopolitical system that one happens to regard as reactionary. More justifiable, perhaps, is the Marxist usage denoting the type of society that is built upon "precapitalist" modes of production and exchange, or its use by comparative historians and sociologists to denote a phase in the development not only of European society but of a whole series of societies: Byzantine, Islamic, Chinese, Japanese, and so on. Whatever the merits of these various usages (and there are others), some sort of definition is clearly a first priority. In the pages that follow, therefore, *feudalism* will be used to denote a set of political institutions, legal relationships, and military arrangements that emerged between the ninth and thirteenth centuries in western Europe and in the Latin principalities established in those parts of the Near and Middle East that fell under western European control. There was a considerable degree of local variation within this large area and the characteristics described will apply most accurately to the heartland of the Carolingian Empire, to the lands of the north between the rivers Loire and Rhine. Nonetheless, if J. R. Strayer's description is followed,[11] the fundamental characteristics of feudalism everywhere can be summed up under three headings: first, "the fragmentation of political power," with the county as the largest really effective political unit in much of western Europe and itself, even then, riddled with independent jurisdictions that eluded the count's control; second, "public power in private hands," the fragmented political power being itself regarded as a property right, a private possession to be sold, inherited, divided, and so on; third, a state of affairs in which "a key element in the armed forces—heavy-armed cavalry—is secured through individual and private agreements," through private contracts between the lord and his knights, even if that lord happened also to be king.

Thus defined, feudalism appears not as an economic arrangement but as "a method of government, and a way of securing the forces necessary to preserve the method of government." Thus defined, too, it refers to a set of political and military arrangements in which only the aristocratic minority—in medieval parlance, "those who fought"—directly participated. This is not to suggest that the military aristocracy existed in a vacuum or to deny that the aristocracy, like the clergy ("those who prayed"), depended upon the economic efforts of others ("those who worked") to sustain its own expensive and nonproductive activities. But the agrarian system of great estates farmed by a dependent peasantry long predated the rise of feudal institutions. Similarly, feudal institutions survived under the changed conditions of an expanding money economy. Thus the relationship between manorialism and feudalism was one of congruence rather than necessity. To define feudalism as a set of political and military arrangements is not to deny that congruence; it is simply to insist that what was novel about the European society of the ninth and tenth centuries was its mode of government, not its economic system.

Nor does such a definition deny that some of the features characteristic of that European society have appeared in other civilizations or that most of them appeared in Japan during the fourteenth and fifteenth centuries, when the parallels with medieval European institutions were particularly strong. In their totality, however, those factors occur in Europe alone, and in the context of any concern with the roots of Western cultural peculiarity it is the *dissimilarities* rather than the similarities between even analogous conditions in non-Western societies and the medieval West that appear, in retrospect, to have been significant. The identification of those dissimilarities, then, is an important task, one that calls for a closer look at feudalism and at the way in which it emerged.

Its roots, of course, lie deep in the centuries predating the rise of the Carolingian Empire. During those centuries, with the disruption or decline of tribal bonds among the invading peoples and the decay among their Roman subjects of loyalty to the state, there was a growth in the practice by which lesser men, some of them warriors, attached themselves by bonds of personal loyalty to the most powerful men in their local communities. This practice, with precedents in both the

Roman and the Germanic past, was the source of the first and most basic component of feudalism, that of the personal dependence of the warrior or vassal upon his lord. The Germanic precedent was an aristocratic one: it had been customary for a great war leader to surround himself with a small band of aristocratic followers who, having pledged to him fidelity unto death, formed the elite troops in his army. The Roman precedent, on the other hand, was by no means aristocratic. In this case the personal followers had been recruited from the lower classes; and the vassals of Merovingian Gaul in the sixth and seventh centuries—strong-arm men who fought on their lord's behalf in return for maintenance, protection, and a share of the spoils—appear to have been somewhat closer in social status to their Roman than to their Germanic forerunners. Nonetheless, they rose in status throughout the seventh and eighth centuries, and that process was accelerated when vassalage came to be linked with the second basic component of feudalism, fief holding.

In its inception, vassalage had had nothing to do with landholding. Like the retainers who formed the private armies of the great aristocrats later on in the fifteenth century, vassals had been maintained in their lord's household. Such landless "household knights" were to be found throughout the feudal era, and, even as late as the tenth century, they may have far outnumbered their fief-holding brethren. Side by side with vassalage, however, had grown up the institution of dependent land tenure. In a time of troubles the less powerful landholders had often found themselves unable to protect their property and had had to resort to the stratagem of surrendering the full ownership of the land to a powerful aristocrat, receiving it back from him as a protected tenant who, in return for stipulated rents and services, could continue to cultivate it and enjoy its fruits. At the same time, it had become common for the great landowners to lease out parts of their land to dependents who would render to him rents and perhaps also stipulated services in return for protection and the right to enjoy the fruits of that land. In both cases the property title remained with the lord and the tenancy was for a restricted period of time; but such dependent tenancies were usually renewable and a tendency for them to become hereditary was quickly established.

118

The service that the dependent tenants owed was not military service and there was at the outset no connection between their tenancies and the institution of vassalage. Indeed, had the nature of Frankish warfare not changed, such a connection might not have been established. Before the mid-eighth century the Franks had usually fought on foot. By that time, however, the introduction of larger horses capable of carrying heavily armored knights and of the stirrup, which greatly increased the effectiveness of those knights, had led to a realization of their superiority in battle to infantry. By that time, too, and during a period of Muslim invasion, it had led to the conviction that it was vital at least to stiffen the mass army of free peasant foot soldiers with a strong knightly contingent. In theory it was easy enough to turn vassals from foot soldiers into mounted knights; in practice, however, it was forbiddingly expensive. Mounts, remounts, attendants, complex equipment, and years of training—all of this cost a great deal. In a period of scarce money but abundant land it is therefore understandable that a solution was worked out from the mid-eighth century onward by making the vassal a dependent tenant, by endowing him with a manorial estate cultivated by its own peasantry from which he could obtain the revenue necessary to maintain himself as an effective cavalryman in the service of his lord. Again, full title to the land—or fief, as it came to be called later on—remained in the hands of the lord, but there was an immediate tendency for son to succeed father and for the arrangement to become in fact hereditary.

The immediate effect of this combination of vassalage with fief holding was to enhance the social status of those warriors who had been elevated to the status of lords of the manor. The long-term effect was to remove any lingering social stigma attached to vassalage itself, which, as a result, increasingly came to be apprehended as a form of personal dependency about which there was nothing ignoble. During the course of the ninth century, therefore, as the Carolingian Empire came under attack and the Carolingian rulers sensed the weakening of their control over the dukes, counts, and margraves who served as their great imperial officials in the localities, they attempted to strengthen their control by the formal establishment of a more personal bond, that of lord and vassal. The dukes and counts became, therefore, royal vassals, but whatever gains accrued from that transformation were more than offset by a comparable transformation of the way in which the public offices of those dukes and counts came to be understood. It appears to have been increasingly difficult for men to keep in mind the old distinction between the office itself and the affiliated properties that supplied the officeholder's income. Kings themselves began to speak of granting a benefice or fief to a vassal when what they were actually doing was bestowing a countship (an office akin to that of the modern military governor) on an appointed public official. The old distinction between office as a focus of public duty and property as a source of private income was breaking down. Office itself was coming to be thought of as property, and, like property, inheritable. When Charles the Bald, king of West Frankia, set off in 877 on an expedition into Italy, he issued a decree that reveals that he himself was willing to concede that the office of count was normally to be regarded as hereditary.

Officeholding, then, came to be assimilated to vassalage, and the office to the fief. The result was the dispersal of royal governmental authority among the dukes, counts, and margraves, who now ruled, however, in everything except theory, as independent magnates, dominating their districts from fortified strongholds, providing military protection for its inhabitants, administering justice, collecting taxes, and keeping the proceeds. In order to do so, however, they themselves had to depend on the loyalty and military prowess of their own personal vassals. As more and more of those vassals came themselves to be fief holders and important men in their own lesser and more easily defensible localities, it became concomitantly harder for great public officials to retain their monopoly over the governmental power they had made their own. The outcome was a further fragmentation of that power and the dispersal of part of it into the hands of a whole range of lesser members of what was now emerging as a feudal military aristocracy.

By the eleventh century, then, one can discern at least the dim outlines of the familiar entity so dear to the older textbooks—namely, the feudal hierarchy, the structure of lord-vassal relationships reaching from the myriad of lowly fief-holding knights at its base, via their immediate lords and the lords of those lords, all the way up to the king, who, as feudal suzerain or supreme lord of lords, presided over the whole system in lonely and no doubt uncomfortable eminence. The realities, of course, were a good deal more complex than such a symmetrical picture would suggest. It was not until the twelfth century that the type of systematization presupposed in our usual notion of the feudal hierarchy took place. Even then not all vassals were fief holders; not all important landowners were necessarily involved in the feudal nexus. A single knight often accumulated more than one fief from several different sources, thus becoming the vassal of more than one lord, and so on; but even before the process of systematization, administrative, fiscal, and judicial powers that had once been public and that we today would classify as governmental had passed into a multitude of hands and were being wielded in a myriad of jurisdictions, ranging from that of the small-time knight in his manorial court right up to that of the king himself in his own high court.

There has been much argument about the political consequences of this state of affairs. They are, however, obvious enough. While feudalism did itself undoubtedly sponsor a degree of anarchy, it also represented a creative response to the daunting challenge of how to get the basic political tasks done in a period of invasion, confusion, and public disorder. But that it should have had the long-range constitutional consequences it did is a good deal less obvious. Those consequences depend in no small degree on the possession by European feudalism of two particular characteristics that are more remarkable than is usually assumed: the contractual nature of the feudal relationship and the personal involvement of the king himself in the feudal nexus.

Two ceremonies customarily signaled a man's assumption of the status of vassalage: that of homage and that of fealty. By the former, the would-be vassal indicated his submission to the lord by kneeling before him, placing his hands within the lord's hands, and promising that he would be the lord's man, serving and defending him for the rest of his life. By the latter, the vassal swore on the Gospels or on a collection of relics an oath of fidelity to the lord. Unless he went on in a further ceremony to invest the vassal with a fief, the lord's role on this occasion was limited to that of publicly accepting the pledge of vassalage. In the early days, when most vassals lived as household knights or retainers, the obligations they incurred were onerous and ill defined. They were to serve their lords at all times and in whatever manner consonant with their own status as free men. The arrangement, nonetheless, was a reciprocal one. The lord was committed, in return, to protect and maintain his vassals. As the grant of a fief became the customary way to discharge that obligation of maintenance, and as it became common for men of high social status to accept the bonds of vassalage, there was a corresponding inclination on their part to define with some precision the nature and extent of the services they owed their lords, and to do so restrictively.

By the twelfth century, then, the feudal contract was generally held by custom to involve, on the lord's part, the maintenance and protection of his vassal and, on the vassal's part, the giving of "aid and counsel" to his lord. By counsel was meant both advising the lord on governmental matters and participating in the hearing and settling of cases that came before the lord's court. By aid was meant, above all, personal military service, usually not to exceed forty days a year, and in the case of powerful vassals the supplying of a contingent of knights for a similar period of service in the lord's army. By aid was also meant, however, the financial assistance the vassal was expected to extend to his lord on those occasions when the latter's financial burden was recognized by local or regional custom to be heavy—as, for example, the marriage of the lord's eldest daughter. Beyond such customary aids, and especially when he was involved in war, a lord might wish to levy further aids, and powerful lords were indeed able to do so; but such aids were regarded as "gracious aids"—that is to say, they had to be asked for; they were to be conceded only (theoretically) at the goodwill of the vassals; they were, in fact, contingent upon their consent. There were other more "incidental" though often very lucrative ways in which the lord might make money out of the feudal relationship, but they are not important to the present discussion. Suffice it simply to add that the contract was bolstered by legal sanctions. If the vassal failed to live up to his obligations, he was subject, after trial by his peers in the lord's court, to the forfeiture of his fief. If the lord, on the other hand, failed in his duties to the vassal, the latter had the right formally to break faith with the lord (*diffidatio*), thereby dissolving the feudal bond. That such legal sanctions could rarely be invoked without resort to arms should not obscure the importance of the fact that they existed at all.

The bilateral nature of the feudal contract and the legal possession by the vassal of a "right of resistance" against a faithless lord was significant enough. Its significance, however, was enhanced immensely when the lord in question happened also to be king. Without the latter's involvement in the feudal hierarchy, without his assumption of the role of paramount lord, legally bound by contractual relationships with his principal subjects, feudalism would have lacked the enduring constitutional importance it actually attained. By that involvement the king, regarded already among the Germanic peoples as in some sense subordinate to the customary law of the *folk*, was burdened with the further weight of legal obligations and restrictions that such a relationship involved: the subordination to feudal law, the rights and liberties guaranteed to his vassals (including freedom from taxation without consent), and the undermining presence of a right of resistance to his commands should those commands be judged illegitimate.

It is easy enough to take all of this for granted, but less easy if we call to mind the contrast afforded by the non-Western society that in its feudal phase came closest to the western European model, namely, Japan. That society, despite all the remarkable similarities to the medieval West, lacked a truly bilateral contract between vassal (*gokenin*) and lord (*tono*). The vassal's submission to the lord was much more marked than was that of his European equivalent, and the nature of the lord's obligations towards his vassal was not clearly defined. Indeed, the whole relationship was far from being defined in the precise legal terms characteristic of western European feudalism. Instead, "the relationship rested strongly on unwritten custom publicized by ceremonial observance; it relied less on written or oral contract which specified individual duties or privileges." [12] Again, in Japan the feudal hierarchy culminated not in the emperor but in the *shogun,* the generalissimo to whose office accrued for centuries nearly all the real functions and actual powers of the imperial government.

Nonetheless, however powerless in day-to-day practice, an imperial court and a civil nobility, survived side by side with the feudal warrior structure, the emperor remaining in theory the sovereign of his people and the source of the merely delegated authority possessed by the *shogun*. The divine emperor, it seems, was too sacred a figure either to be dispensed with altogether or to be domesticated within the network of feudal relationships, despite the noncontractual nature of those relationships. As in Europe, monarchy and feudalism existed side by side; but in Japan the two failed to interpenetrate, and the isolation of the emperor foreclosed the possibility of the type of constitutionalist legacy that European feudalism bequeathed to the West.[13]

Of course, had the roughly comparable duality between Merovingian king and Carolingian mayor of the palace persisted, a similar situation might have arisen in Europe. By 751, after all, the king, who was still endowed with some sort of sacral aura, wielded no power; whereas the mayor, about whose position there was nothing sacred, was the true possessor of power. In contrast to Japan, however, the sacral status of the king was rooted in a pagan past by then half-forgotten. It had survived the triumph of Christianity but had been able to derive no ideological support from that religion. Moreover, in the favorable judgment of the papacy and the introduction at his own coronation of the ceremony of unction, Pepin the Short, in contrast to the Japanese *shoguns,* was able to find the type of independent and countervailing spiritual sanction he seems to have needed in order to displace his Merovingian rival and assume the kingship himself; but the kingship he assumed and to which his descendants succeeded was now—at least by archaic or Oriental standards—comparatively desacralized. It was therefore susceptible later on to being drawn into the network of feudal relationships and regarded as restricted by the obligations arising from the feudal contract. Indeed, the type of specifically ecclesiastical sanction that the Carolingians and other European monarchs came to enjoy, while it conspired on the one hand to confer upon them some sort of sacral status, on the other had implications that comported very well with the obligations imposed by feudalism. While teaching that the authority of the king was of divine origin, ecclesiastics were quick to insist, even in the ninth century, that precisely because of that it could not be exercised in an irresponsible fashion but only in accord with the norms of justice, divine or natural, of which they themselves were, of course, the rightful interpreters.

It is not surprising, then, that when in the late eleventh century the Gregorian reformers launched their attack on the priestly pretensions of the German monarchy, they did not hesitate by appealing to those norms even to justify the deposition of kings. Nor is it too surprising that one of their propagandists, Manegold of Lautenbach, moved no doubt by feudal notions, argued that a king is bound to his subjects by a contract and that if he breaks the provisions of that contract they can regard themselves "without any breach of faith" as being freed from his lordship.[14] More than once in the course of subsequent history, ecclesiastics were willing to combine with the great feudal magnates of the realm, to wrest from their kings some sort of formal recognition of his obligation to govern with their advice and in accordance with the laws of the land. The role played by Stephen Langton, archbishop of Canterbury, in uniting the English barons and leading their opposition to the policies of King John is only the most important of those instances; the Magna Carta, the Great Charter of liberties to which John appended a reluctant signature in 1215, only the best known of their end products.

It is easy, of course, to read far too much into Magna Carta, and much that is not there has at one time or another been read into it—including, indeed, most of those constitutionally guaranteed liberties that only as a result of centuries of subsequent effort did Englishmen actually secure. Because of this, it has become customary to post warnings to the effect that the charter was essentially a feudal document, one designed by feudal magnates to define and restrict the rights of the king in his capacity as feudal suzerain, one intended, therefore, above all to protect their own interests as members of a feudal aristocracy that constituted only a small and highly privileged minority of the population. The charter, it is insisted, had very little to say about the rights of all Englishmen; it did not establish a constitution; it made no provision for representative government; and the machinery of enforcement described in its last chapter depended on nothing less crude than a legalized resort to arms against a recalcitrant king.

All of this is true. Despite the dramatic circumstances surrounding its signing and the more than symbolic importance attached to it in England from the seventeenth century onward, there was little in the Great Charter that was entirely novel and much that reflected assumptions about the powers of kings that were no more than feudal commonplaces; but precisely because of that, the charter stands as an eloquent witness to the importance of the feudal contribution in the development of Western constitutionalism. To the older Germanic belief that the king was responsible for the welfare of his people and in some sense accountable if he failed in that responsibility, and to the novel Christian insistence on separating the realm of the religious from that of the political, feudalism added the precise legal conviction that the king was bound by the laws and customs of his kingdom. Admittedly, it gave pride of place to the laws and customs that protected the property rights of the aristocracy; but, then, those same rights blocked the free exercise of royal taxing powers in whose absence no king could aspire to despotic authority. The Magna Carta affirmed in quite unambiguous terms, for example, the characteristic feudal insistence that no "gracious" or extraordinary aids could be raised without consent. In the thirteenth and fourteenth centuries it was, above all, their urgent need to acquire that consent that led rulers everywhere in Europe to create representative assemblies, and it was those assemblies that were ultimately to provide the means whereby the theoretical limitations on executive power that most accepted might be enforced without recourse to the armed violence that most apparently deplored.

Romano-Canonical Law, Representation, and Consent

"IT was assuredly no accident," Marc Bloch has said, that representative institutions "originated in states which were only just emerging

126

from the feudal stage and still bore its imprint. Nor was it an accident that in Japan, where the vassal's submission was much more unilateral and where, moreover, the divine power of the emperor remained outside the structure of vassal engagements, nothing of the kind emerged." [15] One must agree that it would be hard to imagine the emergence of such representative institutions without the prior existence of feudal arrangements of the specifically western European type. One must also insist, however, on other factors equally lacking in Japan but no less vital to the shaping of the representative procedures that lie today at the heart of the political process in modern liberal-democratic constitutionalist regimes and appear to have been uniquely the creation of medieval Latin Christendom. Central among those factors are the legacy of Roman law, greatest of the Roman intellectual achievements; the recovery in the West during the latter part of the eleventh century of the full body of that law; and the particular ways in which the medieval lawyers applied it.

At first glance, there is nothing odd about such a suggestion. Given the prevailing conditions of political life, it is understandable that early medieval theorizing about matters political should be dominated by the simple dichotomy between ruler and ruled, that it should focus characteristically on the relationship between king and subject, and that it should be concerned above all with their respective rights and duties, as those rights and duties were understood within the context of the customary law of the community. Only in the twelfth century, with the revived study of the highly sophisticated law of classical Roman antiquity, does the idea of the state reappear, the idea of a corporate body of citizens organized under a sovereign executive power, the idea, in effect, of a political community geared to the achievement of the public interest. Of course, in the absence of such an idea it is hard to imagine kings as feeling the need to seek, via representatives of "the community of the realm," the approval of the people for their policies or taxes.

At second glance, however, some troubling difficulties arise. The systematization of Roman law had taken place under imperial, not republican, auspices. The *Corpus Juris Civilis*, the definitive sixth-century compilation of that law, which, from the twelfth century onward was to become the object of much anxious scrutiny in western Europe and the subject of whole wastes of prolix commentary, had been the work of an official legal commission. That commission had been charged with its task by the emperor Justinian himself. He had encouraged it to make on his own sovereign authority such changes in the original texts as seemed necessary. It had proved itself demonstrably inclined to select or tailor those ancient texts to minimize the republican memories that so many of them conveyed and to maximize whatever in them was supportive of its imperial master's autocratic proclivities. That such a body of law should in any way serve to sponsor the development of representative machinery designed to elicit popular consent to royal policies would seem, then, inherently improbable. Certainly, the survival and continuing cultivation of the Roman legal tradition at Byzantium had no such effect. Representative institutions remained as foreign to the political life of the Byzantine Empire as they had been to that of its ancient Roman forerunner. It is revealing, moreover, that when the "new monarchs" of early modern Europe were striving in their respective nation-states to eliminate traditional feudal obstacles to their exercise of an absolute executive power, their lawyers and propagandists were able to find much support in the texts of the Roman law, deploying on behalf of their royal masters such famous absolutist assertions as "the prince is unfettered by the laws" or "what has pleased the prince has the force of law." [16]

On this matter, however, as on others, it appears that what one finds in an ancient text depends very much on what one brings to it. When the lawyers of the medieval Latin West approached the Roman legal texts, unlike their Byzantine counterparts or their Renaissance successors they appear to have been impressed less by the absolutist formulations of the late imperial period than by the republican spirit that so often underlay those formulations. In particular, they appear to have been impressed by the principle that the distinguished political scientist Charles Howard McIlwain once described as "the true essence of Roman constitutionalism," the principle that it is in the people itself that one must seek the ultimate source of political authority.[17] Thus, if Henry of Bracton, the great English jurist of the thirteenth century, may serve as a guide, they were less impressed by the Romanist assertion that the will of the prince "has the force of law" than by the subsequent statement in the text itself that gives the reason for assigning such a legislative authority to the ruler: namely, because by a sort of fundamental law concerning the imperial position itself the people have conferred upon him all their authority and power.

What, then, did these medieval lawyers bring to the Roman texts that their Byzantine contemporaries or Renaissance successors did not? In the first place, they brought minds tinged with prevailing ideas grounded either in Germanic customary law or in feudal practices and institutions, notably the beliefs that the king's power was not an irresponsible one, that he, too, was limited by the law, and that the people retained some sort of residual power to resist him if he lapsed into tyranny. In the second place, some of them at least—and a very influential group at that—were clerics who brought to the texts minds influenced by the study of ecclesiastical law, for the revival of interest in the Roman law went hand in hand in the late eleventh century with a comparable intensification of interest in the ancient canon laws of the church. Already in the twelfth century, Bologna had emerged as the leading center for the study of both laws. At first, instruction in the two laws was usually kept separate, and its beginnings are associated with the names of two distinguished teachers: the "civilian" Irnerius (d. c. 1130), who taught the Roman or civil law, and Gratian (d. c. 1160), who taught the canon law. The church, however, was very much a Roman institution; its early law had been deeply influenced by Roman law; and, as Gratian's great textbook, the *Decretum* (or *Concord of Discordant Canons*), makes very clear, Roman law played a considerable part in the development of medieval canon law. The importance, therefore, of studying both laws in conjunction quickly became evident, and in the thirteenth century, when both laws had become subjects of university study, it was not uncommon for the same professor to lecture on the two laws or for students to take the degree of "doctor of both laws" (*Juris utriusque doctor* or LL.D.).

The resulting intellectual interchange was a fruitful one and some of its most important consequences touched upon the very constitutional-ist issues discussed here. On the one hand, the canonists did not hesitate to treat the church as a kingdom, with the pope as its king or emperor, or to apply to him Romanist notions of imperial absolutism—including the maxim that "the prince is unfettered by the laws." On the other hand, they were moved also by St. Paul's insistence that ecclesiastics were given their power to build up the church, not to destroy it; and they were influenced by the degree to which the early texts incorporated in Gratian's great work pictured the church as a community of believers participating in the decisions that affected them and in the choice of the officials who were to lead them. While conceding vast powers to the pope, therefore, the canonists were anxious to prevent the abuse of those powers and were led "to seek in the consensus of the whole Christian community, in the indefectible Church guided by the Holy Spirit, norms of faith and order which could define the limits within which the pope's supreme legislative and judicial powers were to be exercised" [18]—hence the concern with the functions and powers of general councils representing the universal church and the relationship they bore to papal functions and preroga-tives; hence, too, their preoccupation with the elements in the Roman law that linked popular consent with public authority; and, again, the creative contribution they were able to make to the development of those viable representative mechanisms without which the eliciting of consent in large territorial states would have been impossible. By the thirteenth century, then, they had been led to teach that the pope, acting alone, was bound by the decisions reached by pope and general council on matters concerning the faith and well-being of the church. By the fourteenth century, an increasing number of them were being led to insist that a pope guilty of heresy or of crimes endangering the well-being of the church could be judged by a general council acting alone, corrected, and even deposed. Before the first two decades of the fifteenth century were over, the two general councils of Pisa (1409) and Constance (1414–18), by taking their stand on that teaching and by deposing the rival claimants to the papacy, had succeeded in bringing to an end the Great Schism of the West. But however important these developments—and they will appear again before the end of this chapter—it is the canonist contribution to theories of representation that is the first concern.

The need that representative assemblies initially met was the need of the ruler to secure for his policies as large a degree of public support as possible. It was a need that all rulers have felt, but one felt with particular acuteness by medieval rulers—and by popes as well as kings. The impact of feudalism, the political conditions of the day, and above all, if he really hoped to see his policies implemented, the dependence of the ruler upon the more powerful men and the more privileged groups among his subjects all conspired to increase his need to maximize the degree of consent among them to his policies; but how to do so? In a small city-state where it was possible to assemble in one place at least the more important citizens the problem could be solved by much the same means as those employed by the city-states of the classical world. This was out of the question, however, in the larger territorial states, where, between the thirteenth and eighteenth centuries, rulers turned for a solution to the new mechanism of the representative assembly. Of course, as harried university officials in our own day, anxious to maximize student participation in policy decisions, have all too frequently learned, "representation" can mean more than one thing. In particular (and simplifying considerably), it can mean either "personification"—the symbolic embodiment in its "natural" leaders or in its ruler of the authority of the community, or it can mean the conscious and legal delegation of that authority by the community to persons who represent it (make it present). It is in the latter sense of the word that the new assemblies were representative.

As long as the leading men of the day—the great feudal magnates in secular society and the bishops and abbots in ecclesiastical—could claim successfully to represent by personification those whom they ruled, the need for new machinery was not felt. It was entirely feasible, for example, for a king to assemble at his court the great barons of the realm or the bulk thereof, or even for a pope to summon the bishops of the universal church to attend a general council; but as a multitude of corporate bodies began to emerge, ecclesiastical or urban communities whose cooperation their bishops or barons could not claim to guarantee, it became necessary to seek their consent in a less indirect fashion, and especially in matters pertaining to taxation. To do so it was also necessary to create new machinery, and it was at this point that the

131

canonists, by a creative manipulation and development of certain elements drawn from the Roman law of corporations, were able to make their creative contribution.

A corporation is an association that the law recognizes as being constituted by one or more persons, as possessing various rights and duties, and as being capable of acting as a single (if fictitious) person in legal matters. Corporate bodies of one sort or another had proliferated in the Roman world and the Romans had developed a sophisticated body of corporation law to regulate their activities. Among other things that law laid down precise procedures whereby such corporate bodies could delegate authority to the lawyers whom they frequently needed to represent them in court—delegate, in effect, what we would call "powers of attorney." When it came to coping with the increasing amount of litigation involving such ecclesiastical corporations as monastic communities, cathedral chapters, and so on, the canonists initially did little more than draw upon this body of corporation law and its procedures. In their imaginative transference of the same principles and procedures from the restricted realm of the private law relating to property matters into the public constitutional sphere, however, they took a creative step that it does not seem to have occurred to their Roman predecessors to take, making it possible for popes to seek directly the counsel of powerful ecclesiastical corporations or at least their assent to church-wide policies via representatives possessed of a legally mandated authority "to advise and consent." Thus, as early as 1215, Innocent III, greatest of the medieval popes, summoned proctors from all over Europe to represent convents and cathedral chapters at the Fourth Lateran Council.

During the next three centuries similar procedures were increasingly adopted by the kings and territorial princes of Europe. Embarking, as they were, on increasingly vigorous and ambitious governmental activities whose success depended on the cooperation of their subjects, they needed more than ever to secure for their policies and for the mounting taxation necessary to finance them the consent of the governed, the consent, that is, not only of the baronage but also of the other and increasingly powerful propertied groups in the land.

These centuries, then, both on the national and provincial levels, saw an extraordinary flowering of representative assemblies, assemblies that functioned at one time or another all over Europe—from Sicily to Sweden, from Portugal to Poland, from England to Austria. At the beginning, it is true, such assemblies were very much a tool of government, a means by which the ruler could more easily achieve his goals—so much so, indeed, that one modern investigator of the English medieval parliament coined the felicitous description "self-government at the king's command." By the mid-fourteenth century, however, representative procedures were becoming less exclusively at the service of the ruler. At one time or another, most assemblies were able to make their weight felt in a whole range of governmental activities, notably in the legislative process, and the English Parliament was far from being alone in using the power of the purse, its control over taxation, in order to enhance its legislative authority and to limit the ruler's freedom of maneuver.

If, however, as has already been said, it was the instrumentalities of representation that were ultimately to provide the means whereby theoretical limitations on executive power could be enforced without recourse to armed violence, it cannot be claimed that this happy state of affairs was achieved during the Middle Ages. The activity of medieval representative assemblies was too intermittent, the restraints they imposed too dependent on special circumstances. Moreover, by the sixteenth and seventeenth centuries, the age of their greatness was over. Almost everywhere in Europe, the power of the prince was ascendant; monarchical absolutism was coming to be regarded as the "modern," fashionable thing, the most civilized governmental form; and the constitutional theories and practices inherited from the Middle Ages were being dismissed as archaic hindrances to the achievement of efficient government. Because of this a particular historical importance attaches to the great general councils of the Latin church that were assembled during the course of the fifteenth century, quasi-representative assemblies that, more dramatically than any other, exemplified in practice the constitutionalist aspirations of the Middle Ages. A particular importance attaches also to the Conciliar theorists who so influenced the work of those councils and in whose writings those aspirations found their clearest and most notable expression. The

Conciliar theorists "raised the constitutionalism of the past three centuries to a higher power; expressed it in a more universal form, and justified it on the grounds of reason, policy and Scripture." [19] As a result, long after the Conciliarist program of transforming the papal monarchy into a constitutionalist regime had ceased to be a viable possibility, and at a time when national constitutionalist traditions, too, had fallen into decay or were faltering on the brink of desuetude, Conciliarist ideas still retained the power to fuel the arguments and strengthen the resolution of hard-pressed constitutionalists or advocates of resistance to tyranny.

This was true in England as late as the 1640s in the early days of the first civil war, when the royalist supporters of Charles I confronted the forces of Parliament. It had been equally true a century earlier, when the restoration of Roman Catholicism in England and the persecution launched by Queen Mary had driven the more committed English Protestants into exile, opposition, and advocacy of resistance to tyranny. Later on in the same century, it was again to be true of both Protestant and Catholic advocates of lawful resistance when, during the convolutions of the French religious wars, they each confronted monarchs intent upon imposing on them a religious allegiance they could not in conscience accept. Thus in the *Vindiciae contra tyrannos,* the most famous and influential piece of constitutionalist literature spawned by those wars, the anonymous Protestant author argued that if

according to the opinion of most of the learned, by decrees of Councils and by custom on like occasions, it plainly appears that the Council may depose a Pope, who notwithstanding vaunts himself to be the King of Kings, and as much in Dignity above the Emperour, as the Sun is above the Moon . . . [then] . . . who will make any doubt or question, that the general Assembly of the Estates of any Kingdom, who are the representative body thereof, may not only degrade and disthronize a tyrant; but also, even disthronize and depose a King, whose weakness and folly is hurtful or pernicious to the State.[20]

Small wonder, then, that the conciliar movement has been described as "the culmination of medieval constitutionalism," and as forming "the real watershed between medieval and modern politics," or that the road from the Council of Constance to the English Revolution of 1688 has been said to have been "a direct one." [21] Nor, if the fundamental theme pursued in the first part of this chapter is recalled, should it escape attention that it was in the wake of the Protestant Reformation and with the onset of the Counter-Reformation that Conciliarist theories were being exploited and Conciliarist memories evoked. These things were occurring, that is to say, at a time when, in one country or another, religious minorities of either Protestant or Catholic persuasion were finding their consciences coerced by rulers of a different faith, were being forced to qualify the loyalty they owed to those rulers, and were hedging about with historic limitations the allegiance they owed to their states. They were finding, in other words, that if they were indeed to render to God the things that were God's, they would be unable to render to Caesar the things that he was currently claiming to be his. Rarely had the tension and instability engendered by the New Testament separation of religion and politics been more threatening; rarely was it to be more fruitful.

V

REASON AND FAITH

The Direction of Mediaeval
Intellectual Life

Of the great scientific revolution that culminated in the seventeenth century one of its recent historians has written that it "outshines everything since the rise of Christianity" and looms large "as the real origin both of the modern world and of the modern mentality," not simply because it ended with the dismantling of so much of the older natural science, ancient as well as medieval, but also because it ultimately "changed the character of men's habitual mental operations even in the conduct of the nonmaterial sciences, while transforming the whole diagram of the physical universe and the very texture of human life itself." [1]

Few today—not even the most apocalyptic antitechnocrats of the counterculture—would care to dispute that claim, nor would many wish to question the uniqueness of the Western scientific achievement or the critical importance of the scientific revolution to that achievement—the less so, indeed, in that there is clearly nothing unique about the Western *interest* in understanding the processes of the natural world. Other civilizations pursued the same interest to the point of producing promising natural sciences. None of these sciences, however, succeeded in developing beyond the embryonic stage. In the course of his massive inquiry *Science and Civilization in China*, Joseph Needham, while emphasizing the impressive nature of early Chinese science, puzzled over its failure to make the critical breakthrough that European science achieved in the sixteenth and seventeenth centuries. A similar problem attends upon the history of science in Islam—the more acute, indeed, in that Islam, like Byzantium, was for centuries in possession of the bulk of Greek scientific work without breaking through to anything approximating a Newtonian physics. Historians have sometimes spoken as if the scientific revolution was the outcome of the late medieval and Renaissance recovery of contact with the riches of the Greek scientific achievement; but the history of science in the Roman, Byzantine, and Islamic worlds gives the lie to such historiographic shortcuts. The truly important thing was not the possession by western Europeans of Greek scientific or philosophical writings: others had possessed them and had often been content with doing little more than repeating or elaborating upon what they said. The important thing, instead, was what Europeans made of those texts, what they brought to them, what was on their minds, and the fact that, by the later Middle Ages and in some very crucial respects, it differed from what was on the minds of their Roman predecessors or their Byzantine or Islamic contemporaries.

The scientific revolution was an exceedingly complex event. As such, it presupposed the working and interaction of a baffling multitude of factors: mathematical, technological, educational, economic, socio-logical, philosophical. Among the most fundamental of those factors, however, was a prior shift in the thinking of the scientific inquirer himself, one that led him to ask different questions, use different methods, seek different solutions from those of his classical predecessors or their counterparts in other civilizations. No less than other successful revolutions, in fact, the scientific revolution presupposed a revolution in the minds of men.

Concede that claim, of course, and the intellectual history of western Europe in the centuries immediately preceding the scientific revolution must certainly possess an interest far more compelling than the merely archaeological. If a fundamental shift did indeed occur in the thinking of those concerned with understanding the world of nature, it must surely have occurred subsequent to the twelfth-century quickening in the tempo of intellectual life, when Western philosophers and theologians strove above all to comprehend and come to terms with the newly translated philosophical and scientific works of Aristotle and his Muslim commentators. Concede that claim, too, and a particular interest attaches also to the philosopher Alfred North Whitehead's provocative advocacy of the idea that the development of modern science was inconceivable in the absence of the habits of mind inculcated by medieval scholastic theology—as also to his characteristically perceptive remark that "the sort of person who was a scholastic doctor in a mediaeval university, today is a scientific professor in a modern university." [2] Later on in this chapter we will return to Whitehead's argument. Before we can do so, however, it is necessary to be clear both about the nature of scholasticism and about its place in medieval intellectual life.

Humanists, Lawyers, and Universities

NOT long ago an unguarded conversational reference to medieval intellectual life would almost invariably evoke ribald remarks about angels dancing on the heads of pins, a reference to the debate, allegedly endemic among medieval scholastic theologians, concerning the number of angels who could comfortably be accommodated on the head of a (presumably medieval) pin. It is an interesting reaction, not so much because it reveals the condescension with which medieval intellectual pursuits were customarily viewed in some circles—though it does that, too—but rather because it reflects the belief that theology was *the* intellectual pursuit and the scholastic theologian *the* intellectual figure most characteristic of the Middle Ages.

It is easy enough to understand the grounds for this belief. For those who shared the older, negative view of the Middle Ages, it was precisely the dominance of sterile theological speculation that helped account for the intellectual torpor taken to be characteristic of the whole period. For those who reacted against that negative view, the Middle Ages were seen, above all, as "the Age of Faith," and, for such an age, what more appropriate a subject of study than theology itself? But if theology in general was indeed *the* prestige subject in the Middle Ages and scholastic theology "the Queen of the Sciences," it is important to realize how small a percentage of the total student population actually studied it, and how short was the period during which what we call "scholasticism" actually dominated the medieval intellectual scene.

In the absence of seminaries for the education and formation of priests (for those were to be introduced only in the sixteenth century), few of the medieval clergy can have pursued any formal studies in theology. Both before and after the emergence of universities in the late twelfth and thirteenth centuries, the bulk of those pursuing a more advanced education were involved in the study of the liberal arts, which, though regarded as preparatory to the study of theology, did not include it—no more, indeed, than it included law or medicine. Of the minority who went on to pursue such "postgraduate studies," the greater part, understandably enough, were attracted to law and medicine, which, though they lacked the overriding prestige attached to theology, held greater promise of leading to careers crowned by prominence and rewarded by wealth.

If theologians, then, formed something of a small elite group in the Middle Ages, the body of scholastic theologians constituted an even smaller elite, and one restricted also to a fairly limited period of time. *Scholasticism*—a word used in a variety of ways—can best be taken to denote the rather technical fashion of thinking, teaching, and, therefore, writing that developed in the medieval schools during the course of the twelfth century, dominated the academic scene in the thirteenth and fourteenth centuries, and began to slide into disrepute during the course of the fifteenth. Scholasticism no more represented the "norm" in medieval intellectual life, then, than does the highly technical and "scientific" approach to matters intellectual that characterizes our own era represent the "norm" in the postmedieval period. Taking the history of European intellectual and educational life as a whole, indeed, the thirteenth and fourteenth centuries on the one hand and the nineteenth and twentieth centuries on the other stand out somewhat as exceptions to the norm. They both do so by virtue of the highly professionalized and technical nature of their most characteristic intellectual pursuits. For in the modern as well as in the medieval period it is the broadly humanistic range of studies in the liberal arts that has constituted the dominant educational tradition and most persistently shaped European intellectual life.

Like so much else, the roots of this tradition are thrust deep into the world of classical antiquity where the study of the "liberal" arts was considered to provide the type of general education most appropriate to

142

the needs of a *liber homo*—a free man, or, perhaps more accurately, a gentleman. Plato and Cicero had regarded such an education as the proper introduction to the more intensive study of philosophy, and it was to be extremely important for the future of Western intellectual life that St. Augustine sympathized with their point of view. In his influential work *On Christian Doctrine*, he urged Christian scholars to retain what amounted to the old Roman curriculum in the liberal arts as a necessary preparation for the more important and higher studies in Christian philosophy and theology. Given the turbulent political conditions of the early medieval period, the disappearance of the traditional educational institutions, and the concomitant decline of learning, it is even more important that educated monks like St. Jerome (d. 620) and Cassiodorus (d. c. 575) should have succeeded in making the study of the liberal arts an integral part of the monastic life.

Education implies schools, schools imply libraries, libraries imply books and, at that time, the copying of books. All of these were eventually to become intimately associated with the great monasteries of the early medieval West, despite the fact that they had little to do with the religious aspirations that had originally given rise to monasticism and could find little positive sustenance in the influential guiding *Rule* that St. Benedict of Nursia (c. 480–543) had originally drawn up for his monastery at Monte Cassino. There was nothing in that *Rule,* for example, about the copying of books; it was Cassiodorus who appears to have initiated the process that was ultimately to make it an almost quintessential part of the monk's duty. "Oh, blessed the perseverance," he wrote, "laudable the industry which preaches to men with the hand, starts tongues with the fingers, gives an unspoken salvation to mortals and against the iniquitous deceits of the Devil fights with pen and ink. For Satan receives as many wounds as the scribe copies words of the Lord." [3] Cassiodorus speaks here, of course, of copying the Bible, but in order to maintain the type of educational program he had bequeathed to them, the monks had to copy much else besides, and to their efforts we owe the preservation of the bulk of the classical Latin literature that has survived into the modern world.

The independence, economic self-sufficiency, and frequent rural isolation of the great landed monasteries fitted them admirably to be

the principal bearers of learning during the turbulence of the early
Middle Ages, and the monastic schools retained their preeminence in
educational matters until the beginning of the twelfth century. At that
time, with the restoration of public order, the increase in population,
and the revival of town life, the need for the monastic role in education
and the very appropriateness of such a role to the monastic vocation
was called into question. The initiative in educational matters was
already passing to the secular clergy (and even to the laymen) who
were teaching at the new schools connected with the cathedrals or with
other prominent churches in the more important urban centers. And as
the numbers of students increased, these schools began to grow in
number and size.

With that shift came also, as the twelfth century wore on, a shift in
the type of education dispensed. By the end of the fourth century it
had become customary to regard the liberal arts as seven in number and
to divide them into two groups: the *trivium,* which consisted of
grammar, rhetoric, and logic, and the *quadrivium,* which included
music theory, astronomy, arithmetic, and geometry. In early medieval
study of the liberal arts some attention was given to all of these
subjects, but it would be fair to say that most attention was lavished
upon the subjects of the *trivium* and, of those (at least until the second
half of the twelfth century), upon grammar and rhetoric. This
represents a less restricted curriculum than the names themselves might
suggest to us. Between them, grammar and rhetoric were taken to
include not only Latin grammar, syntax, written composition, and oral
delivery, but also the study of the literature of classical Rome. The
twelfth century was to witness, in fact, not only the recovery of an
almost classical command of Latin prose and poetic style among its
leading humanists at Chartres, Paris, Orléans, and elsewhere, but also a
distinct flowering of interest in classical Latin literature.

Whatever the strengths of this type of education, its limitations are
also readily evident. Indeed, its dominance is explicable only if one
recalls that the knowledge of Greek had long since been lost in the
West and that direct contact with the Greek philosophical and
scientific tradition was limited for centuries to the merest handful of

translated fragments. However Platonic the sympathies of many medieval thinkers, they were largely dependent for their Platonism upon what they learned indirectly from such authors as Cicero or St. Augustine. Before the late fifteenth century, only three of Plato's dialogues were available in Latin translations, and one of those, that of the *Timaeus*, was incomplete. Before the mid-twelfth century, Aristotle was even less well known, and the masters of logic were forced to exercise their talents upon the rather thin dialectical fodder provided by the merely introductory treatises to Aristotle's logic that were available in the Latin translations made by Boethius (d. c. 525), like Cassiodorus one of Theodoric the Goth's Roman civil servants. By mid-century, however, this had come to be known as the "old logic" because, by then, the remaining portions of Aristotle's logical work had been translated and were being avidly studied as the "new logic."

The dialectical techniques that had become authoritative in the ancient world were now at the disposal of medieval teachers and the result was a progressive shift of curricular emphasis within the *trivium*. Thus by the early thirteenth century grammatical and literary studies had been whittled back to an almost irreducible minimum, and the curriculum at the University of Paris in the faculty responsible for the study of the liberal arts was almost wholly given over to logic. But not for long. The renewal of direct contact with the philosophical writings of Greek antiquity was not limited to works concerned with logic. In Syria (from the time of the first Crusade onwards), at Constantinople, in Sicily, and above all in Spain, the translators were at work throughout the twelfth century. At Toledo (since its recapture in 1085 an important center of contact between Christian, Muslim, and Jew), the archbishop, indeed, had set up something approximating a translation factory. For the world of Latin Christendom the outcome of all this activity was a great influx of ancient Greek philosophical and scientific writings, along with more recent Jewish and Arabic work in the same fields. During the late twelfth and early thirteenth centuries, via translations made from the Greek itself, or from Arabic translations of the Greek, or, not infrequently, via both, the Latin world was gradually put into contact for the first time not just with Aristotle's logic but with the whole body of his writings and with an extensive array of Arabic commentaries on those writings, especially those of the great Muslim philosopher Averroës (Ibn Rushd, 1126–98).

The effect of this reception of Aristotle was very dramatic. If logic had earlier pushed grammar and rhetoric to one side, it was now the fate of logic to be put in its place as simply one part of the first complete philosophic and scientific system Western thinkers had encountered. By 1255 the faculty of arts curriculum at Paris included the whole corpus of Aristotle's writings. Henceforth, no other ancient thinker could rival his prestige. He was now simply "the philosopher." He was the great authority on whom budding philosophers and natural scientists were required to cut their intellectual teeth. His were the philosophical categories in terms of which professional theologians were trained to think, and with his scheme of things medievals struggled henceforth to harmonize their Christian beliefs. But if the recovery of Aristotle was to make a very dramatic and profound impact upon medieval educational and intellectual life, the precise nature of that impact was in no small measure to be determined by two roughly contemporaneous developments. The first concerned educational methods; the second, educational institutions.

Medieval students would appear to have been no less manic-depressive, riot-prone, or financially indigent than are their modern counterparts, and they also shared—at least with modern American students—a marked degree of dependence upon anthologies of extracts from the great authors of the past. It is at once the great strength and weakness of such collections—*florilegia,* as they were called in the Middle Ages—that the authors whose words are cited in order to throw light on a given topic do not always agree one with another. In an age, however, that revered the great authorities of the past—legal, philosophical, theological—one during which oral discussion and public disputation played a central role in the educational process, such discrepancies would necessarily have been much more disquieting than fruitful had not a methodology or mode of inquiry been devised to cope with them. It is that methodology, rather than any system of ideas, that the word "scholasticism" is most properly taken to denote, for "the scholastic method was a development of the *florilegium.* In its simplest

146

form, it was an attempt to solve by infinitely patient criticism and subtlety of distinction, the problems posed by the juxtaposition of related but divergent passages in the works of the great Christian writers." [4] The method involved was hammered out during the course of the twelfth century, and it should be noted that it was not only logicians and theologians like Peter Abelard (1079–1142) or Peter Lombard (1100–1160) who contributed to its formation, but also lawyers like Gratian, in whose *Decretum* conflicting legal authorities are balanced against each other and a systematic attempt is made to harmonize them. Indeed, the full title of that great work, the *Concord of Discordant Canons*, suggests at once the intellectual dilemma that gave rise to scholasticism and the means proposed to resolve it.

The rise to prominence of scholasticism also coincided in time with the rise to prominence, first at Paris and Bologna and then elsewhere, of the new institutional forms to which we refer simply as "universities" but to which contemporaries referred as "universities of masters or scholars." The difference is a revealing one. For us the word *university* denotes simply the institution of advanced learning that has come everywhere to dominate our systems of higher education. With a carelessness that is no less anachronistic for all its generosity, we are apt also to apply the word to the great schools of the ancient world and even to those that flourished in civilizations untouched by the influence of Western educational models. Strictly speaking, however, such usage is quite improper. Universities were a medieval invention, and when medievals spoke of them they were referring not to the great schools or *studia generalia*—where at least one of the advanced professional disciplines was taught and to which students resorted from all over Europe—but to the guilds or *universitates* of masters and students, which, from the last quarter of the twelfth century onward, began to appear at those great schools. Those guilds were simply sworn societies or corporations of masters or students who had joined together for mutual protection. Modeled on the commercial and craft guilds of the medieval cities, they were a response to the need of the growing numbers of masters and students congregated in those cities to protect their own interests against the pressures being put on them by townsmen and civic authorities, perhaps also by ecclesiastical authorities—though it should be noted that the bulk of masters and students in the great northern universities were themselves clerics of one sort or another.

Given the fact that the classes at the urban schools of the twelfth and thirteenth centuries were conducted in leased or borrowed buildings, the fledgling universities (i.e., guilds) were unembarrassed by the extensive property holdings that are both the presupposition and the burden of their modern descendants. In their battles with hostile civic authorities, then, their trump card was the ability to declare a strike or cessation of studies, or even to move the whole operation to another less hostile city, thus emptying the offending town of its rent-paying student population, which in some cases must have constituted as much as one-tenth of the total populace. For "protective reactions" of this type to be effective, however, it was necessary for the masters themselves to control who could teach in the schools. This they did by regulating entry into their own ranks, by imposing on the schools what amounted to a closed-shop policy, and by establishing control over the granting of the *licentia docendi,* or license to teach, which was the forerunner of all academic degrees. Degrees were to be given only to the qualified; that a candidate was qualified was to be determined not simply by length of studies but also by examination; and examinations to be both effective and equitable presupposed coherent curriculum, systematic teaching, and a regulated course of studies. "Curriculum, examinations, commencement, degrees, are all part of the same system; they are all inherited from the Middle Ages, and in some form they go back to the twelfth century." [5]

If it would be possible to exaggerate the importance of the emergence of universities in the twelfth and thirteenth centuries, it would be hard to do so. By institutionalizing higher education in western Europe, they created a stable academic context in which large intellectual endeavors could be, if not more readily undertaken, at least more systematically pursued and more nearly brought to fruition. By securing for scholars a highly privileged position in society and a reasonable degree of independence from nonacademic pressures, they also created the conditions (lacking so notably, for example, in Islam) under which such endeavors could be pursued over long periods of time

148

and with a minimum of interference from those uninformed outsiders whose fate it was to dwell in the outer darkness beyond the perimeters of the guild. Together with scholasticism, which provided a methodology geared to rendering compatible the contradictory and harmonious the dissonant, the universities made it possible for medieval intellectuals to come remarkably close to achieving the impossible: namely, to domesticating within the alien confines of the Christian world view the "naturalistic" and at many points incompatible philosophy of the pagan Aristotle. The ecclesiastical authorities might raise obstacles to this process—as they did at Paris in 1210, 1215, and again in 1231—but they could only delay it; and differ though they might in their presuppositions and solutions, the great scholastic theologians of the medieval universities were at one in their insistence on coming to terms with the new Aristotle, and on incorporating within their systems as much as possible of his thinking. If they disagreed about what it was to reason, or about the nature of the relationship between philosophic reason and the Christian revelation, they did not doubt that such a relationship existed or that the form it took was one of interdependence rather than of mutual exclusion. And in this they remained faithful to the position adopted centuries before, when the early Christian thinkers first had to confront the palpable tensions between the biblical teachings to which they were committed in faith and the Greek philosophical doctrines that framed the educated common sense of their day.

Reason and Revelation

THAT the dominant Christian attitude toward the Greek philosophical tradition in general should have been one of openness is no more to be taken for granted than that monasteries should have become centers of learning and promoters of the liberal arts. In both cases it is only our familiarity with the outcome that suggests the necessity of the process. To the medieval cultivation of the literature produced by pagan Rome we owe not only the very survival into the modern world of so many of the Latin classics but also the existence of so many elements of classical inspiration to be found in the modern European vernacular literatures. Cultivation of a pagan literature was not undertaken without misgivings, however. There was much in the classics, after all, to provoke and offend Christian sensibilities. St. Jerome, fine classicist though he was, had himself expressed such misgivings, even if he succeeded admirably in overcoming them. So had St. Benedict of Nursia; so, too, Pope Gregory the Great.

If moral sensibilities were bruised by the worldliness and eroticism of so much of the classical literature, it was the purity of the faith itself, however, that appeared threatened by the insidious paganisms of a philosophic tradition that knew nothing of Yahweh, the personal God of Abraham, Isaac, and Jacob, the biblical God of power and might. Had not the New Testament itself warned against the seductions of that tradition? "See to it," St. Paul had written to the Colossians, "that no one makes a prey of you by philosophy and empty deceit, according to human tradition, according to the elemental spirits of the universe and not according to Christ" (Col. 2:8); and to the Corinthians: "The foolishness of God is wiser than men"; God has "made foolish the wisdom of the world" (1 Cor. 1:20, 25). Whenever in subsequent centuries the purity of the biblical teaching seemed threatened by the incursions of the fashionable philosophies of the day, those warnings were to succeed in starting echoes, and never more dramatically than in the writings of Tertullian, who, in one famous passage, having identified philosophy as "the material of the world's wisdom" and denounced Aristotle as "unhappy" for having equipped philosophers with the art of dialectics, exclaimed: "What . . . has Athens to do with Jerusalem? What concord is there between the Academy and the Church? What between heretics and Christians? . . . Away with all attempts to produce a mottled Christianity of Stoic, Platonic and dialectic composition! We want no curious disputation after possessing Jesus Christ, no inquisition after enjoying the Gospel! With our faith, we desire no further belief." [6]

Tertullian's fundamentalism, like that of Tatian (b. c. 120) before him, represents something of an extreme, but misgivings about the philosophical pursuit of the sort he felt have frequently been expressed by Christian thinkers, not only by ecclesiastics or followers of the monastic life, but also, paradoxically, by Christian laymen who were themselves philosophers—thus, for example, Blaise Pascal (1623–62), for whom "all philosophy" was "not worth one hour of pain";[7] or even, for that matter, Søren Kierkegaard (1813–55), who so profoundly influenced the development of modern existentialism.

The note these writers struck cannot simply be ignored. If it remained a subdominant, as it were, in the intellectual life of the medieval Latin West, the ultimate fate of philosophical and scientific reasoning in the intellectual worlds of medieval Jewry and medieval Islam suggests the ease with which, had conditions been otherwise, it might well have assumed greater prominence. Jewish and Muslim thinkers, like their Christian counterparts, faced the problem of reconciling with their religious beliefs a philosophical tradition that, while it represented the noblest intellectual achievement known to them, was at odds on some very critical points with the vision of God, of man, and of the universe conveyed to them in the sacred writings they believed to have been divinely revealed. Like their Christian counterparts, they failed to agree among themselves either about the desirability of undertaking such a reconciliation, or, admitting it to be indeed desirable, about the means whereby it could be engineered. Again, as with the Christians, many of them might be called "Tertullianists"—fundamentalists, that is, who took their stand on the intellectual sufficiency of the revealed word of God and of the ethical and legal tradition constructed therefrom. Others, however, argued for the need to assimilate the philosophical wisdom of the Greeks and set out to construct systems of ideas that would incorporate that wisdom and use it to deepen the fundamental insights conveyed by Bible and Koran. Of the latter, one need refer only, for the Jews, to Philo of Alexandria (d. c. A.D. 40), who, by reconciling Platonic teachings with Judaism, blazed the trail that the Christian theologians of the Alexandrian school were to follow, or to Moses Maimonides (1135–1204), whose attempt at harmonizing Aristotelian and biblical thinking served as an inspiration especially to Thomas Aquinas (1225–74), by common agreement the greatest of scholastic theologians, when he later on made a similar attempt. For the Muslims, it is necessary to do no more than cite the two philosophers whose writings exerted so profound an influence on Latin Christendom: Ibn Sina (980–1037), a Persian known in the Latin world as Avicenna, and Averroës, the Spaniard whose authority as the leading interpreter of Aristotle medievals acknowledged so strikingly when they referred to him simply as "the Commentator."

In any history of philosophy that is not parochially European in its orientation (and in some, indeed, that are), these men stand out as figures of the utmost importance. Yet, by the thirteenth century, the fundamentalists and legalists were winning the day in both the Jewish and the Muslim worlds. In subsequent years, ironically enough, Maimonides, Avicenna, and Averroës were in many ways to enjoy a better press among Christian thinkers than among their Jewish or Muslim counterparts. That this should have been the case with the Jews reflects the discrediting of the more "liberal" and philosophic Judaism of the Philonic or Alexandrian mold that followed in the wake of the first Crusade, the concomitant spread of violent anti-Semitism across western Europe, and the progressive loss by Jews of the political security, social standing, and economic well-being that had often been theirs in the early medieval period. As a result, the later medieval centuries saw, in the inward-looking ghetto communities to which Jews had been increasingly confined, the triumph under rabbinical sponsorship of the more rigid and legalistic Talmudic form of Judaism that did much to discourage any further pursuit of the old attempt to bring philosophic reason and sacred revelation into fruitful and harmonious juxtaposition.

Changes in political conditions also had much to do with the comparable shift in attitude that occurred in the Muslim world and brought to a halt the promising philosophic and scientific ventures of the early medieval centuries. The rise to power of fanatical Berber dynasties in North Africa and Muslim Spain and the triumph of the Seljuk Turks in the old heartlands of the Islamic Empire did much to strengthen the hold of the religious legalists throughout *Sunni*, or orthodox, Islam. It also did much to sponsor acceptance of the authoritarian theology of al-Ash'arī (d. 936), with its insistence on unhesitating acceptance of Koranic revelation and of the *sharī'a*, or divine law, that it contained and its marginalization within theology of the role of philosophic reason. Asharism, however, might well have achieved its final victory even without such changes in the political sphere, for that victory also represents the culmination of a struggle that had been going on for centuries between the Mu'tazilite or philosophically inspired rationalists and the fundamentalist defenders of an orthodoxy grounded in the Koran and in the *Hadīth*, the officially accepted body of recorded traditions about the life and sayings of Mohammed.

In the context of this struggle, al-Ash'arī's views represent something of a compromise. What he did—and it was initially suspect to the more rigidly legalistic exponents of orthodoxy—was to apply "the methods of Greek dialectic to the support of the Koran and the Hadīth," thus evolving "a new orthodox scholasticism" and defeating "the Mu'tazilites on their own ground." [8] In this system the function of philosophy was strictly a subordinate and apologetic one. There was in Asharism no more genuine an interpenetration of Koranic revelation and Greek philosophical doctrines than there was in the thinking of the great scientists and philosophers of the Islamic world, so many of whom were no less unorthodox to Muslims than they were to Christians. In the thinking of those men (and Averroës and Avicenna may serve as good examples), there is a persistent tendency to segregate Koranic religious teaching from their more properly philosophical doctrines, to categorize the former as a rather crude approximation of the truth of things, though one admirably designed to foster the moral formation of the ignorant and credulous masses; and to regard the latter as conveying the true vision of reality, though one accessible only to that small illuminated elite endowed with the gift of philosophic insight.

This tendency was ultimately to account for some of the most striking characteristics of Islamic society, and it has been suggested that the social environment in which Muslim thinkers had to work helps account for it. Nowhere in Islam does one find ecclesiastically sponsored institutions like the Latin universities in which large bodies of clerics worked side by side (and often successively) on philosophical and theological questions in a privileged and protected society

153

conducive, on the one hand, to cross-fertilization between the two fields, and secure, on the other, from coercion by ignorant religious fanatics. Even had this not been the case, the very nature of the Koran and the extraordinary status accorded it by Muslims would have served as formidable obstacles, in any intellectual circles that could be called orthodox, to bringing its teachings into intimate contact with Greek philosophical ideas; for Muslims are "a people of the book" in a way that Christians can never be, and the New Testament is no more to be aligned with the Koran than is Muhammed with Christ. At the very base of Christian belief and worship lies the Incarnation; it is in the person of Jesus Christ that Christians claim to encounter the divine: Christ, the incarnate God, the eternal Word (*Logos*) "who became flesh and dwelt among us." At the base of Muslim belief, on the other hand, lies the divine law of righteousness, preexisting in God in an eternal archetype and entering history (one is tempted to say "becoming incarnate") in the revelations that Mohammed received from the angel Gabriel and committed to writing in the work known as the Koran. Thus, if Mohammed is to be compared with anyone, it is with Paul rather than with Christ, and the New Testament is to be aligned with the *Hadīth* rather than with the Koran. Indeed, the Koran comes as close as anything in Islam to occupying the place the person of Christ occupies in Christianity. It is "the glorious Koran," "the noble Koran," a sacred object to be touched by "none but the purified," itself a miraculous event, the focal point of man's communion with the divine.

This being so, Muslim hesitancies about subjecting Koranic teaching to philosophical analysis—just as the continuing absence in the Islamic world of anything comparable to modern Western biblical criticism[9] —is entirely understandable. The Koran was a revelation complete in itself, the source along with the *Hadīth* of a law (the *sharī'a*) that shaped not only what we would call the religious but many other aspects of life in Islamic society. Had the New Testament occupied in Christian belief so similarly exalted a position it is very doubtful, for example, if the Roman law would have been so enthusiastically received or would have played so fundamental a role in either Byzantine or Latin Christendom. Had it occupied such a position it is also doubtful if that critical encounter between Greek philosophical thinking and biblical teaching, which has done so much to shape the contours of the Western intellectual tradition, could ever have taken place.

However revered, the New Testament did not, of course, occupy that sort of position. Moreover, it suggested (in words cited again and again by church fathers and medieval philosophers) that God manifests himself not only to the believers who encounter him in the word of Scripture, but also to all who care to scrutinize the fabric of his creation. "For what can be known about God is plain to them, because God has shown it to them. Ever since the creation of the world his invisible nature, namely his eternal power and deity, has been clearly perceived in the things that have been made." (Rom. 1:14–20). Christians, then, could regard the exercise of philosophic reason as the exploration of God's natural revelation, and the highly philosophical tone of the prologue to the Gospel according to St. John positively invited such an exploration and the correlation of its results with the truths revealed in the Scripture itself. Philo of Alexandria had already shown the way, blending the cosmogony elaborated in Plato's *Timaeus* with the account of Creation set forth in Genesis. The most influential among the Greek and Latin fathers of the church were to follow in his footsteps: Clement of Alexandria (d. c. 215) and Origen (d. c. 254), for example, in the East; St. Augustine, above all, in the West. Augustine, himself a Neoplatonist, says in the *Confessions* that he had found in the "books of the Platonists" all the fundamentals of his Christian belief except the doctrine of the Incarnation.[10] So dazzled was he by the apparent coincidence of viewpoint between the Bible and Plato that he was led to toy with the idea that Plato may have been conversant, at one remove or another, with parts of the Old Testament.

On this attitude toward philosophic reason, as on so many other matters, Augustine's attitude proved to be decisive for the Latin West. The authority of Aristotle might succeed that of Plato, the philosophical options might change, and with them the nature of the claims made for the range of human reason; but whatever the shifts in the current of intellectual life, and whatever the misgivings voiced by the Tertullians or Tatians of the day, the dominant Christian attitude toward the exercise of philosophic reason and toward the Greek philosophical tradition that so nobly manifested its achievements remained one of openness. In the thinking of the medieval philosophers and theologians, then, Jerusalem continued the encounter with Athens that it had long since begun in the pioneering work of Philo; and from that historic encounter neither party emerged unchanged.

God, Philosophy, and Science

ABOUT the impact of Athens upon Jerusalem much has been written. Some have lauded as an enrichment of the primitive Christian vision the penetration of Christian modes of thought by philosophic ideas of Greek provenance. Others, moved by nostalgia for an original purity—real or imagined but certainly long since gone—have deplored it as a lamentable distortion; but none have doubted that such a penetration did indeed occur. Trinitarian, christological, and eucharistic doctrines, the very creedal statements of the ancient and medieval church, the formulations of Christian theologians belonging to widely differing persuasions and periods and ranging from Justin Martyr (d. c. 167) to Paul Tillich (1886–1965)—all of these betray a profound indebtedness to the Greek philosophical tradition.

About the impact of Jerusalem upon Athens, however, much less has been said. Many a historian of philosophy, indeed, still contrives to give the impression that modern philosophy began *de novo* with the work of Descartes, Locke, Leibniz, and the other great philosophers of the early modern period, or that the palpable differences between the thinking of such men and that of the classical Greek philosophers owe nothing at all to the reshaping of ancient patterns of philosophic thought by ideas and preoccupations of Judaic and Christian provenance. In the absence of such a reshaping, however, and without the long centuries of tension between biblical and philosophical conceptions, it would be hard indeed to account for the fundamental assumptions upon which the early modern philosophers chose to erect their systems, or, for that

156

matter, the assumptions basic to the work of such great architects of the scientific revolution as Sir Isaac Newton (1642–1727) or Robert Boyle (1627–91). As Whitehead rightly implies, the theological component in the thinking of these men is far more crucial than we usually tend to suppose. The tension in question, then, deserves close examination. It manifested itself most acutely during the medieval period, and it was around the problem of God that it came most sharply into focus. If the reasons for this are easy enough to isolate, they are extremely difficult to articulate in small compass and in a manner readily accessible to the layman. They are, moreover, impossible to render intelligible without a brief foray into the history of Greek philosophy.

Both Plato and Aristotle had elaborated distinctive and highly sophisticated conceptions of God. Behind those conceptions, however, lay a prephilosophical understanding of the divine, which, in its broad characteristics, the early Greeks shared in common with the other peoples of the archaic world. It is the point of view that underpinned notions of sacral monarchy, one that failed to differentiate the divine from the world of nature, or, to the extent to which it did achieve such a differentiation, did so by regarding the natural world in general and natural things and processes in particular as in some sense a manifestation of the divine. Though Plato and Aristotle both advanced beyond that point of view, they did so without wholly abandoning it. Thus Plato could speak of the universe as "a blessed god," and Aristotle could characterize as "inspired" the old myth that the first substances "are gods and that the divine encloses the whole of nature." [11]

Translated onto the philosophical plane, however, this archaic point of view found more characteristic expression in the notion of the divine as being immanent in nature, related to it as an indwelling and organizing principle, the source at once of the order of its movements and the unity of its disparate parts. The analogy invoked was the relation of mind to body in man, and the universe was conceived as a great organism permeated by mind or soul; but if the Greeks saw in the orderliness of natural processes the working of an intelligence, eternal and divine, it was not a divine intelligence that transcended nature, nor was it any more eternal than was the material world itself. When Plato

157

sought to vindicate philosophically the belief in the presence of mind in the universe, he did so without questioning the eternity of the matter out of which that universe had been fashioned. Thus in the *Timaeus* (an extremely problematic work but the Platonic dialogue that the early Christian Fathers and the medieval theologians both knew best), he depicts the Demiurge or World-Maker as a sort of cosmic artisan fashioning an intelligible universe out of preexistent matter in accordance with the eternally subsistent "Forms," essences, arche-types, or "Ideas" that serve him as exemplars, patterns, or blueprints for all things.

The *Timaeus*, therefore, has something in common with such archaic Creation myths as the Babylonian *Enuma elish*, myths that are concerned not with Creation in the sense Christians usually ascribe to that word, but rather with the emergence of a "cosmos" or ordered, harmonious system out of a preexisting chaos. The Demiurge is no omnipotent Creator-God. Neither the Ideas nor matter owe their existence to him—far from it, indeed, for both by their existence impose limits on his creative activity, the former in that they serve as the pattern he must strive to realize in matter, the latter in that it resists his attempts to impose that pattern. Nowhere is it suggested that the Demiurge should be an object of worship, and Plato may well have intended him not to be understood literally but rather as a mythical symbol standing for the presence in the universe of a divine reason analogous to man's and "working for ends that are good." Something similar may be said of Aristotle's *Metaphysics*, in which he presents no Creation story, it is true (for his universe is eternal), but the notion of a First Principle, which while it transcends the universe is also immanent in it "as the order of the parts." Aristotle himself calls this First Principle "God," but it is neither a Creator-God, nor a personal God, nor an object of worship. Indeed, it is not even a God who acts directly upon the universe as efficient cause, but rather an Unmoved Mover, the final and highest good that, because all things aspire and ceaselessly strive to emulate its perfection, serves as the cause of motion or change in the universe. As Dante tells us in the profoundly Aristotelian words with which he concludes the *Divine Comedy*, it is "love that moves the sun and the other stars."

158

Put in this way, both Plato's and Aristotle's understanding of the nature of the divine, of the universe, and of the relationship between the two, would appear to be wholly incompatible with the parallel Judaic and Christian views; but then neither Plato nor Aristotle put these things quite so simply. The *Timaeus* and the *Metaphysics* are both extremely difficult works, fraught with ambiguities and posing problems of interpretation over which modern scholars continue to wrangle. By stressing some aspects of their thinking more than others, therefore, there was room for subsequent philosophers to develop Platonic and Aristotelian views in a fashion less difficult to reconcile with biblical notions. Moreover, during the years after Aristotle's death, most of his major works appear to have been lost, and he was known only through his early and highly Platonic dialogues. For centuries, then, he was honored as the master of logicians but regarded as a Platonist. So it was Plato alone with whom first the Hellenized Jews of Alexandria and then the Christian Fathers had to come to terms; and, even then, not so much the original Plato as one whose thinking had been combined with or reshaped by philosophic ideas of Stoic, Pythagorean, and even Aristotelian provenance to produce the increasingly religious and frequently mystical systems of thought leading up to the position that nineteenth-century scholars called Neoplatonic and that found its most coherent and distinguished expression in the writings of the Egyptian philosopher Plotinus (d. A.D. 270).

There are few developments in the history of philosophy more tangled than the movement of ideas that culminated in Plotinus. For present purposes, however, it must suffice to say that this movement involved a persistent tendency to understand Plato's Demiurge not as a mythical symbol but literally as a World-Maker, to conflate him with the Transcendent Unmoved Mover of Aristotle—the final and highest good whom he himself called "God"—and to treat Plato's eternally subsistent Ideas or Forms not as independent entities but as thoughts or ideas *in the mind* of the supreme God resulting from that conflation. Thus emerged the notion of a transcendent God, at once the Highest Good to which all things aspire, the First Cause to which all things owe their being, the Supreme Reason from which all things derive their order and intelligibility, and, increasingly (for Neoplatonism was as much a path of salvation as a philosophy), the object of a lively devotional sentiment.

Given this development, it is not too hard to understand how St. Augustine, following the trail first blazed by Philo Judaeus and later broadened by the Greek Fathers, was able to engineer in a fashion that proved to be definitive for Western Christian philosophy the further conflation of the Neoplatonic God—the God of the philosophers, as it were, in its final and most developed version—with the biblical God of Abraham, Isaac, and Jacob, the personal God of power and might who not only transcends the universe but of his omnipotence creates it out of nothing. In so doing, he closed the way to any further Christian flirtation with the Greek notion of the eternity of the world such as that indulged in by the Alexandrian theologian Origen two centuries earlier. At the same time, by agreeing with Philo, the Neoplatonists, and many of his Christian predecessors that the creative act was indeed an intelligent one guided by Ideas of the Platonic mold, but Ideas now located in the divine mind, he responded to the Greek concern to vindicate philosophically the order and intelligibility of the universe. By virtue of his authority, then, he ensured for the doctrine of the divine Ideas an enduring place in Christian theology.

That very doctrine, however, itself witnesses to the internal tensions that Augustine's synthesis involved. The retention of the Ideas manifests the enduring influence of the Greek identification of the divine with the rational order of the universe. The denial of their independent existence and their location in the mind of God, on the other hand, reflects the desire to make room for the biblical conception of the divine as almighty power and unimpeded will; but was it room enough? If the universe was truly rational and ultimately intelligible, could God ever be willful? If God could really be willful, could the universe fully be rational? What had guaranteed the rationality of Plato's universe, after all, had been the control of the Demiurge's creative activity by the patterns presented in the Ideas or Forms. When Job, however, had sought some justification, comprehensible in human terms, for the disasters that his Hebraic God had brought down upon him, God's only reply was not a rational vindication of his justice but a disdainful and terrifying vindication of his omnipotence: "Where were you when I laid the foundation of the earth? . . . Have you commanded the morning since your days began? . . . Can you bind the chains of the Pleiades, or loose the cords of Orion? . . . Shall a fault-finder contend with the Almighty?" (Job 38:4, 12, 31; 40:2).

The tensions, then, were already present in Augustine, but the troubled political conditions of the early medieval world and the concomitant decline in the vitality of intellectual life precluded their being subjected to close theological or philosophical scrutiny. When they did finally come to the fore, it was above all in the form of that strenuous debate concerning the priority in God of reason or will that was to engage the attention of so many of the scholastic theologians from the thirteenth century onward, most notably St. Thomas Aquinas, Duns Scotus (1266–1308), and William of Ockham (c. 1300–1349)—an abstruse disagreement, perhaps, but one of considerable importance in the history of science, for, as we shall see, it did much to promote the particular conception of the laws of nature that was central to the thinking of the early modern scientists.

That debate presupposed, however, the recovery of the works of Aristotle and, with them, the most systematic and thoroughgoing of ancient attempts to comprehend reality—including the world of physical reality that had not been of compelling interest to Plato. Aristotle's thought forced upon the attention of the scholastic philosophers and theologians what was to them a novel understanding of the divine and of its relationship with the natural world. It was also one much harder to reconcile with the biblical vision than the Platonic and Neoplatonic viewpoint with which the church fathers had succeeded in coming to terms. The difficulties involved, moreover, were exacerbated by the fact that the crucial portions of Aristotle first arrived in Arabian guise, interwoven with the paraphrases and commentaries of Avicenna and Averroës to such a degree that for some time Latin thinkers were unable to determine which ideas were actually Aristotle's and which those of his commentators—men, after all, whose thinking was by no means purely Aristotelian in inspiration.

Thus, the modified Aristotle with whom the scholastics first had to cope, and the Aristotle whom the ecclesiastical authorities at Paris at first condemned, was one who appeared to teach not only the eternity of the world but also its necessity; that is to say, his world was not a *created* world presuposing a free decision of the divine will, but a world that eternally and necessarily flowed from the divine principle, on the analogy of a stream pouring ceaselessly from its source or of a logical conclusion proceeding necessarily from its premises. As such it was a determined world in which everything had to be what it was and in which there was no room either for the providence of God or the free will of man. To the extent, moreover, that the Aristotle encountered was that of Averroës, he was also an Aristotle who denied to man any form of individual immortality.

With such an Aristotle it was possible for those scholastics who taught philosophy in the faculties of arts to come to terms, though by so doing they left themselves open to the charge of espousing the so-called Latin Averroist doctrine of the double truth. They made their peace with Aristotle by digging in along the lines of professional departmentalism and separating what they taught as philosophers, or as commentators on "*the* philosopher," from what they believed (or claimed to believe) as Christians. For the theologians, however, no such option existed. They had either to turn their backs on Aristotle's metaphysics and natural philosophy, and by so doing to cut themselves off from the most advanced intellectual trends of their day, or, somehow or another, they had to make him acceptable. After a certain amount of hesitation and disagreement, most of them opted for the latter course, seeking first to penetrate the veil of commentary and to ascertain how much of the troublesome material had with certainty to be ascribed to Aristotle himself. It was out of such attempts to isolate the authentic teaching of Aristotle and to reconcile it with Christian belief that there emerged the synthesis that is by common consent regarded—and rightly so—as the greatest of medieval philosophic-theological achievements: the system that St. Thomas Aquinas elaborated and that found its most impressive statement in the marvelously architectonic structure of his *Summa Theologica.*

More bold in his rationalism than many of his more conservative contemporaries, Aquinas set out to demonstrate on rational grounds the validity of such ideas as creation out of nothing, the immortality of the individual soul, the providential activity of God, and the freedom of the human will. We have seen, however, that the Arabian-Aristotelian negation of the two last propositions was simply a conclusion that followed from the prior commitment to the notion that the world was both produced and ruled by necessity. Aquinas's vindication of those propositions, then, hinged upon his own prior commitment to the opposite notion that the world was itself the work of "an active cause acting voluntarily" and that it "did not proceed or emanate from God of necessity. God created for a purpose, and that the world exists at all and that this particular world exists is the result of divine choice." [12] Behind that commitment, as also behind his arguments for creation out of nothing, lay his more fundamental attempt to establish as a *philosophical* doctrine the Judaic and Christian belief in a transcendent and omnipotent Creator-God which Augustine before him, less prone in any case to distinguish between philosophy and theology, had been more willing to accept simply as a matter of faith.

At the same time, by retaining the Platonic Ideas in their Augustinian and Neoplatonic guise as creative archetypes in the mind of God, Aquinas was able to assert that the creative act was not only a free but also a rational one, thus vindicating the rationality and intelligibility of the universe. Being fully convinced, it seems, that it was Aristotle who had most profoundly explored that intelligibility and most successfully explained the rational order of the visible world, he sought, therefore, while blending Augustinian and Aristotelian ideas, to base his own understanding of that world upon a remarkably thoroughgoing assimilation of Aristotelian rationalism in general and Aristotle's philosophy of nature in particular—but only at a price, the price, in the eyes of many a contemporary, of having assimilated Aristotelian rationalism somewhat more successfully than any Christian theologian should.

Nowhere is the price more evident than in the effect of that rationalism in leading him to assume the primacy of reason over will, not only in man but also in God. It was an assumption with far-reaching consequences for the whole manner in which he conceived the world of nature, and, in particular for the specific way in which he conceived those observable uniformities in natural occurrences that the early modern scientists called "laws of nature." In accordance with that assumption (and unlike Newton or Boyle later on), Aquinas regarded such laws not as having been imposed upon nature from outside by God's legislating will, but in a much more "Greek" fashion as the external manifestations of an indwelling or immanent reason. Thus he speaks of an "eternal law" that orders to their appropriate ends all created things, irrational as well as rational, and defines it as "nothing other than the idea of the divine wisdom insofar as it directs all acts and movements" and governs "the whole community of the universe." [13]

It is the advantage of this way of looking at things that it enabled Aquinas to regard the whole of being—including the realm of nature as well as of man—as in its own fashion subject to the dictates of the same law. The disadvantage, however, is that subjection to law would appear to extend to God himself, thus threatening his freedom and omnipotence, since the eternal law is nothing other than one aspect of the divine reason itself, and in God reason is prior to will. It would appear, therefore, that the old discord between the Greek and biblical notions of the divine, far from being resolved in the new combinations spawned by medieval scholastic theologizing, was simply transposed into another key, reappearing on the level, as it were, of the divine psychology. With Aquinas's doctrine of eternal law, the tensions involved have not only survived but have been sharpened to breaking point.

After Aquinas's death that breaking point came with surprising rapidity. In 1277, Etienne Tempier, bishop of Paris, formally condemned as contrary to the Christian faith a host of philosophical propositions, including some that could be attributed to Aquinas. Behind those condemnations lay the fear, widespread earlier among the more orthodox Muslim and Jewish thinkers and strongly felt by many scholastic theologians of the day, that the thoroughgoing rationalism of Aristotle and his Christian followers endangered the fundamental belief in the freedom and omnipotence of God that was common to all three religions. The "honeymoon of philosophy and theology," as Etienne Gilson put it, was over. The condemnations marked the formal beginning of a theological reaction that was to vindicate the freedom

and omnipotence of God at the expense of the ultimate intelligibility of
the world. Subsequent theologians had to do their thinking in the full
glare of this persuasive clarification, and it is not surprising that many
of them tended to take the divine omnipotence as their fundamental
principle, to set God over against the world he had created, and to
regard the order of that world as deriving not from any sort of
participation in the divine reason or from the realization of the divine
Ideas, but rather from the peremptory mandate of an autonomous
divine will. This tendency was manifest already in the primacy over
the divine intellect that Duns Scotus accorded to the divine will. It
became dominant in the thinking of those philosophers and theologians
who aligned themselves with the "nominalist" school that became so
very powerful in the later Middle Ages. Notwithstanding its great
diversity, that school owed its fundamental inspiration to the works of
William of Ockham.

Ockham's thinking has been described as being "dominated by the
first words of the Christian creed: I believe in one God, the Father
Almighty," [14] and not improperly so, for he rejected the doctrine of the
divine Ideas not only as dissolving the unity of the Christian God into a
heathen multiplicity, but also as implying an inadmissible qualification
of the divine omnipotence and freedom. As a result he was led to deny
that created things participate, even by virtue of their intelligible order,
in the being of God. If it is permissible to speak of laws of nature, then,
those laws are not the manifestations of an immanent reason but rather
"the laws ordained and instituted by God." His world, accordingly, is
not so much a "living" organism possessed of its own inherent
intelligibility and order as an inanimate machine operating in accordance with the norms of behavior imposed upon it by its maker.[15] It is a
stark world in which all existents are radically dependent upon the
decisions of a free and omnipotent God whose will is prior to his
reason. Being what he is, God could have chosen to create otherwise
than he did. Certainly, he could have chosen to impose a different order
on those things he actually did create. Even as it is, he can still himself
effect directly whatever normally occurs through the agency of what
we call natural causes. There are simply no necessary relations or
connections between distinct things in nature, not even between cause

and effect. If man is ever to know the order of the world he can only expect to do so by examining in an inductive fashion what is *de facto*, for being completely dependent on the divine choice it cannot be deduced by any *a priori* reasoning. He can know individual things but he cannot reason beyond them to any unchanging and necessary world of intelligible essences or forms; so that, linked with Ockham's fundamental insistence on the omnipotence of God, and at least in part dependent upon it, is also the empiricism that is so manifest in his thinking.

One may well wonder a little, however, about the nature of Ockham's empiricism. Historians of philosophy have frequently depicted him as a radical skeptic, and his universe as a miraculous universe arbitrarily peopled with unpredictable events. May it not be, then, as some indeed have claimed, that the very violence of his theological reaction renders even empiricism redundant and carries him into a world so thoroughly impregnated with the divine will that the very idea of a *natural* order becomes a quasi-blasphemous intrusion?

Such a possibility should not be dismissed out of hand. In the fourteenth century one nominalist theologian at least came close to such a point of view, and, centuries earlier, moved by similar religious worries in the Islamic world, al-Ash'arī and his school appear to have arrived at it. In their attempts to protect the freedom and omnipotence of God, the Asharites had denied the necessity of cause and effect, ignored the idea of natural law, and made God directly responsible for everything that happens at every moment in time. In a world thus conceived, a miraculous world in which all "natural" processes were in fact sacramental rather than natural, there could be no threat to the freedom and omnipotence of God, and the doctrine of creation out of nothing was easily vindicated against all comers.

But, then, to return once again to the issue raised at the beginning and alluded to more than once in the course of this chapter, in a world thus conceived there was also no room at all for the development of any sort of natural science. In this it was the direct antithesis of the Greek view of the universe as an organism permeated with mind, an intelligible and ordered universe open to penetration by human reason. At the same time, however, the intelligible universe of the Greek philosophers had been in a sense *too* open to rational investigation to be able to sponsor the type of empirical natural science that emerged in the scientific revolution and is classically represented by the work of Sir Isaac Newton. It is important to realize that there is a distinction not simply of degree but also of kind between the Newtonian science and the natural science of classical antiquity. Such was the confidence of the ancients in the divine rationality of the universe that they believed it possible for the questing mind to penetrate to the very natures or essences of things and to *deduce* therefrom why those things behave in the way they do. The ultimate goal of their investigations, then, was a very ambitious one: nothing less than the discovery and disclosure of the very essences and purposes of things. In this they were followed by the bulk of those scholastic philosophers who sought to investigate the world of nature; but if that particular scientific tradition had many achievements to its credit, it proved ultimately to be incapable of generating a critical breakthrough of the type that occurred during the scientific revolution. One of the central elements of that breakthrough was, in fact, the struggle to overthrow it. What took its place was the more modest project of investigating natural phenomena empirically or experimentally with the object of understanding how things behave in the natural world, and, by discovering and formulating in precise mathematical terms the laws that govern their behavior, to open the way to the accurate prediction of natural occurrences and the concomitant control of natural forces.

While the Newtonian science presupposed, then, the firm conviction that a rational order was indeed present in nature, it regarded that order not as intrinsic to the natures or essences of things, but rather as an extrinsic pattern of natural laws imposed upon it by a sovereign Creator-God whose most striking characteristics were his will and power. That order was of a fundamentally different type, reflecting a different philosophy of nature and presupposing, as a result, a different conception of the divine than those asserted by the philosophers of ancient Greece, or even, for that matter, by such ardent medieval Aristotelians as Aquinas. The difference, it is now time to assert, is to be accounted for by the continuing impact of Judeo-Christian thinking in general and of the late thirteenth-century theological reaction in particular first upon philosophy and hence, in the course of time, upon scientific investigation as well. Whereas the comparable but earlier reaction in Islam culminated in the triumph of Asharism, in Latin Christendom it led to the growing prominence of the nominalist school sponsored by Ockham. It was a reaction, therefore, that stopped considerably short of the extremes of the Asharite school, for it is improper to suppose that Ockham or his nominalist followers conceived of God as a wholly capricious being. If some of them argued that God can, of his *absolute power*, do anything that does not involve a formal contradiction (for example, suspend or transcend the present natural economy as he does in the case of miracles) they also insisted that by his *ordained* or *ordinary power* he normally acts in harmony with the order he has actually ordained in nature and which we apprehend as "the common course of nature."

This characteristically nominalist distinction between differing modes of the divine activity, when used in this fashion (its meaning was unstable), had important implications for the way in which the nominalists conceived of the natural world and for the role they assigned to scientific investigation. It enabled them, at the very moment when they were vindicating the universal sway of God's omnipotent will (as witnessed by the sacraments and by miracles), to preserve, unlike their Muslim predecessors, a clear area within which the human reason, operating empirically, could be expected to achieve valid results. It is true that this area was a vastly reduced one if compared with that envisaged by Plato and Aristotle, or even, for that matter, by Augustine and Aquinas, for the human reason, as envisaged by the nominalists, is in no position to deduce from a rational analysis of things their essence or purpose. Given the presently ordained natural order, however, God, the First Cause, can be said to act via natural causes in accord with those imposed norms which we call the laws of nature and which are accessible to scientific investigation.

When Whitehead argued, then, that the fundamental prerequisite of science was "the inexpugnable belief that every detailed occurrence can be correlated with its antecedents in a perfectly definite manner, exemplifying general principles," and when he argued further that this "faith in the possibility of science, generated antecedently to the development of modern scientific theory," was "an unconscious derivative of medieval theology," there was more evidence in the history of medieval philosophy to support his claim than he can have known. He saw that faith as grounded ultimately in the scholastic notion of God as being both personal and rational. That notion he contrasted with those prevailing elsewhere—as, for example in Asia, where, he says, "the conceptions of God were of a being who was either too arbitrary or too impersonal for such ideas to have much effect on instinctive habits of mind. Any definite occurrence might be due to the fiat of an arbitrary and irrational despot, or might issue from some impersonal, inscrutable origin of things." [16] If the history of philosophy both in the world of Latin Christendom and in that of Islam lends support to his position, so, too, it seems, if Joseph Needham is correct, does the lack of anything approaching a scientific revolution in China. In the course of his massive study *Science and Civilization in China* Needham argues that one of the crucial reasons for the failure of the Chinese to develop a natural science comparable to that of the West was their prior failure to produce a comparable concept of laws imposed upon nature; this latter failure was, in turn, the outcome of their lack of any conception of a personal, legislating Creator-God. It was not, he says, that the Chinese lacked the idea of an order in the universe, but that they regarded it as a "harmonious cooperation of all beings" arising "not from the orders of a superior authority external to themselves, but from the fact that they were all parts in a hierarchy of wholes forming a cosmic pattern, and what they obeyed were the internal dictates of their own reason." Speaking of the Taoist thinkers in China, he adds that "with their appreciation of the relativism and subtlety and immensity of the universe they were groping after an Einsteinian world-picture without having laid the foundations for a Newtonian one," and that "by that path science could not develop." [17]

The last assertion, of course, is predicated on a recognition of the startling facts with which this chapter began: the uniqueness of the Western scientific achievement and the critical importance of the scientific revolution to that achievement. No one, I assume, would wish to assert that the sole factor accounting for that great intellectual revolution was the fundamental shift in the philosophy of nature engineered in the later Middle Ages by the renewed and disturbing pressure upon Greek modes of thought of the alien idea of an omnipotent Creator-God; but none, I would urge, need hesitate to regard it as a *necessary* factor, and as a very important one at that. For anyone who concedes that claim but remembers the ultimately abortive nature of natural science in Byzantium and Islam where Athens also encountered Jerusalem, though not in quite the same way, the odds against the appearance in history of anything like the scientific revolution can only seem immense, and the peculiarity of the Western cultural tradition, even more profound.

VI

PASSION AND SOCIETY

The Texture of Mediaeval Sentiment

HELMER: To forsake your home, your husband, and your children! And you don't consider what the world will say.

NORA: I can pay no heed to that. I only know that I must do it.

HELMER: This is monstrous! Can you forsake your holiest duties in this way?

NORA: What do you consider my holiest duties?

HELMER: Do I need to tell you that? Your duties to your husband and your children.

NORA: I have other duties equally sacred.

HELMER: Impossible! What duties do you mean?

NORA: My duties towards myself.

HELMER: Before all else you are a wife and a mother.

NORA: That I no longer believe. I believe that before all else I am a human being, just as much as you are—or at least that I should try to become one.[1]

This scene, written by Ibsen in 1879 and now destined, it would appear, to become a *locus classicus* in the burgeoning literature of feminism, may serve to introduce the two main themes around which this chapter revolves. The first is the slow emergence of Western individualism; the second, the even slower process by which, in the West, the dignity, status, and self-esteem of women has been raised to a degree rarely matched at other times or in other parts of the world. Nora's words suggest that these two developments are not unrelated, and rightly so. If the woman's liberation movement has set itself a multitude of goals, the most significant, for the intellectual historian at least, is surely its attempt to sponsor among women a proud rejection of the "sexual politics" of self-effacement and the firm appropriation of an independent sense of selfhood, one shadowed no longer by the defining identities of mother, wife, or lover. That attempt constitutes yet another stage in the restless quest for the attainment of autono-

173

mous, self-subsistent individuality that has long since become one of the distinguishing features of Western life. If, in our own age, the drawbacks to that quest—social and psychological as well as philosophical—have become increasingly evident, the benefits that have already accrued from it should no more escape us than they escaped the pioneer advocates of Westernization in the non-Western countries or the early supporters of feminism in Europe and North America. Nor should we miss its fundamental oddity. Autonomous individuality is a notion that would have been as alien to our primitive and archaic ancestors as, by and large, it has continued to be to those whose patterns of thought and feeling have been framed by the great Oriental cultural traditions, and, if the philosopher Hegel is correct, one not much less alien to the ancient Greeks, even those of the classical era. Hegel regarded that notion as "historically subsequent to the Greek world," as "the pivot and centre of the difference between antiquity and modern times," and as sponsored in part by the Roman law but above all by the Christian religion.[2]

On this point, as on so many others, not even the numbing obscurity of Hegel's philosophical discourse can dim the acuteness of his historical insight. If some would be unhappy with his suggestion that Plato himself had not yet embraced "the principle of the self-subsistent inherently infinite personality of the individual," few would wish to deny that the ordinary inhabitant of the Greek city-state was conceived (and, like his primitive and archaic forebears, probably conceived of himself) less as an individual possessed of a personal history and standing ultimately alone, than as an integral part of society, deriving therefrom his identity and whatever value he possessed. Nor would many want to question the strategic role Hegel ascribed to Christianity in the undermining and ultimate subversion of that archaic pattern.[3] Discussing "the right of the subject's particularity, his right to be satisfied, or in other words the right of subjective freedom," he says that "[t]his right in its infinity is given expression in Christianity and it has become the universal effective principle of a new form of civilization." It is true that the Christianity he has in mind is above all the Protestantized or secularized Christianity of the early modern and Enlightenment eras. It is also true that he sees "the right of subjective freedom" as finding expression especially in the realm of what we would call morals and politics. Nonetheless, he lists "love, romanticism and the quest for the eternal salvation of the individual" as among "the primary shapes which this right assumes," and these are characteristically medieval themes. His remarks, then, prompt the claim that in the world of sentiment, secular as well as religious, the later medieval centuries constitute, if not necessarily a definitive, at least an important phase in the emergence of the peculiarly Western and modern spirit of individualism. And individualism, it is appropriate to insist, as it has come to shape the lives of women as well as those of men.

The Love of God

THE untrammeled power of God, capable of calling forth from nothingness the mystery of individual existence; [4] the providence of God, so particular as to sustain the life of even the most insignificant of his creatures; the generosity of God, so extensive as to endow the highest of those creatures with a reflection of his own autonomy and freedom; the love of God, so all-pervasive and undiscriminating as to transcend the categories of race, sex, and status and to touch the lives of each of his children—these are powerful notions, and like many another Christian teaching, their relevance to the idea of individual human personality is evident. So little are we tempted to minimize the contribution of Christianity to the emergence of that idea, however, that it is its exile to the margins of the early medieval religious sensibility that is likely to escape our attention. Nonetheless, it is only in the late eleventh century that spiritual writings once again demonstrate the intense preoccupation with the mysteries of the individual psyche that St. Augustine had already betrayed so strikingly at the end of the fourth century in his *Confessions*. In the subsequent centuries, that preoccupation was to deepen considerably and to take on an emotionalism of a type lacking even in Augustine, but before the late eleventh century—and especially from the seventh century onward—the characteristically Christian concern with the relationship

175

of the individual soul to God was to a remarkable degree submerged in the collective rhythms of a devotional life that was communal rather than personal, external rather than internal, public rather than private.

The reasons for this hiatus are not too hard to find. They are rooted in the social and intellectual changes consequent to the barbarian invasions, the loss of that sophistication of life without which St. Augustine's psychologizing would have been impossible. They are rooted also in the mind set characteristic of the Germanic conquerors and of their clerical descendants, upon whose shoulders fell the task of constructing from the remnants of their own religiocultural heritage and the legacy of Roman Christianity a mode of religiosity congruent with the conditions of life in early medieval Europe. Moreover, given those conditions of life, deurbanized and localized to a degree well-nigh unthinkable in the Mediterranean world of the early Christian era, it is hardly surprising that religious life took on an overwhelmingly communal cast, clearly linked in its solemn liturgical celebrations with the collective destiny of the *folk* and closely integrated in its more routine devotions with the seasonal needs and aspirations of an almost wholly agrarian people. Equally, given the central role played by the Germanic kings in pre-Christian times as sacral mediators between their folk and the gods, and given, too, the role of so many of those kings in the conversion of their peoples to the new religion, it is not surprising that their Christian successors should occupy so prominent a position in early medieval religious life.

The degree to which the liturgical calendar corresponded with the ancient cycle of festivals geared to the religions of nature lent itself to such a development; so, too, did the old patristic and "collective" understanding of the Eucharist as a corporate offering made by the church—itself still conceived, moreover, not as the body of the clergy alone but as at once the body of the faithful and the body of Christ. Thus, for example, it has been pointed out that "the three principal high feasts of English paganism—Winter's Day, Midwinter's Day, and Summer's Day—with which the king was undoubtedly associated as performer of the sacrifice are paralleled in the later high and crown-wearing occasions assimilated to the Christian seasons." [5] Similarly, the early medieval coronation rites, in many ways the most

176

striking liturgical creations of the period and regarded for centuries as conferring a sacrament, accorded to the consecrated king a quasi-priestly, mediatorial role as representative of his people before God. In Germany and England alike, the king, after his coronation, joined the priests within the sanctuary of the church, offering the elements of bread and wine for his own Communion. At least one medieval commentator appears to have regarded that offering as being made on behalf of the collective Christian people, so that the role of representative communicant is assigned to the king.

None of this is too startling if one recalls the place in the economy of salvation that Eusebius of Caesarea had been willing to accord to the emperor Constantine; but, then, one of the reactions in the fourth century to that and other overeager accommodations of the church with the world had been a marked strengthening of the monastic impulse. That impulse was in origin an unambiguously sectarian and nonclerical one. Lay people by the thousands had fled "the world," seeking in the Egyptian desert the solitude, rigor of life, and freedom from worldly temptation they believed necessary if their anxious quest for individual spiritual perfection was to succeed. During the course of the next three centuries the embryonic monastic communities that had soon appeared underwent considerable development and expansion, adopting various rules of life and spreading out to the west as well as the east until their presence was felt in almost every part of Christian Europe—but not without responding, as had the church at large, to the collective needs of society, undergoing a transformation that did much to dampen their original sectarian fervor.

The change involved was a gradual one. By the early ninth century, however, when the emperor Louis the Pious set out to impose the Rule of St. Benedict upon all monasteries within the empire, monasticism had well-nigh ceased to be a vocation for the few, lived out on the margins of society. Instead it had become a widely influential mode of life, appealing to a broad segment of society and frequently pursued in large and wealthy houses deeply involved in the day-to-day life of the countryside. At the same time, the *raison d'être* of the monks had ceased, by and large, to be the pursuit of personal sanctification and had become instead that of interceding with God on behalf of the rest of society and of completing as substitutes the burdensome penances their aristocratic benefactors felt themselves unable to discharge. Their role, then, had become a clerical one, and they a class of professional intercessors, the dischargers of a daily round of corporate worship, performing in choir the successive phases of the Divine Office, which, particularly at the great houses of the Cluniac family, developed into an elaborate, onerously lengthy, but impressively beautiful ceremonial of divine praise. For this calling professional competence and commitment was enough; personal sanctity was not necessarily a prerequisite. The monastic ranks, accordingly, were replenished increasingly, not by individual seekers after perfection, but through the practice whereby aristocratic parents placed children as oblates in the monasteries they or their ancestors had founded. Thus the monks came to conceive of themselves, and to be conceived by others, as soldiers of Christ, struggling by their ceaseless round of prayer against the numberless forces of evil, and striving to preserve the well-being of clergy and faithful, king and kingdom. As King Edgar's foundation charter of 966 for the new minster at Winchester put it: "The abbot is armed with spiritual weapons and supported by a troop of monks anointed with the dew of heavenly graces. They fight together in the strength of Christ with the sword of the spirit against the aery wiles of the devils. They defend the king and clergy of the realm from the onslaughts of their invisible enemies." [6]

Public, impersonal, communal, heroic—that is the sense one gets of the monastic piety of this period. More than ever before, it was the monasteries that molded the spirituality of the church at large, and one should not underestimate the degree to which that form of piety answered to the spiritual aspirations of the times. Later on, it is true, the great German mystic Meister Eckhart (1260–c. 1328) could say that "to seek God by rituals is to get the ritual and lose God in the process." [7] It would appear, however, that it was precisely through losing themselves in the anonymity of corporate ceremonial ritual, the noble routine of an awesome liturgy carried out amid surroundings of beauty and splendor, that his earlier medieval ancestors achieved their own intimations of immortality and felt themselves bathed in the effulgence of the divine majesty. This is a little hard to grasp, perhaps, particularly for modern Christians who, in the intense privacy of their own religious moments, owe far more to the individualism of later medieval and Reformation Christianity than to anything that had gone before. No single statement can fully convey to us the sense of that earlier communal piety; but if there is one that comes close to so doing, it is surely the passage that concludes the "little book" which the great Abbot Suger (c. 1081–1151), patron of the arts and archrepresentative of the older monastic tradition, wrote about the consecration of the new choir at his monastery of St. Denis.

After the consecration of the altars all these [ecclesiastical dignitaries] performed a solemn celebration of Masses, both in the upper choir and in the crypt, so festively, so solemnly, so different and yet so concordantly, so close [to one another] and so joyfully that their song, delightful by its consonance and unified harmony, was deemed a symphony angelic rather than human; and that all exclaimed with heart and mouth: "*Blessed be the glory of the Lord from His place. Blessed and worthy of praise and exalted above all* be Thy name, Lord Jesus Christ, Whom God Thy Father has anointed the Highest Priest with the oil of exultation above Thy fellows. By this sacramental unction with the most holy chrism and by the susception of the most holy Eucharist, Thou uniformly conjoinest the material with the immaterial, the corporeal with the spiritual, the human with the Divine. . . . By these and similar visible blessings, Thou invisibly restorest and miraculously transformest the present [state] into the Heavenly Kingdom."[8]

Suger writes, of course, as one for whom all of this still worked; but already in his own day there were those for whom it did not, and they, too, were to be found in the monastic life, which was once more, therefore, to function as the spiritual pacesetter for the church at large. For centuries now, as we have seen, the main stress in that life had been on an impersonal and external routine geared to the fulfillment of a communal role; supportive though that routine could be, it appears to have responded but little to the personal spiritual aspirations of the individual monk. Toward the end of the eleventh century, then, there began to appear within the world of Benedictine monasticism a certain uneasiness with the established order of religious life, a restless desire for a life once more of greater solitude and heightened rigor, a revived yearning for an existence geared less to the needs of the community at large than to the exploration of that interior space wherein the individual seeker could hope to encounter the divine. The teachings of St. Romuald (c. 950–1027) and St. Peter Damiani (1007–72) south of the Alps, and, above all, that of St. Bernard of Clairvaux (1090–1153) to the north, were at the same time a manifestation of that yearning and a response to it; so, too, was the flurry of new monastic orders in the latter part of the eleventh century and the first part of the twelfth. Notable among these new orders were the Carthusians, so rigorous from the start that they were never to be accused of relaxation; and the Cistercians, the order to which St. Bernard himself belonged and which owed to his guiding inspiration so much of its influence and extraordinary success.

It is, indeed, to St. Bernard in particular, to the Cistercian example in general, and to the spiritual literature they both produced that may be ascribed the dissemination across Europe in the twelfth century of a new type of spirituality, more private, more personal, more emotional than that cultivated during the great age of Benedictine monasticism that had drawn to a close. Self-knowledge, the interior life of the committed individual, the thirst of the soul for God—these are the dominant themes, along with the ecstatic affirmation that God had clothed himself in our humanity in order (as St. Bernard put it) that he "might draw the affections of carnal men, who could only love carnally, to a salutory love of His Flesh, and then on to a spiritual love." [9] If the accent lay on the individuality of man, it lay also on the humanity of God. The God of early medieval devotional life had been conceived in a manner congruent with the magnificence of the great liturgical acclamations: mighty Lord of the universe, terrifying judge of men, royal Christ reigning in glory, heavenly analog of our greatest earthly kings; but the God who now came to the fore was one with whom the humblest of mortals could feel a saving kinship: the God-made-man who endured the helplessness, suffering, and death that are the measure of man's mortality, the human Christ whose very name has the power to heal.

The change involved is clearly signaled by a comparable shift in religious iconography. The representations of Christ on the cross as triumphant king, which had been dominant in earlier centuries, were now edged to one side by crucifixes or crucifixion scenes that dwelt on the humanity, pain, and suffering of the dying Savior. A parallel change took place in Marian iconography, for along with that more tender and compassionate devotion to the human life and suffering of Christ there had developed also a similar devotion to his earthly mother, apprehended now not so much in her remote majesty as Mother of God but in her humility and vulnerability as Blessed Virgin. By these changes can be charted the dissemination beyond the cloister of what had been at first a new form of monastic spirituality and its penetration into the broader world of clerical and lay piety.

In that process St. Francis of Assisi (1181/82–1226) and his followers played a central role. Practicing a novel form of monastic life that left them committed with new fervor to the traditional vows of obedience, chastity, and, above all, poverty, but tied no longer to residence in a particular monastery or even locality, these Franciscan friars brought the new more personal and emotional piety and the simple religious devotions that went along with it into the homes of the comparatively unchurched urban masses of Europe. Through their example, spiritual direction, popular preaching, and "third order," which opened even to lay people a life of penitential dedication, they made themselves felt as a vital spiritual force everywhere in Europe until well into the fourteenth century. And in the two centuries that followed, at a time when the public corporate structures of the church, monastic as well as secular, had entered a period of decay, the type of individual, affective piety that first the Cistercians and then the Franciscans had nourished continued to flower and even to put forth new shoots.

That piety manifested itself in multiple ways—especially among the laity—from the emergence of dedicated sectarian groups, anticlerical and sometimes heretical, some of which maintained a tenuous existence right on into the era of the Reformation, to the emphasis on individual extraliturgical devotions at the expense of the public corporate worship of the church, which was to pass over into the spirituality of modern Roman Catholicism. It manifested itself, too, in the process whereby the older collective understanding of the eucharistic celebration was progressively undercut by the notion of the mass as a private thing to be watched with reverent awe but calling for no congregational participation, a sacrifice offered by an officiating priest on behalf of the individual or individuals for whom it had been requested or who had themselves requested it. It manifested itself, again, in the great flowering of mysticism that occurred in the Rhineland, the Netherlands, and England during the fourteenth century. If the next century was to produce no great mystics of the stature of a Meister Eckhart—that stalwart colonizer of the interior frontiers of the soul—something of their spirit lived on in the fervent, affective piety cultivated by the Brethren of the Common Life in their quasi-monastic communities and passed on to the schoolboys with whom they came into contact in the discharge of their pastoral work in the schools.

The Brethren practiced a sort of monasticism without vows. Their communities were composed of laymen as well as clerics who strove to pursue in common an austere life of work and prayer, with a strong emphasis on individual devotions rather than the corporate chanting of the sacred office usual in the older monastic orders. The bulk of their houses were concentrated in the Rhineland and the Netherlands, but during the course of the fifteenth century the influence of the *devotio moderna* (as their particular brand of spirituality came to be called) reached out right across northwestern Europe. In later centuries, moreover, it was to reach still farther—in Protestant as well as Catholic Europe—for it left as its enduring monument one of the most widely read and certainly the best-loved of all Christian spiritual writings, the little manual known as the *Imitation of Christ* and attributed to Thomas a Kempis.

The second book of that work consists of "Admonitions Tending to Things Internal," and its first chapter conveys a clear sense of the personal and inward nature characteristic, if not of all late medieval piety, at least of much that was most vital in it:

"The Kingdom of God is within you," saith Christ our Saviour. Turn thee therefore with all thy heart to God, and forsake this wretched world and thy soul shall find great inward rest. Learn to despise outward things, and give thyself to inward things, and thou shalt see the kingdom of God come into thyself. . . . If thou wilt make ready for Him in thy heart a dwelling-place, that is all He desireth to have in thee, and there it is His pleasure to be. Betwixt Almighty God and a devout soul there are many ghostly visitings,

sweet inward speaking, great gifts of grace, many consolations, much heavenly peace, and wondrous familiarity of the blessed presence of God.[10]

"The Kingdom of God is within you"—the contrast with the glorious vision of a Suger and with the more public, communal, and impersonal piety of the early Middle Ages could scarcely have been more complete.

The Love of Man

THE change in religious sensibilities that became increasingly evident in the course of the twelfth century was not an isolated phenomenon. At about the same time a shift of comparable magnitude was occurring in what may perhaps be called the "secular sensibilities" of the era—the complex of shared aspirations, honored values, and emotional attitudes that was clearly reflected in the contemporary literature, and especially in the narrative literature of epic and romance that was so popular in the great aristocratic households. The temptation to essay a correlation between these changes in religious and secular sensibilities is an immediate one. If they have sometimes been distinguished more by vigor than discretion, such attempts at higher synthesis have by no means been lacking. The difficulties involved are undoubtedly formidable. "These changes are hard to define and their connexion [with one another] can more readily be felt than explained";[11] but felt they certainly should be, even if satisfactory explanation may indeed prove elusive.

It has long been the practice among literary historians to divide the more ambitious forms of narrative poetry of the Middle Ages into the two major groupings of epic and romance. That practice generates its own problems, but, for present purposes, the distinction is a relevant one, and it should help convey some sense of the shift in secular sensibilities that became evident during the course of the twelfth century.

Medieval epic is usually taken to comprehend a broad group of poems ranging from the Anglo-Saxon *Beowulf*, written probably in the first half of the eighth century, to the Icelandic literature written down in its present form during the thirteenth. Among other things it includes not only such Continental Germanic epics as the *Hildebrands-lied* (ninth century) or the *Nibelungenlied* (thirteenth century), but also the *chansons de geste,* the French national epics of which the greatest and most influential was the *Chanson de Roland* (twelfth century). Varied though they are, these works have in common several features that serve to distinguish them from the romance. Of these, the most fundamental (and the one most germane to this discussion) is the fact that, unlike the romance, they were not regarded as belonging to a fictional genre by the authors who wrote them or the audiences who heard or read them. In however modified a form and however encrusted with legend or invention, at their heart lay embedded incidents that even today we can identify as historical. Thus we can date to 520 the raid that, the poem tells us, Hygelac, king of the Geats, made on the Franks during Beowulf's youth. Similarly, from sober historical sources of ninth-century provenance, we can identify the pivot of historical fact upon which the central action of the *Chanson de Roland* turns—namely, the slaughter in 778 in the Basque Pyrenees of the rear guard to Charlemagne's retreating Spanish expedition. That rear guard included a certain Roland, duke of the Marches of Brittany.

The epic, then, possesses a certain quasi-historicity. More important, during the Middle Ages it possessed a *felt* historicity, and one that must have imposed upon its author's freedom of creative maneuver restrictions with which the author of the romance did not have to cope. What were believed by author and aristocratic audience alike to have been traditional ideals honored by the founders of their nation could hardly be slighted, and their epic heroes clearly had to exemplify those ideals. The temptation, therefore, to endow those heroes with attributes that were idiosyncratic or personal was understandably a small one; and the temptation may have been the smaller because of the degree to which epic poetry with an oral tradition behind it tends to preserve and embody archaic modes of thinking about matters psychological. On this point, the Homeric analogy is instructive.

An important group of Homeric scholars, most prominent among them Bruno Snell,[12] have focused attention upon the markedly external ways in which the Homeric poems depict internal psychological processes. They have pointed out the degree to which those poems use what is common, public, and external to represent psychological states that we today would regard as inherently private, as pertaining to the individual in the isolation of his internal mental operations—thus the reliance, where we would think soliloquy appropriate, upon externalized dialogue, upon "personified interchanges" between, for example, a hero and his horse, or a hero and a god. Some have further suggested that what is reflected in such stratagems is the survival in the Homeric psychology of archaic patterns of thought that lacked a clearly differentiated concept of individual identity, that saw no sharply defined boundaries between the self and the collectivity to which it belonged, and that was therefore prone, in its depiction of mental activity, to ignore the idiosyncratic and merely personal and to stress the communal and public.

Of course, the leap from the Homeric to the medieval epic is a long and perilous one. While it is plausible to assume that the modes of thought characteristic of the archaic phase in different parts of Europe possessed a certain commonality, in so doing one clearly runs the risk of imposing upon other parts of the world a mind set that may in part have been peculiar to the ancient Greeks. Nonetheless, one cannot help being struck by the parallels between the externalizing stratagems one encounters in the medieval epic and those employed in the Homeric poetry. If Achilles's decision whether or not to kill Agamemnon is presented externally in the form of dialogue between himself and the goddess Athena (*Iliad*, 1. 181 ff.), the decision making that goes into Roland's refusal to sound his horn and summon Charlemagne's help is rendered in a similarly external way in the form of a debate with Oliver (*Roland*, ll. 1049–1109). Similarly, if Homer reveals Achilles's state of mind on another occasion by having him address his horses (*Iliad*, 19. 400 ff.), in the *Chanson de Roland* we are also given a valuable glimpse into Roland's values and self-conception when he addresses his sword, Durandel (*Roland*, ll. 2284–2354).

Whatever weight may properly be placed on parallels of this sort, it remains indisputable that the dominating ethos of the epic was one of communal values and group loyalties, values and loyalties signaled or affirmed by representative deed and symbolic gesture in a highly external fashion readily apprehensible by a (presumably) sympathetic audience. Thus the several characters in *Beowulf* are given no complex inner core; they are quasi-abstract, easily recognizable types. Moreover, despite the veneer of Christian belief on the poem, it is significant that Beowulf's ultimate reward would appear to be that of living on by virtue of his heroic deeds in the memory of posterity, an essentially pagan form of immortality that Homer would have recognized, and one that for its efficaciousness presupposes the absence of any idea of a unique personal identity capable of establishing clear boundaries between the individual and the group to which he belongs. If such a notion of immortality is, of course, lacking in the *Chanson de Roland*, a much more Christian poem, there again the characters portrayed are types, and Roland in particular emerges less as a courageous individual than as an ideal hero, a figure of universal and symbolic value.

The *Chanson de Roland* in its present form was probably composed during the opening years of the twelfth century. The romances of Chrétien de Troyes (fl. c. 1170) date to the last thirty years or so of the same century. The contrast in tone between the two may serve as well as anything to illustrate the shift in secular sensibilities that had begun to occur in the intervening years. Being romances, Chrétien's poems are works of fiction, since the authors of the romances, while making use of cycles of legend concerning the Trojan War, the exploits of Alexander the Great, and, above all, the shadowy ruler of Celtic Britain who had come to be known as King Arthur, neither felt themselves nor were felt by their readers to be relating truly historical stories. As a result, an author like Chrétien enjoyed the freedom to shape his traditional materials in such a way as to set up an idealized world and to create for that world an equally idealized code of behavior that did not necessarily have to correspond either with the mores actually prevalent among his aristocratic readers or with those believed to have prevailed in an ancestral past. He also enjoyed the freedom to create characters who, while responding to that idealized code of behavior, could be more than merely typical figures, could be endowed with those idiosyncratic traits and other manifestations of an internal

186

life unique to them that we can recognize as truly individual. More important still, Chrétien and the other writers of romances who came after him chose in fact to exploit that freedom.

Here, then, as in the religious life of the twelfth century, one sees evidenced a marked concern to cultivate the inner space of the individual psyche. By twentieth-century standards, it is true, Chrétien can hardly be regarded as a particularly subjective poet. Despite the use of soliloquy and the presence of passages of psychological analysis, most of the action in his poems concerns the "common stuff" of knightly adventure; but he often treats these adventures in a rather lighthearted way, and even when he does not do so they remain subordinate to his dominant interest. That interest must have struck his contemporaries as extraordinarily subjective, for it concerned psychological matters, the inwardness of the individual heart, the action that is not externalized but takes place in the human soul. If that is true of Chrétien's poems, and particularly of his *Cligès*, it is even more true of Gottfried von Strassburg's version of the *Tristan and Isolt* story, composed about 1210, or, again, of Geoffrey Chaucer's *Troilus and Criseyde* composed over a century and a half later. Indeed, if the brilliant analysis in C. S. Lewis's *Allegory of Love* is correct, the new feeling for inwardness, the new preoccupation with psychology and sentiment, is present even where we would least expect to find it, in the seemingly stilted, artificial, and wholly objectified world of late medieval allegory to which belonged one of the most popular and influential of all medieval literary works: the *Roman de la Rose*, the first part of which was composed by Guillaume de Lorris around 1235. Asserting that allegory is "the subjectivism of an objective age" Lewis argues that despite its allegorical form "the *Roman de la Rose* is a story of real life," that it would be "a work not of creation, but of mere ordinary dexterity, to strip off the allegory and retell this story in the form of a novel," and that what we would then discover would be a "love story of considerable subtlety and truth." [13]

A *love* story, of course. In the medieval romances as in the greater part of modern European literature and of the various national literatures that can trace their line of descent from Europe, love stories of one sort or another provide most of the compelling interest. Running through the Arthurian romances—and Wolfram von Eschenbach's *Parzival* (c. 1210) can be taken as archetypical—is another compelling theme: that of the service of the mysterious Grail, a symbol variously interpreted. That itself implies another type of love story—the story of the unquenchable yearning of the human soul for contact with the divine—and the two loves, religious and secular, are woven into a single fabric. In any case, preoccupation with the love of man for woman, no less than with the love of man for God, necessarily focuses the attention of author and reader alike upon the inner space, upon the psychological. Without that preoccupation it would be hard indeed to account for the intense subjectivism of so much of our modern literature.

Precisely because of that, however, we should not take for granted the strength and endurance of the romantic preoccupation. It was lacking entirely, after all, in the epic literature examined earlier. There the role that women play is a marginal one, having little impact either upon the movement of the story or the behavior of their men. Instead, the center of emotional gravity lies elsewhere. If any human beings truly engage Roland's affections, they are Charlemagne, his liege lord, and Oliver, his friend. If their ranks were to be expanded, they would appear to include before Aude, his betrothed, the fallen comrades in arms whom he reverentially seeks out in the battlefield and ranges around the dying Bishop Turpin. Instead of love between the sexes, the "deepest of worldly emotions in this period is the love of man for man, the mutual love of warriors who die fighting against odds, and the affection between vassal and lord." [14] In all of this there is little of the inwardness of the heart. Like the reverential awe or fear of the Lord God ("the glorious King," "Ruler of Victories," as he is called in *Beowulf*), these are essentially public emotions, societally cohesive and communally endorsed. They represent a world of sentiment differing in its very texture from that which came increasingly to preoccupy itself with the loneliness of the individual quest for the beloved, be it the religious quest for the ineffable moment of encounter with the divine or the ecstasies attendant upon the romantic love of woman. The nature and previous history of Christianity would lead one to expect that the former should finally make its appearance on the

188

medieval scene. That the latter should do so, however, and should come so to dominate the European literary imagination, is somewhat more startling and calls for some attempt at explanation, or, failing that, since "explanation" is an ambitious word, for some attempt at least to explore the historical conditions that made its emergence possible.

The Status of Woman

ARGUING in 1845 that "the friend of Woman [should] assume that Man cannot by right lay even well-meant restrictions on Woman," Margaret Fuller, the pioneer American feminist, went on to assert: "If the negro be a soul, if the woman be a soul, apparelled in flesh, to one Master only are they accountable. There is but one law for souls, and, if there is to be an interpreter of it, he must come not as man, or son of man, but as son of God." [15]

Given the social conservatism and male chauvinism so frequently characteristic of the modern Christian churches, that assertion may well appear surprising. It should serve to remind us, however, of the explosive potential of so many New Testament teachings—in this case, that of the irrelevance before God of sexual, racial, and social distinctions. "[A]s many of you as were baptized into Christ have put on Christ," St. Paul wrote to the Galatians. "There is neither Jew nor Greek, there is neither slave nor free, there is neither male nor female, for you are all one in Christ Jesus" (Gal. 3:27–28). If this has always been a man's world, as Simone de Beauvoir has insisted, rarely has it been so much so as it was in the essentially patriarchal societies of classical Greece and Rome. There, despite changes over the course of time, the dignity and status accorded to women remained particularly low, so low, indeed, that Mithraism, the popular mystery cult that in the early fourth century vied with Christianity for imperial favor and could easily have become the official religion of Rome, was a man's religion that entirely excluded women—a far cry from the New Testament insistence upon the equality of male and female in the eyes of God, or from the degree of honor accorded to women in the early church, or, indeed, from the deepening conviction that, after Christ, it was a woman, Mary, Mother of God, to whom mankind was most deeply indebted for the graces bestowed upon it.

Again, given the attitude of suspicion toward human sexuality so frequently evinced by the Christian churches, suspicion sometimes bordering on the pathological, we must also be at pains to remind ourselves that the central strand in the teaching of both Old and New Testaments on sexual matters is one of affirmation rather than negation. Nowhere do we encounter the notion, widespread at the close of antiquity, that procreation is an evil and marriage accordingly to be eschewed. On the contrary, the Old Testament says that God, having created mankind male and female, commanded them to "be fruitful and multiply" (Gen. 1:27–28), and, in contrast with the classical world, it is to marriage rather than to virginity or temple prostitution that a sacred, religious character is attached. Nor does the New Testament abandon this basic conviction that man's sexuality is a gift to him from God, that it is therefore fundamentally good—even though its use must be subordinated to God's providential purposes, the propagation of the species and the confinement of the sexual function within due limits, which are to be realized in the married state alone. Marriage is also accorded great dignity—so great, indeed, that St. Paul uses the loving relationship of Christ to his church as an image for the proper relationship of husband to wife (Eph. 5:23–33). Any infidelity to the marriage bond on the part of either partner—husband no less than wife—is roundly condemned; that bond is portrayed as lifelong; and divorce, if not necessarily totally inadmissible, is clearly regarded as altogether deplorable.

While the early Christians, then, certainly struggled to distance themselves from the generalized eroticism and lasciviousness of the pagan societies within which they dwelt, they also felt it necessary to polemicize against those fellow Christians whose denigration of sexuality extended to the prohibition of marriage as an evil. During the course of the second century, under the influence of Oriental, neo-Pythagorean, and Gnostic convictions concerning the impurity of matter and the concomitant evil of procreation, that attitude continued, nonetheless, to spread among Christians. The church fathers were forced, as a result, to marshal their arguments in defense of marriage. Even as they did so, however, a certain irresolution began to be evident in their thinking, and on this whole issue their doctrinal legacy to the Middle Ages ended by being an ambivalent one.

At the very root of that ambivalence lay the fact that St. Paul's own teaching had also been ambivalent. Side by side with the more positive attitude that has been stressed lay a less positive appraisal of the status of women and some reservations about the desirability even of marriage itself. If husbands should love their wives as Christ loves the church, so, too, should wives "be subject in everything to their husbands." Moreover, if marriage is certainly not to be forbidden, Paul clearly regarded celibacy as the better state. "He who marries his betrothed does well; and he who refrains from marriage will do better" (1 Cor. 7:38). As the context of this particular admonition makes clear, Paul's own reasons for making it were his conviction that Christ's Second Coming was nigh and his belief that those who married were more likely to be caught up in worldly concerns and less able than the unmarried to be "anxious about the affairs of the Lord." If, as time went on, the first of those convictions understandably lost its hold on Christian thinking, the second did not. The precarious nature of the Christian hold upon public toleration in a pagan empire doubtless helped perpetuate the sense that familial ties might constitute a drag upon full religious commitment; but it is also clear that the Gnostic disparagement of the flesh left an enduring mark upon patristic teachings concerning sex, women, celibacy, and marriage. However great the respect accorded to that second Eve, Mary, Mother of God, the faithful were also reminded that it was, after all, through the deviousness of another woman, the first Eve, that sin had entered the world. However legitimate procreation, they were also taught that the sexual act was invariably accompanied by sinful passion, and that it was only the sacramental graces of matrimony that reduced the nature of that sin to venial proportions. However worthy the married state, they were also assured, again and again, that it was much less honorable than virginity. Lifelong celibacy, then, came to be regarded among

Christians as a calling higher and holier than marriage, and as an almost necessary prerequisite for any thoroughgoing attempt to enter the narrow way that led to perfection.

The spread of monasticism across Europe and the great prestige that attached to the monastic life during the early Middle Ages witness to the strength of such attitudes; but the drawbacks did not become fully evident until the late eleventh and twelfth centuries, in the wake of the attempt by the Gregorian reformers to extend the monastic rule of celibacy to the secular clergy, too. Monasticism, after all, was a way of life open to women as well as men, but the only access or quasi-access women had had to the ranks of the secular clergy had been via the widespread practice of clerical marriage. That route to partnership in one of the elite groups of medieval society was now officially closed to them, even if the struggle to impose celibacy was a bitter one and never fully successful. Moreover, the very harshness of that struggle helped sponsor among the reformers a hostility toward women that was to leave its mark, in turn, upon other predominantly clerical institutions, including the new universities. "With some notable exceptions," it has been said, "the world of formal scholarship in the Middle Ages was a bastion of male chauvinism." [16] Certainly, the climate of opinion during the later Middle Ages when the universities were being established was one characterized increasingly by anti-feminism, and it was the very prevalence in the literature of the period of anti-feminist strictures that provoked the poetess Christine of Pisa (c. 1363–c. 1431) to launch her pioneering counterattack against the male supremacists of her day.

Insofar as it was determined by ecclesiastical attitudes, then, the status of women during the Middle Ages was a lower one than a reading of the New Testament might lead one to expect; but insofar as it was also determined by the attitudes and practices traditional to the invading Germanic peoples and by the exigencies of a mode of life that was overwhelmingly land oriented, it was lowered still further. Whereas the Romans had emphasized the role of consent of the partners in marriage, Germanic custom treated the wife as a property transferred from father to husband. As in traditional Indian society today, marriage had nothing to do with "love." Indeed, it had little to

192

do at all with the personal desires of the respective partners; betrothal frequently occurred at too early an age for such desires to be relevant. Like the monasticism of the early Middle Ages, it served familial needs—though in this case the need to cement alliances or to consolidate or extend property holdings. The prospective bride, therefore, was in a position somewhat analogous to that of a boy placed by his parents as an oblate in a monastery. That is to say, she was, like him, a conscript serving in a cause that it was not hers to choose, but a conscript, it should be added, serving at a lower rank and in a capacity a good deal less honored than his.

Nor should the other side of the coin, the heavy responsibilities for estate management that wives in the higher social ranks were frequently expected or even forced to undertake during the prolonged absences of their husbands at war, court service, or the like, lead us to believe that the successful discharge of such responsibilities necessarily sponsored any improvement in the general status or self-image of women. The *Paston Letters*—a superb collection of correspondence full of precious information concerning the attitudes and activities of a prominent Norfolk family during the troubled era of the Wars of the Roses in fifteenth-century England—leave no room for doubt either that Agnes and Margaret Paston were women of considerable managerial capacity or that their menfolk regarded them as such. Those letters also leave no doubt, however, that that capacity extended as well to the intricate business of selling off their own daughters to the highest matrimonial bidder. Thus Agnes did not hesitate to confine her daughter Elizabeth in solitude for a period of over three months, beating her (a cousin tells us) "sometimes twice in one day" so that "her head is broken in two or three places." The reason? Elizabeth, a girl of about twenty, was proving difficult about marrying a certain Stephen Scrope, the heir, it seems, to a valuable property, but a widower of almost fifty who himself writes that he had "suffered a sickness that kept [me] a thirteen or fourteen years ensuing; whereby I am disfigured in my person and shall be whilst I live." [17] There is no reason to believe that in this respect the eleventh or twelfth centuries were any less insensitive than the fifteenth.

Under such conditions it is not surprising that women who aspired to the dignity and self-esteem that marriage could not be relied upon to afford should have looked beyond that state, either by eschewing it altogether or by seeking outside it the emotional sustenance it could not be expected to give. The first of those alternatives was that chosen by the numerous women of distinction who sought fulfillment in the religious (i.e., monastic) life. The second was that chosen by the even larger group who sponsored, sustained, encouraged, or responded to the cult of romantic or "courtly" love.

During the early Middle Ages the provisions made at least for aristocratic women who wished, or whose families wished them, to enter religious life were quite extensive. The seventh and eighth centuries, in particular, saw the foundation of a large number of convents for nuns. Those convents, many of them ruled by aristocratic abbesses of formidably independent spirit, enjoyed a very considerable measure of jurisdictional autonomy. So far, indeed, was male domination from being the rule that not infrequently in these centuries one finds double monasteries, twin communities of monks and nuns both subordinated to the rule of an abbess. One of the most distinguished of these was the large and influential congregation of men and women at Whitby in what is now Yorkshire, which, during the seventh century, was presided over in succession first by the great Abbess Hilda, kinswoman to Oswiu, king of Northumbria, and then by Aelfflaed, his daughter.

During the great period of monastic expansion stretching from the tenth to the twelfth centuries, however, provision for the needs of women aspiring to enter the religious life failed to keep pace with that for men. At the same time, the recovery of a sense of ecclesiastical order and propriety in what had always been a male-dominated church led to attacks upon the independence enjoyed earlier on by the great convents. The double monasteries were suppressed, and the later medieval centuries saw a growing tendency to limit the expansion of the communities of nuns. They saw also a persistent drive to place those communities firmly under the control of the male religious orders, and that at a time when women were beginning to live longer than men, to outnumber them, and to seek entry into religious life in ever-increasing numbers. "Disgust at the recollection or prospect of marriage seems to have played a very large part in recommending the monastic life to women," [18] and, as time went on, that disgust certainly did not diminish. Indeed, the advent of the Gregorian reform and of the new religious sensibility worked if anything to heighten it and to render the celibate state even more attractive to women.

The needs, however, that the established convents were not sufficiently numerous to cope with were met in many ways less acceptable to the official ecclesiastical authorities; they were met, that is, by some of the heretical sects in which women appear to have played a disproportionately important role, and, still more, by the communities of Beguines that multiplied at an extraordinary rate during the thirteenth and early fourteenth centuries in northwest Germany and the Netherlands. These were communities of religious women who belonged to no monastic order, lived in accordance with no official rule, took no formal vows, but, while continuing to pursue ordinary occupations, committed themselves to a community life of simplicity and celibacy. Their vows being private, their life unclois-tered, their work in the world and their connection with the ecclesiastical authorities minimal, they provoked among those authori-ties a good deal of hostility, some of which arose from fear of heresy, but much of which was grounded in the same drive toward male dominance that had already curtailed the independence of the official monastic communities for women. Thus, as early as 1273, asserting that "I would have them married or thrust into an approved Order," Bruno, bishop of Olmütz in eastern Germany, complained to the pope that the Beguines were exploiting their independence in order to avoid due submission to their priests and to escape "the coercion of marital bonds." [19]

This type of clerical hostility led to the imposition of restrictions upon the lives of the Beguines, but it did not result in their demise. In Cologne, indeed, some of their communities survived as late as the eighteenth century. While they endured, they continued to provide for at least some of those who were unable or unwilling to marry or remarry an opportunity for the life of dignity and self-esteem denied by society to those of their single sisters who did not choose to consecrate their unmarried state or were unable to do so. For those already subject to "the coercion of marital bonds," of course, the route to that dignity and self-esteem had necessarily to be of a very different type, and it is with that in mind that we return once more to the great shift in secular sensibilities that occurred during the course of the twelfth century.

The Love of Woman

THAT change involved, as we have seen, the development of an intense preoccupation with the romantic love of man for woman. Evidence on such matters is not easy to come by, but the circumstances surrounding the origins and dissemination of that preoccupation powerfully suggest that it owed much of its intensity to female influence and, in particular, to the influence exerted by those aristocratic ladies who presided over and molded the more sophisticated court life that began to flourish in the great feudal centers of western Europe during the eleventh and twelfth centuries.

So far as the Christian world is concerned, those origins lay to the south, in the great noble courts of the French Midi, where the court poets (*troubadours*) made romantic or "courtly" love the central theme of the lyric poetry they composed in the Provençal vernacular, the *langue d'oc*. That type of poetry flourished in the Midi from the time of William IX, duke of Aquitaine (1070–1127), first of the troubadours known to us, to that of Peire Cardinal (c. 1225–72), the poet who, during his own lifetime, saw the cultivated court life of the region destroyed by the Albigensian Crusade. Already by that time, however, the forms, techniques, and, above all, the central theme of the troubadour poetry had become the property of the *trouvères*, their counterparts in northern France. The troubadours had also left an enduring imprint on German and Italian lyric poetry, and, via the latter, influenced deeply such great lyric poets of the English Renaissance as Sir Philip Sidney and Edmund Spenser.

It is no longer fashionable, as it once was, to assign to Eleanor of Aquitaine (c. 1122–1204), granddaughter of William IX and sometime queen of both France and England, the sole responsibility for having introduced the notion of courtly love into the north of France. The lines of influence between north and south were undoubtedly more numerous than that would imply; but Eleanor was certainly an esteemed patroness of the troubadours—including Bernart de Ventadorn (fl. 1150–80), one of the greatest of them all—and it was at her court at Poitiers that her daughter, Marie, countess of Champagne (b. 1145), set up for some years a veritable academy of love. Later on, at Troyes, Marie's household appears to have included both Andreas Capellanus (Andreas the Chaplain, fl. 1180), author of the *De amore*, the highly influential theoretical treatise that has been called the textbook of courtly love, and Chrétien de Troyes, who, more than anyone else, can be credited with having engineered the union between the narrative form and the love psychology of the lyric poets. In his treatise Andreas cites both Eleanor and Marie as authorities for some of the opinions he records concerning matters of love, and we have it on Chrétien's own express insistence that he himself composed his Lancelot romance, an influential embodiment of courtly love principles, at the bidding of Marie, out of materials she provided and around the theme she indicated.

If the circumstances surrounding the diffusion of the notion of romantic or courtly love point to the guiding influence of prominent married women, so, too, do some of the specific characteristics that notion came to possess in the course of the twelfth century. Those characteristics would appear to reflect the social distance between the usual sort of troubadour—unlike William IX no nobleman himself but simply a court poet in the service of a great family—and the lady patroness whom he served and to whom his songs were typically addressed—none other, in fact, than his lord's wife. If the romantic love of which the romances treat is by no means always adulterous in nature, that which the Lancelot-Tristan group glorifies certainly is, and the romances belonging to that group were the most enduringly popular ones of all. So, too, certainly in inspiration, perhaps also in aspiration, was the love idealized in most of the troubadour lyrics. C. S. Lewis points out that "[a]ny idealization of sexual love, in a society where marriage is purely utilitarian, must begin by being an idealization of adultery." [20] Though the poet Marcabru (fl. 1129–50) rebukes his fellow troubadours as fosterers of adulterous "letching-after-love," Andreas Capellanus blandly insists to the contrary that true love is of necessity extramarital. No warmth of affection between marital partners is to be confused with it, for that affection is not freely given. It is, instead, a matter of duty in a relationship in which there is between the partners an equality of obligation and in which there is no room for the furtiveness and jealousy that lovers "should always welcome as the mother and nurse of love." Nor, given the security of possession that the marital state affords the partners, is there any room for the anxious yearning and desire on which true love feeds. [21]

These remarks point already to the principal characteristics of courtly love, but to discern those characteristics one does not have to rely on the somewhat tongue-in-cheek textbook definitions of an Andreas. They can be observed, instead, in the poems of the troubadours themselves. Those poems employ a whole range of stylistic formulas and literary conceits, many of them familiar to the poets of classical antiquity; but the features essential to the ideal of courtly love, and which together constitute its originality, are few in number and can, in fact, be summed up under three headings.

The first is the idealization of woman. In sharp contrast to the subordinate status ordinarily accorded by medieval men to their women, the beloved lady is represented here as a being superior to her lover who is possessed of qualities of mind and virtue inferior by far to hers. *She* plays the lord, therefore, he the vassal; and in the poems she is even addressed as "my lord" (*midons*). The second is the portrayal of love as ever insatiated desire, a longing and yearning for a "distant love" that is best sustained not by complete sexual gratification, but by the incomplete and fleeting favor, the stimulus of distance and denial. The third is the concomitant ascription to such love of a uniquely ennobling force. It is for the lover a transforming anguish, a cathartic ecstasy, the source of all virtue and of all good.

Of course, the troubadours differed in temperament and there are concomitant differences of nuance in the ways in which they handled the love theme that is common to all. Nonetheless, the type of love they had in mind throughout is "pure," "good," and "true" love (*fin' amors*), which they were at pains to distinguish from the false or "pied" love (*amars*) that was nothing other than a sort of undifferentiating lechery pursued for its own sake. If there is a clear line of thematic development from the early troubadours to the later, it is one that moves away from the robust, even crude, sexuality of a William IX ("Let my hands 'neath her mantle meet/ And I'll have done with sorrowing") and in the direction of a Bernart de Ventadorn's more ethereal celebration of the transforming effect of desire: "By nothing is a man made so worthy as by the love and courting of women, for thence arises delight and song and all that pertains to excellence. No man is of value without Love."[22]

"No man is of value without Love"—here Bernart expresses the dominant sentiment of the troubadours. Given the fact that their moving inspiration was usually adulterous, given, too, the contemporary idealization of celibacy, it is surely unnecessary to belabor the extent to which their conception of love, however supportive of feminine self-esteem, ran counter to the church's teachings on sexual morality. Nor is it hard to perceive the threat it posed to the role of marriage in the property arrangements of the feudal aristocracy, arrangements that could ill survive the type of doubt about the legitimacy of heirs that the suspicion of *wifely* infidelity could be expected to sponsor. Less readily evident, however, is the essential novelty of that conception. It has recently been urged that "the feelings and conceptions of *amour courtois* are universally possible . . . in any time or place and on any level of society";[23] but the opinion commonly received among scholars runs to the contrary and it appears unshaken by such allegations, and rightly so. If properly perceived, with due attention paid to these precise distinguishing characteristics, courtly love emerges, historically speaking, as a very improbable possibility—indeed, as a distinct novelty. We have already seen that it had no place in the early medieval epic. To that it must now be added that it was a sentiment with only the most tenuous of roots in the classical past, when the consuming love of woman had generally been regarded either as a tragic insanity or an occasion for hilarity; and, with the exception of the medieval Arab world where some very striking parallels have been found, it was also a sentiment with no real counterpart in the non-Western cultures either. Never has the point at issue been more clearly formulated than it was by C. S. Lewis, and his appraisal can hardly be bettered. "If the thing at first escapes our notice," he said,

this is because we are so familiar with the erotic tradition of modern Europe that we mistake it for something natural and universal and therefore do not inquire into its origins. It seems to us natural that love should be the commonest theme of serious imaginative literature: but a glance at classical antiquity or at the Dark Ages at once shows us that what we took for "nature" is really a special state of affairs, which will probably have an end, and which certainly had a beginning in eleventh-century Provence. It seems—or it seemed to us till lately—a natural thing that love (under certain conditions) should be regarded as a noble and ennobling passion: it is only if we imagine ourselves trying to explain this doctrine to Aristotle, Virgil, St. Paul, or the author of *Beowulf*, that we become aware how far from natural it is. Even our code of etiquette, with its rule that women always have precedence, is a legacy from courtly love, and is felt to be far from natural in modern Japan or India. . . . French poets, in the eleventh century, discovered or invented, or were the first to express, that romantic species of passion which English poets were still writing about in the nineteenth. They effected a change which has left no corner of our ethics, our imagination, or our daily life untouched, and they erected impassable barriers between us and the classical past or the Oriental present.[24]

This being so, historians of literature have understandably struggled hard with the problem of origins. None of the numerous theories that have been advanced can be sustained by evidence of a conclusive sort, but the steady accretion of supportive material has at least conferred an increasingly higher degree of plausibility on the oldest theory of them all. As long ago as the sixteenth century it was claimed that the lyrics of the troubadours had been influenced by Arabic love poetry, and recent evidence has done much to bolster that claim.

It now seems clear, for example, that the structural forms and stylistic traits of the Provençal poetry owed something, perhaps a great deal, to Arab influence. Only a little less clear is the indebtedness of the troubadours to their Arab predecessors for some of the most striking aspects of their notion of love. Two works produced in the early eleventh century by Arab poets from Andalusia, *The Book of Flowers* by Ibn Dawoud and *The Dove's Neck-Ring* by Ibn Hazm, have frequently been canvassed as possible sources. The most complete and striking Arab parallels to the Provençal conception of courtly love, however, have been found in Arabic philosophy rather than in Arabic poetry, and Avicenna's *Treatise on Love*—a mystical work that treats of love, both human and divine—has been identified on quite compelling grounds as the single most likely source. There is no documentary evidence that the work was translated into Latin before 1130 and it has not proved possible to establish specific lines of influence. Nonetheless, the parallels in this case are especially striking and the general thesis of Arabic origins would appear to be a sound one. The points of contact between Muslim Spain and the Provençal-speaking regions of Spain and France were multiple. The travels of some of the most prominent troubadours in Muslim territory are well attested. We are told, indeed, that the troubadour Cercamon (c. 1100–1152) bore that name because "he visited the whole world [*E cerquet tot lo mon*] wherever he could get to." We are also told by another contemporary that translations of Arabic poetry and prose had become available via those Christian states in northern Spain that had mixed Muslim-Christian populations.[25] Moreover, the precise way in which a theoretical writer like Andreas Capellanus handled the blatant contradiction between the ideology of courtly love he expounded in his *De amore*, and the Christian sexual morality he professed as a priest is powerfully reminiscent of the way in which heretical Muslim philosophers like Avicenna and Averroës handled the parallel conflicts between the doctrines they taught as philosophic truth and the official Islamic teachings to which they were professedly committed as believers. Nor, interestingly enough, does that fact appear to have escaped the ecclesiastical authorities.

In an earlier chapter it was noted that the solution adopted by those Muslim philosophers to their faith-reason difficulties, as also that adopted later by the "Latin Averroists" of Paris, had been strictly to divorce philosophical teachings grounded in natural reason from religious teachings grounded in Koranic revelation. In his own work, Andreas proceeds in like fashion. In the first two books, which constitute the *De amore* proper, he expounds the ideology of courtly love, grounding his judgments (and the judgments he reports) in reason and nature. The last book, however, is a *De reprobatione amoris*; it concerns, that is, the rejection of love, and in it he repudiates the romantic ideology and the judgments of the first two books. Here he argues on the level of faith and supernatural grace, teaching "the avoidance of women as weak and vicious, [and] the cultivation of the love of God as the sole source of virtue and good." [26]

Some have seen in the contrast between the sentiments expressed by Chrétien de Troyes in *Lancelot* and in *Percival* and by Chaucer in the main body of *Troilus and Criseyde* and in the palinode appended to it, the choice of a similar tactic by men who had perceived the incompatibility of the fashionable romantic ideology they had written about as poets with the religious beliefs they had adhered to as Christians. If so, however, the tactic was not one that recommended itself to the guardians of orthodoxy. At the beginning of the condemnations of 1277, Bishop Tempier of Paris, in the context of condemning those "Latin Averroists" who were allegedly saying that some things were "true according to philosophy but not true according to the Catholic faith, as if there were two contrary truths," specifically singled out for censure Andreas's *De amore.*[27] A dramatic setback, it might seem, to the rise of the new romantic ideology; but insofar as it was effective at all, it may have done nothing more than close off a potential blind alley in the history of European sentiment.

On this matter, as on the problem of reason and revelation, the attitude that became dominant in Latin Christendom differed from that characteristic of the Islamic world. Again, as in that case, it was an attitude distinguished not by continued determination to segregate in separate compartments new ideas and traditional religious commitments, but by the willingness to permit encounter between them and to pursue a policy of mutual accommodation. Had that not been so, indeed, it is doubtful if the complex of emotions connected with the cult of courtly or romantic love could ever have spread so widely beyond the restricted aristocratic circles of court life or become so tightly woven into the very texture of European sentiment.

Of course, the process of accommodation was a laborious one, and one that remained incomplete until well into the modern period. The prevailing ecclesiastical views of woman and of human sexuality were too harshly negative, the institution of marriage too deeply entangled in the intricacies of property arrangements, the whole ideology of courtly love too bound up with an alien idealization of woman and an immoral glorification of adultery for things to have been otherwise. Nonetheless, accommodation began early and progressed steadily during the later medieval centuries. During those centuries the literature of romance began to reach a growing literate public beyond the ranks of the aristocracy and, by diffusing abroad a more elevated conception of feminine qualities, undoubtedly served to enhance the dignity of women, perhaps also to heighten their own self-esteem, and certainly to begin the transformation of marriage. The medieval period had seen the institution of the bartered bride hallowed by social custom and sanctioned by religious ceremony. It was now to see, if not the consummation, at least the initiation of the fateful union between Christian monogamy and romantic passion.

That Andreas Capellanus should have felt it necessary to refute, and at such length, the idea that true love could exist between marital partners would seem to indicate that by the end of the twelfth century there were already those who were willing to modify the new conception of love to such a degree as to render it compatible with marriage and to modify, it should be added, prevailing conceptions of the marital relationship to such a degree as to render them, in turn, compatible with courtly love. Among the writers of the great romances neither Chrétien de Troyes nor Wolfram von Eschenbach would appear to have been unsympathetic with that point of view, and there are enough instances in the later medieval literature of romantic love finding its ultimate fulfillment in marriage to suggest that the love match, though undoubtedly quite exceptional in practice, was now coming in theory to be regarded as the ideal. That ideal, destined ultimately to become a tired cliché of Western story, song, and film, found its noblest expression only after the close of the Middle Ages in the *Faerie Queene* of Edmund Spenser (1522–99), and perhaps also its warmest affirmation in his *Epithalamion*—written in celebration not of any unquenchable yearning for a "love from far away" but of his own wedding to a girl endowed at once with "celestial treasures," "unrevealed pleasures," and "lips lyke cherryes charming men to byte."

That Spenser himself "lived happily ever afterwards" should not blind us to the fact that the ideal he celebrated was predicated on a compromise between the courtly ideal of romantic love and the Christian ideal of lifelong monogamy, a compromise characteristically Western in its dynamics not simply because it involved an accommodation between Christian values and notions of alien provenance but also because of its inherent instability. The "proprietary" marriage of the standard medieval type had proved compatible enough with the church's sacramental approach, but the romantic view was destined to generate tensions of a novel kind. If falling in love, ideally speaking at least, was to be regarded as a prerequisite for marriage, then, presumably, falling out of love, ideally speaking again, could be taken to indicate that marriage was dead at least in spirit. If the open love that is crowned with wedded bliss has for the last three centuries been one of the dominant themes of Western literature, we should not forget that the subdominant has been what amounts almost to an obsession with the secret passion that finds its consummation in adultery.

Moreover, if the advent of the love match certainly worked to refine the marital relationship, suffusing it with a greater tenderness and mutual esteem, it did not necessarily eliminate "the coercion of marital bonds." Instead, the literature of contemporary feminism would suggest that it may in some ways have rendered those bonds more destructive by making them less visible, denying to woman, thereby, not merely her selfhood but even the sense that such is properly hers to claim. It was the startled perception of that denial (or something close to it) that led Ibsen's Nora to defy convention, to flee the doll's house that had permitted her no identity other than the one shaped for her by her husband's self-regarding fantasy. It is, again, the institutionalization of that perception that many a consciousness-raising group struggles today to promote.

Yet, the unenviable status of women even today, for example in modern India, and the nature of the marital relationship in that country (by modern Western standards, chillingly remote),[28] should serve to remind us how subtle, in particular, is this preoccupation with woman's identity, how extraordinary, in general, is modern feminism, and how special are the historical conditions that both presuppose. They should also serve to underline, should that indeed be necessary, how very great a significance attaches to the emergence of romantic love in twelfth-century Europe, its subsequent transformation of European attitudes toward women, and its insertion into the marital relationship of enhanced expectations and the seeds of a more divine despair. How difficult, after all, to imagine a Simone de Beauvoir without a Bernart de Ventadorn or without a Marcabru a Kate Millett!

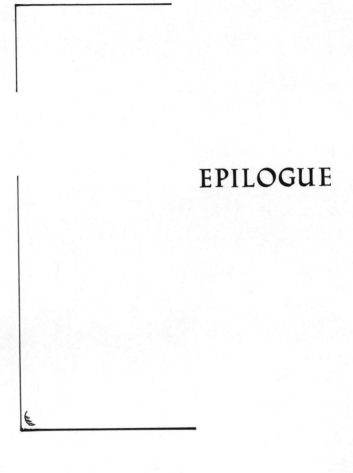

EPILOGUE

Of the Middle Ages medieval men and women knew nothing—least of all, it need hardly be insisted, that in their own era they were witnessing the beginnings of the laborious process by which the edifice of Western cultural singularity was to be erected. How could they, indeed? Only in the sixteenth and seventeenth centuries, during the upheavals spawned by the advent of the Reformation, did the individualism nurtured in the later Middle Ages begin to bear full fruit. Only in the first years of the eighteenth century, again, did it really become clear to contemporaries that a great breakthrough had occurred in the study of the natural world. Only in the latter half of that same century did England's prototypical industrial revolution get under way and the European constitutionalist tradition begin once more to put out new shoots. Only in the mid-nineteenth century did the sheer pressure of events finally bring home to Chinese, Indians, and Japanese alike that the Western challenge confronting them posed a threat of an order wholly different from anything with which their previous histories had acquainted them and one which their own ancient cultural traditions equipped them ill to meet. Only in the course of the twentieth century, finally, has it become clear to us in the West that the tide of history does not necessarily flow in our direction, that there was nothing inevitable about the process that led our civilization to dominate and reshape so much of modern world history, that it is not so much the differing destinies or apparent peculiarities of the non-Western cultures that cry out for historical explanation as the achievements of the West itself and the truly singular concatenation of factors—social, economic, political, religious, and intellectual—without which those achievements would have been inconceivable.

In the course of this book we have found that such explanations are by no means easy to come by. Even if we abandon the pursuit of sufficient explanations and content ourselves instead with the more modest attempt to isolate necessary conditions, that attempt has still to be made in the teeth of a stubborn complexity in the relevant factors themselves, in the intricacies and timing of their interaction with one another, in their vulnerability to the intrusion of chance events and their exposure to the contingencies of human decision. This complexity is such as to induce vertigo in those who attempt to surmount it, and our own explanations constitute little more than lifelines strung to encourage those bold enough to make that attempt. That fact should not be forgotten if the essential modesty of the claims made for those explanations is not to be missed. Nor should it be forgotten if the assertions we have frequently made about the importance of religious factors are properly to be understood; and, by way of conclusion, it is to this last issue that we must briefly address ourselves.

Even at their most limited those claims are fraught with burdensome difficulties. In the early eighteenth century, it is true, the great philosopher of history Giambattista Vico (1688–1744) argued that "among all peoples the civil world began with religion" and that "if religion is lost among the peoples, they have nothing left to enable them to live in society." [1] This is true enough, we may well be prepared to admit, of the other great civilizations of the world, which historians have certainly not hesitated to characterize in terms of their dominant religious traditions; but, Vico to the contrary, not so convincing with reference to our own, and understandably so, since one of the great distinguishing features of modern Western civilization has been its secularism, its conscious (and unconscious) relegation of the religious to an increasingly marginal position among the multiple components of its cultural tradition. Already in Vico's own lifetime during the Age of Enlightenment that process was far advanced—so far, indeed, that his own views on these things were scarcely typical of his age and certainly not honored by his contemporaries. Far more characteristic was Voltaire's representation of Christianity as a dead-weight of prejudice and corruption holding back man's gradual and beneficent ascent to a higher and more natural plane of existence. More characteristic, too, were his repeated condemnations of the Christian church as an "ancient palace of impostures" that a liberated reason must undermine at its very foundations, or as an "infamous thing" that had to be destroyed if progress were to continue. The ultimate optimism of such eighteenth-century views has a rather odd ring for us today. The history of our own century has not been such as to quicken the faith even of those most nostalgic for the unruffled certainties of the old belief in progress and in man's gradual ascent to a realm of purer light. Nonetheless, scratch a historian and one is less likely, I would predict, to find a firm sympathizer of Vico's than a chastened fellow traveler of Voltaire's. The faith of the Enlightenment, it sometimes seems, has proved less durable than its prejudices.

On this matter, however, if not necessarily on all, my own sympathies clearly lie rather with Vico than Voltaire. They do so, not least of all, because the findings of the anthropologists, the sociologists, the students of archaic and comparative religion would appear to converge on the paradoxical conclusion that the roots of modern Western secularism are themselves engaged in religious soil, that Christianity itself was one of the most powerful forces sponsoring the process of cultural differentiation whereby the realms of nature, of society, and of man were progressively desacralized and the dominion of religion pushed back to the uncolonized frontiers of the modern consciousness. Behind that process lay the remorseless working of the biblical conception of an omnipotent and transcendent God who created out of nothing the world and all that dwelt therein. That conception negated the widespread ancient belief that nature was a necessary emanation of the divine substance and man a fallen part of that substance. By so doing it established the fundamental philosophical precondition both for the emergence of a viable natural science and for a firm grasp on the idea of individual human personality. By so doing it also destroyed the ancient notion of a divine continuum linking man with nature and the "state" with the cosmos, undercutting, thereby, the very basis for the archaic pattern of divine kingship, for the notion of the "state" as the "embodiment of the cosmic totality," the focus of a lively religious sentiment.

This being so, the ultimate failure of the medieval church to establish in Europe a viable sacral civilization analogous to the great Oriental cultures was itself a necessary prerequisite for the emergence of that most singular feature of modern Western civilization: its secularism. To have established such a sacral civilization it would have had to blunt too drastically the fundamentally desacralizing thrust of its own biblical message by compromising too thoroughly with the pre-Christian order. Compromise, of course, it did, and on many fronts—with the nature worship of the pagan past, with the archaic pattern of sacral kingship, with the Roman ideal of imperial universalism, with the Greek philosophy of divine immanence, with the Provençal ideology of courtly love. But in terms of its fundamental Christian commitments, those compromises always stopped short of the wholly compromising; and, as I have more than once urged, it is in the new forms created by those compromises and in the instability characteristic of them that we must seek the roots of so much that is singular about our modern civilization—including, I cannot now refrain from adding, not only its markedly dynamic quality but also the precise tone of its secularism.

Failure, then, as well as success—the historical process is an irremediably ironic one. No less than other periods, the medieval bears witness to that truth. It was not of the Middle Ages alone, after all, that medieval men and women knew nothing.

212

NOTES

Introduction

1. Cotton Mather, *American Tears upon the Ruines of the Greek Churches* (Boston, 1701), pp. 42 ff.; quoted in Wallace K. Ferguson, *The Renaissance in Historical Thought: Five Centuries of Interpretation* (Cambridge, Mass., 1948), p. 55.

2. Also, addressing the German emperor-elect, Henry VII, then descending on Italy, as "by Divine Providence King of the Romans, and ever Augustus," he could urge "that the glorious dominion of the Romans is confined neither by the frontiers of Italy, nor by the coast-line of three-cornered Europe. For although it has been constrained by violence to narrow the bounds of its government, yet by indefeasible right it everywhere stretches as far as the waves of Amphitrite, and scarce deigns to be circumscribed by the ineffectual waters of Ocean." (Paget Toynbee, ed. and trans., *Dantis Alagherii Epistolae*, 2nd ed. [Oxford, 1966], ep. 7, pp. 100, 102).

3. Thomas Hobbes, *Leviathan*, ed. Michael Oakeshott (Oxford, 1946), pt. 4, chap. 47, p. 457.

4. *Russia i Evropa*, in *Zaria*, no. 2 (1869), pp. 81 ff.; quoted in Pitirim A. Sorokin, *Modern Historical and Social Philosophies* (New York, 1963), p. 55; Oswald Spengler, *The Decline of the West*, trans. Charles F. Atkinson, 2 vols. (New York, 1926), 1:18.

5. Max Weber, *The Protestant Ethic and the Spirit of Capitalism*, trans. Talcott Parsons (New York, 1930), p. 13.

i

1. *The Qur'ān*, 30:1–2; translation in 2 vols. by Richard Bell (Edinburgh, 1939), 2:393.

2. The Donation of Constantine was a document, drafted at the papal court in the mid-eighth century but attributed to Emperor Constantine, according to which Constantine had, among other things, conferred upon Pope Sylvester and his successors "both our palace . . . and likewise all provinces, palaces and districts of the city of Rome and Italy and of the regions of the West." See Henry Bettenson, ed., *Documents of the Christian Church* (Oxford, 1947), pp. 137–42. The provisions of this curious document were variously interpreted during the Middle Ages, but its authenticity was not successfully challenged until the fifteenth century.

3. Hugh Trevor-Roper, *The Rise of Christian Europe* (New York, 1965), p. 24.

ii

1. Ernst Troeltsch, *The Social Teaching of the Christian Churches*, 2 vols., trans. Olive Wyon (New York, 1960), 1:334, 340–41; 2:994.

2. Already in the third century, in search of a life of more rigorous moral commitment than that common to the mass of Christians, men had begun to withdraw to the desert, dedicating themselves to poverty and asceticism. In the fourth century, as their numbers increased, the first monastic communities made their appearance. It was St. Benedict (c. 480–543) who established at Monte Cassino the type of monastic life that was destined ultimately to become dominant in western Europe.

3. Luke 2:1 ff., 3:1 ff.; Acts 11:28, 18:2.

4. Eusebius, *Life of the Blessed Emperor Constantine*, bk. 1, chap. 44; English translation in Henry Ware and Philip Schaff, eds., *A Select Library of the Nicene and Post-Nicene Fathers of the Christian Church* (Oxford and New York, 1890), n.s. 1:494.

5. *Oration*, chap. 6; Ware and Schaff, *Nicene and Post-Nicene Fathers*, 1:591.

6. Bettenson, ed., *Documents of the Christian Church*, p. 87.

7. In this connection the instructions sent in 601 by Pope Gregory to the Benedictine missionaries in England are revealing:

"[W]hen by God's help you reach our most revered brother, Bishop Augustine, we wish you to inform him that we have been giving careful thought to the affairs of the English, and have come to the conclusion that the temples of the idols in that country should on no account be destroyed. He is to destroy the idols, but the temples themselves are to be aspersed with holy water, altars set up, and relics enclosed in them. For if these temples are well built, they are to be purified from devil-worship, and dedicated to the service of the true God. In this way, we hope that the people, seeing that its temples are not destroyed, may abandon idolatry and resort to these places as before, and may come to know and adore the true God. And since they have a custom of sacrificing many oxen to devils, let some other solemnity be substituted in its place, such as the day of Dedication or the Festivals of the holy martyrs whose relics are enshrined there. . . . For it is certainly impossible to eradicate all errors from obstinate minds at one stroke, and whoever wishes to climb to a mountain top climbs gradually step by step, and not in one leap. It was in this way that God revealed Himself to the Israelite people in Egypt, permitting the sacrifices formerly offered to the Devil to be offered thenceforward to Himself instead." (Bede, *A History of the English Church and People*, vol. 1, chap. 30; trans. Leo Shirley-Price [Baltimore, 1965], pp. 86–87).

8. *Confessions*, 6:2; trans. R. S. Pine-Coffin (Baltimore, 1964), pp. 112–13.

9. Otto Höfler, "Der Sakralcharakter des germanischen Königtums," in *Studies in the History of Religions: The Sacral Kingship* (Leiden, 1959), 4:681.

iii

1. William H. McNeill, *The Rise of the West* (Chicago, 1963), p. 732. He adds (p. 733): "The social, political, and cultural possibilities inherent in such a change in the elemental rhythm and routine of human life have not yet been more than partially and perhaps fumblingly explored."

2. David S. Landes, *The Unbound Prometheus: Technological Change and Industrial Development in Western Europe from 1750 to the Present* (Cambridge, 1969), pp. 1–2, 13–14.

3. While hazarding such judgments at this point and later on in the chapter, one should keep in mind the remark attributed to one economist to the effect that, in the absence of decent statistics, there can be no economic history for the centuries prior to the nineteenth—only economic prehistory. For the somewhat precarious estimates from which these comparisons are inferred see Phyllis Deane, *The First Industrial Revolution* (Cambridge, 1965), pp. 5–7, and Landes, *Unbound Prometheus*, pp. 13–14.

4. Tertullian, *Concerning the Soul*, chap. 30; cited in Solomon Katz, *The Decline of Rome and the Rise of Mediaeval Europe* (Ithaca, 1955), p. 7.

5. Edward Gibbon, *The History of the Decline and Fall of the Roman Empire*, 6 vols., ed. Dr. William Smith (New York, 1880), 1:286.

6. Robert S. Lopez, *The Commercial Revolution of the Middle Ages, 950–1350* (Englewood Cliffs, N.J., 1971), pp. 16–17.

7. W. W. Rostow, *The Stages of Economic Growth* (Cambridge, 1960), p. 8.

8. Lynn White, Jr., *Medieval Technology and Social Change* (Oxford, 1962), p. 76, comments: "It was not merely the new quantity of food produced by improved agricultural methods, but the new type of food supply which goes far towards explaining, for northern Europe, at least, the startling expansion of population, the growth and multiplication of cities, the rise in industrial production, the outreach of commerce, and the new exuberance of spirits which enlivened the age. In the full sense of the vernacular, the Middle Ages, from the tenth century onward, were full of beans."

9. The compelling history of harrow and flail may serve as a warning against the dangers of overfacile generalization about the dissemination of new agricultural implements during the Middle Ages. As late as the eighteenth century, it seems, the hinged flail had not yet been adopted in Norfolk, and only in the nineteenth century did the toothed harrow come into general use in the south of France. See Charles Parain, "The Evolution of Agricultural Technique," in M. M. Postan and H. J. Habakkuk, eds., *The Cambridge Economic History*, 6 vols. (Cambridge, 1941–67, 2nd ed., 1966), 1:92–179.

10. Deane, *The First Industrial Revolution*, p. 51. She continues: "By selling abroad goods which are in surplus at home in return for goods which are scarce at home, it is possible both to widen the range of goods and services coming on to the home-market and to increase the value of domestic output, and so to improve the national standard of living both qualitatively and quantitatively. In widening the potential market for domestic producers, foreign trade encourages them to specialize, to develop special skills and techniques of economic organization, and to reap the economies of large-scale production. This broadening of their economic horizons constitutes an incentive to greater productive activity and helps to break up the economic inertia which so often inhibits material progress."

11. Most prominent among these were the Florentine firms of Bardi and Peruzzi, both of which were dragged down to ruin when one of their most distinguished clients, King Edward III of England, repudiated his debts in 1343.

12. Harry A. Miskimin, *The Economy of Early Renaissance Europe* (Englewood Cliffs, N.J., 1969), p. 25.

13. Landes, *Unbound Prometheus*, p. 15.

14. In discussing this whole episode, J. J. L. Duyvendak, *China's Discovery of Africa* (London, 1949), stresses the distaste with which trade had always been viewed. Noting (p. 26) that the consumers of goods being imported "were the wealthy classes, first and foremost the Court and its harem ladies," he comments: "Ideologically, however, this state of affairs was never admitted: in the Confucian theory trade was regarded as something inferior, almost sordid, with which as such the Emperor could never have anything to do. Therefore the form in which relations with overseas nations are always represented is that of tribute-bearing. The barbarians came from afar, recognizing the overlordship of the Son of Heaven and bringing tribute, after which they were graciously allowed to trade."

15. Lynn White, Jr., "Technology and Invention in the Middle Ages," *Speculum* 15 (1940):141–59 at 156.

16. White, *Medieval Technology*, pp. 128–29.

17. Lynn White, Jr., "What Accelerated Technological Progress in the Western Middle Ages?" in A. C. Crombie, ed., *Scientific Change* (New York, 1963), pp. 272–91.

iv

1. Stephen Gardiner, *De vera obedientia,* translated into English, 3rd ed. (Rome, 1553), D III v; Charles H. McIlwain, ed., *The Political Works of James I* (Cambridge, Mass., 1918), p. 307; Jacques-Bénigne Bossuet, *Oeuvres Complètes,* ed. F. Lachat (Paris, 1862–66), 23:558 ff.; translation in James H. Robinson, *Readings in European History,* 2 vols. (Boston, 1906), 2:274, 276.

2. *Patriarcha,* vol. 1, ed. Peter Laslett, *Patriarcha and Other Political Works of Sir Robert Filmer* (Oxford, 1949), p. 53.

3. Citing Adlai Stevenson's observation that "the natural government of man is servitude. Tyranny is the normal pattern of human government," one scholar has recently argued that "the historian cannot fail to discern that the normal story of human government is indeed one of alternation between different forms of tyranny with occasional interludes of anarchy." (Brian Tierney, "Medieval Canon Law and Western Constitutionalism," *The Catholic Historical Review* 52, no. 1 [1966]:3).

4. H. and H. A. Frankfort, John A. Wilson, and Thorkild Jacobsen, *Before Philosophy: The Intellectual Adventure of Ancient Man* (Baltimore, 1964).

5. Henri Frankfort, *Kingship and the Gods: A Study of Ancient Near Eastern Religion as the Integration of Society and Nature* (Chicago, 1948), p. 3.

6. Christopher Dawson, *Religion and Culture* (New York, 1960), p. 116.

7. According to Edgar Snow's account of a conversation with Mao in *Life,* 20 April 1971.

8. T. M. Parker, *Christianity and the State in the Light of History* (London, 1955), p. 7.

9. Honorius Augustodunensis, *Summa Gloria de Apostolico et Augusto;* cited in R. W. Southern, *Western Society and the Church in the Middle Ages* (Baltimore, 1970), p. 37.

10. Tierney, "Medieval Canon Law and Western Constitutionalism," 7–8.

11. Joseph R. Strayer, *Feudalism* (Princeton, 1965), pp. 12–13.

12. John W. Hall, "Feudalism in Japan: A Reassessment," *Comparative Studies in Society and History* 5 (1963):33.

13. See Kan-ichi Asakawa, ed. and trans., *The Documents of Iriki*, 2nd ed. (Tokyo, 1955), doc. 155A, pp. 373–76, for a memorandum prepared by the *shogun's* court probably in 1867 and intended to acquaint the foreign diplomats who had been admitted into Japan with the nature of Japanese "feudal" government. Among other things it says: "The emperors have not concerned themselves in government already for more than six hundred and eighty years. However, as they have been, since the formation of the state, the supreme sovereigns following in a single line of divine succession and forever unalterable, and as they are revered by the nation as heavenly deities, likewise the successive *tai-kun* (shō-gun) on occasions lead *dai-myō* [barons] to pay them court. The emperor entrusts to the *tai-kun* all political powers, and awaits his decisions in silence; the *tai-kun*, holding all the political powers of the country, maintains the virtue of humility, and upholds the emperor with the utmost respect. This is the foundation of the profound peace of the country." It was also the foundation, it should be noted, that made possible a smooth transition in 1867 when the forces of the opposition ended the shogunate, representing the new imperial government (both to themselves and to others) as a "restoration" of the seventh-century imperial regime.

14. Manegold of Lautenbach, *Ad Geberhardum Liber,* translation in Ewart Lewis, *Medieval Political Ideas,* 2 vols. (London, 1954), 1:165.

15. Marc Bloch, *Feudal Society,* 2 vols., trans. L. A. Manyon (Chicago, 1964), 2:452.

16. "Princeps legibus solutus est," *Digest* 1:3, 31; "Quod principi placuit legis habet vigorem," *Digest* 1:4, 1; P. Krueger, Th. Mommsen, and R. Schoell, eds., *Corpus Juris Civilis,* 3 vols. (Berlin, 1899–1902), 1:6–7.

17. Charles H. McIlwain, *Constitutionalism: Ancient and Modern,* rev. ed. (Ithaca, 1958), p. 57.

18. Tierney, "Medieval Canon Law and Western Constitutionalism," 11.

19. J. N. Figgis, *Political Thought from Gerson to Grotius, 1414–1625: Seven Studies* (New York, 1960), p. 47.

20. *Vindiciae contra Tyrannos: A Defence of Liberty against Tyrants . . . being a Treatise written in Latin and French by Junius Brutus and Translated out of both into English* (London, 1689), p. 142.

21. Figgis, *Gerson to Grotius,* p. 41; H. J. Laski, "Political Theory in the Later Middle Ages," *The Cambridge Medieval History,* 8 vols. (Cambridge, 1911–36), 8:636, 638.

V

1. Herbert Butterfield, *The Origins of Modern Science, 1300–1800,* rev. ed. (New York, 1965), pp. 7–8.

2. Alfred North Whitehead, *Science and the Modern World* (New York, 1948), chap. 1; *Adventures of Ideas* (New York, 1955), p. 121.

3. *Institutiones divinarum . . . lectionum,* 30; J. P. Migne, ed., *Patrologiae Cursus*

Completus . . . series latina, 221 vols. (Paris, 1844 ff.), 70:1144D; cited in E. K. Rand, *Founders of the Middle Ages* (New York, 1957), p. 243.

4. R. W. Southern, *The Making of the Middle Ages* (New Haven, 1961), p. 191.

5. Charles H. Haskins, *The Renaissance of the Twelfth Century* (New York, 1957), pp. 370–71.

6. Tertullian, *On Prescription against Heretics,* chap. 7; cited in Etienne Gilson, *Reason and Revelation in the Middle Ages* (New York, 1938), pp. 9–10.

7. Pascal, *Pensées* (Paris, 1961), no. 29, p. 94.

8. H. A. R. Gibb, *Mohammedanism* (New York, 1962), p. 116.

9. Wilfred Cantwell Smith, *Islam in Modern History* (Princeton, 1957), p. 18, n. 13, suggests that the Muslim counterpart to biblical criticism is modern *Hadīth* criticism and adds, "To look for historical criticism of the Qur'ān is rather like looking for a psychoanalysis of Jesus."

10. *Confessions,* 7:18–21; trans. R. S. Pine-Coffin (Baltimore, 1965), pp. 152–55.

11. *Timaeus* § 34B; translated in F. M. Cornford, *Plato's Cosmology: The Timaeus of Plato* (New York, n.d.), p. 58; Aristotle, *Metaphysics* 12:10; ed. and trans. W. D. Ross, *The Works of Aristotle Translated into English,* 12 vols. (Oxford, 1930–52), 12:1074 b, 1–15.

12. F. C. Copleston, *Aquinas* (Harmondsworth, 1955), p. 138.

13. *Summa Theologica,* 1a 2ae, qu. 91, art. 1 and 2; qu. 93, art. 1.

14. Etienne Gilson, *History of Christian Philosophy in the Middle Ages* (New York, 1955), p. 498.

15. It is worthy of note that the habit of likening the universe to a great clock—a cliché of popular scientific discourse in the seventeenth century—already makes its appearance in the writings of some of the nominalist philosophers toward the end of the fourteenth century.

16. Whitehead, *Science in the Modern World,* pp. 13–14. In light of the argument elaborated in the preceding pages, it should be noted, however, that Whitehead's stress is placed far too one-sidedly on the rationality of God. Thus, though he acknowledges the importance of the fact that the medievals "conceived of God as with the personal energy of Jehovah," his principal concern is with the fact that they also conceived of him as possessing "the rationality of a Greek philosopher."

17. Joseph Needham and Wang Ling, *Science and Civilization in China,* 4 vols. (Cambridge, 1954–71), 2:543, 578–83.

vi

1. Henrik Ibsen, *A Doll's House,* Act III; in William Archer, ed., *The Works of Henrik Ibsen,* 6 vols. (New York, 1911), 4:181–82.

2. *Hegel's Philosophy of Right,* trans. T. M. Knox (New York, 1967), pp. 84 § 124, 124 § 185. For subsequent citations see, in addition, Preface, p. 10, p. 133 § 206, p. 195 § 299; cf. pp. 267–68, *Add.* 118: "It was in the Christian religion in the first place that the right of subjectivity arose, together with the infinity of self-awareness."

3. On this matter, see above, chap. 4, pp. 111 ff.

4. Cf. Daniel O'Connor, "The Human and the Divine," in Daniel O'Connor and

Francis Oakley, eds., *Creation: The Impact of an Idea* (New York, 1969), p. 107: "The most fundamental impact of the idea of creation on the theory of man can be very simply formulated: man is not divine nor part of the divine. It is the unanimous verdict of the religious philosophers of the ancient world that man or at least a part of man shares essentially in the divine nature. But this claim is radically negated by the doctrine of creation. . . . [M]an is not a part of the divine substance which has fallen into the dark prison of matter, and not the divine spirit as it becomes self-conscious, but a created and incarnate spirit, conscious and free, made 'in the image and likeness of God.' "

5. William A. Chaney, *The Cult of Kingship in Anglo-Saxon England* (Berkeley and Los Angeles, 1970), p. 65.

6. The foundation charter is printed in *Liber Vitae*, ed. W. de Gray Birch (Winchester [?], 1892), pp. 232–46. I cite this passage from Southern, *Western Society and the Church in the Middle Ages*, pp. 224–25.

7. Sermon 5: "The love of God"; in Raymond B. Blakney, ed. and trans., *Meister Eckhart* (New York, 1941), p. 127.

8. *Libellus alter de consecratione ecclesiae Sancti Dionysii*, ed. and trans. Erwin Panofsky, *Abbot Suger on the Abbey Church of St. Denis* (Princeton, 1946), pp. 119–21.

9. *Sermo XX in Cantica*; cited in H. O. Taylor, *The Mediaeval Mind*, 4th ed., 2 vols. (Cambridge, Mass., 1951), 1:426–27.

10. *Of the Imitation of Christ by Thomas a Kempis as Translated out of Latin by Richard Whytford Anno 1556*, ed. Wilfrid Raynal, O.S.B. (London, 1908), p. 59.

11. Southern, *The Making of the Middle Ages*, p. 219.

12. See especially Bruno Snell, *The Discovery of Mind*, trans. T. G. Rosenmeyer (Cambridge, Mass., 1953), chap. 1, "Homer's View of Man."

13. C. S. Lewis, *The Allegory of Love* (London, 1938), pp. 30, 116, 135. He points out, for example (p. 30), that when in the Lancelot story (*Le Chevalier de la Charrette*) "Lancelot hesitates before mounting the cart, Chrétien represents his indecision as a debate between *Reason* which forbids, and *Love* which urges him on." Pointing out that Chrétien de Troyes tends to become allegorical precisely when he is turning from storytelling to psychological analysis, Lewis notes that "[i]t is as if the insensible world could not yet knock at the doors of the poetic consciousness without transforming itself into the likeness of the sensible: as if men could not easily grasp the reality of moods and emotions without turning them into shadowy *persons*."

14. Ibid., p. 9.

15. Margaret Fuller, *Woman in the Nineteenth Century*; excerpt reprinted in Miriam Schneir, ed., *Feminism: The Essential Historical Writings* (New York, 1972), p. 68.

16. David Herlihy, *Women in Medieval Society* (Houston, 1971), pp. 9–10. He adds that "this particular tradition has been slow in dying."

17. James Gairdner, ed., *The Paston Letters*, 6 vols. (London, 1904), vol. 2, no. 71. For Scrope's remarks, see G. P. Scrope, *History of Castlecombe* (London, 1852), pp. 264–83; cited in H. S. Bennett, *The Pastons and Their England* (Cambridge, 1922), p. 29.

18. Southern, *Western Society and the Church in the Middle Ages*, p. 311.

19. Ibid., p. 329.

20. Lewis, *Allegory of Love*, p. 13.

21. Andreas Capellanus, *The Art of Courtly Love*, trans. John Jay Parry (New York, 1941), pp. 100–107.

22. For William IX's poem "Ab la dolchor del temps novel," see the translation in Angel Flores, ed., *An Anthology of Medieval Lyrics* (New York, 1962), p. 11. Bernart de Ventadorn's poem is cited and translated in Alexander J. Denomy, *The Heresy of Courtly Love* (Gloucester, Mass., 1965), pp. 22, 59.

23. Peter Dronke, *Medieval Latin and the Rise of European Love-Lyric*, 2 vols. (Oxford, 1965–66), 1:2.

24. Lewis, *Allegory of Love*, pp. 3–4.

25. For Cercamon see Jean Boutière and A. H. Schutz, *Biographies des Troubadours* (Paris, 1964), p. 9; A. R. Nykl, *A Book Containing the Risāla Known as 'The Dove's Neck-Ring'* (Paris, 1931), p. lxxviii.

26. Denomy, *Heresy of Courtly Love*, p. 34.

27. There is a translation of all 219 of the condemned propositions in Ralph Lerner and Muhsin Mahdi, eds., *Medieval Political Philosophy: A Sourcebook* (New York, 1963), pp. 335–54; for the words cited see pp. 337–38.

28. Richard Lannoy, *The Speaking Tree: A Study of Indian Culture and Society* (New York, 1971), p. 102, cites a recent study of comparatively Westernized, urban, middle-class Indians in Bangalore which attempted to tabulate the degrees with which affective intensity is felt in familial relationships. In a mixed sample of 157, "emotional attitudes of family members towards each other were rated as follows: mother-son 115, brother-sister 90, brother-brother 75, father-son 74, father-children 24, husband-wife 16, sister-sister 5."

Epilogue

1. *The New Science of Giambattista Vico,* translated from the third edition (1744) by T. G. Bergin and M. H. Fisch (Ithaca, 1948), § 8, p. 7, and § 1109, p. 383.

Map Credits

pp. 13, 16, 19, from C. Harold King, Arthur J. May, and Arnold Fletcher, *A History of Civilization* (New York: Scribners, 1969).

p. 26, from Ernest John Knapton, *France: An Interpretive History* (New York: Scribners, 1971).

SUGGESTIONS FOR FURTHER READING

Readers interested in pursuing a more complete account of the general course of medieval history are advised to consult such tried and trusted textbooks as Joseph R. Strayer and Dana C. Munro, *The Middle Ages, 395–1500*, 5th ed., New York: Appleton, 1970; Carl Stephenson and Bryce Lyon, *Mediaeval History: Europe from the Second to the Sixteenth Century*, 4th ed., New York: Harper & Row, 1962; or Brian Tierney and Sidney Painter, *Western Europe: The Middle Ages, 300–1475*, rev. ed., New York: Knopf, 1970. More specialized treatments of specific regions, periods, or topics may be found in the multiple articles of the *Cambridge Medieval History*, 8 vols., Cambridge: The University Press, 1921–36. All of these works contain extensive bibliographical data and the books listed below represent merely a brief selection of works available in English and in paperback editions.

A. *Works of an introductory nature written in a straightforward fashion and readily accessible to the layman.*

Baldwin, John W. *The Scholastic Culture of the Middle Ages: 1000–1300*. Lexington, Mass.: Heath, 1971.

Barraclough, Geoffrey. *The Medieval Papacy*. New York: Harcourt Brace Jovanovich, 1968.

Dawson, Christopher. *The Making of Europe*. New York: World, Meridian Books, 1956.

Gilson, Etienne. *Reason and Revelation in the Middle Ages*. New York: Scribners, 1938.

Haskins, Charles Homer. *The Renaissance of the Twelfth Century*. New York: World, Meridian Books, 1957.

Hussey, J. M. *The Byzantine World*. New York: Harper & Row, Torchbooks, 1961.

Knowles, David. *Evolution of Medieval Thought*. New York: Random House, Vintage Books, 1962.

Lewis, Bernard. *The Arabs in History*. New York: Harper & Row, Torchbooks, 1960.

Lopez, Robert S. *The Commercial Revolution of the Middle Ages, 950–1350*. Englewood Cliffs, N.J.: Prentice-Hall, Spectrum Books, 1971.

Miskimin, Harry A. *The Economy of Early Renaissance Europe, 1300–1460*. Englewood Cliffs, N.J.: Prentice-Hall, Spectrum Books, 1969.

Morrall, John B. *Political Thought in Medieval Times*. New York: Harper & Row, Torchbooks, 1962.

Painter, Sidney. *French Chivalry: Chivalric Ideas and Practices in Medieval France*. Ithaca: Cornell University Press, 1957.

Russell, Jeffrey B. *A History of Medieval Christianity: Prophecy and Order.* New York: Thomas Y. Crowell, 1968.

Tierney, Brian. *The Crisis of Church and State: 1050–1300.* Englewood Cliffs, N.J.: Prentice-Hall, Spectrum Books, 1966.

Wallace-Hadrill, J. M. *The Barbarian West: The Early Middle Ages, A.D. 400–1000.* New York: Harper & Row, Torchbooks, 1962.

B. *Works of a more advanced nature read most profitably by those already acquainted with the history of the period. All of them are works of generally acknowledged distinction.*

Bloch, Marc. *Feudal Society.* 2 vols. Translated by L. A. Manyon. Chicago: University of Chicago Press, Phoenix Books, 1964. A work of great range that makes a sophisticated use of the comparative method and has been described as "the standard international treatise on feudalism."

Cochrane, Charles N. *Christianity and Classical Culture: A Study of Thought and Action from Augustus to Augustine.* Oxford: The University Press, Galaxy Books, 1957. A penetrating and very learned analysis of "the revolution in thought and action" engineered by "the impact of Christianity upon the Graeco-Roman world."

Huizinga, J. *The Waning of the Middle Ages.* New York: Doubleday, Anchor Press, 1954. A classic evocation of the forms of life, thought, and art in northwestern Europe during the fourteenth and fifteenth centuries. Provocative and illuminating.

Lewis, C. S. *The Allegory of Love: A Study of Medieval Tradition.* Oxford: The University Press, 1936. A brilliant interpretation of the twin themes of romantic love and the allegorical form ranging across the centuries from the eleventh to the sixteenth.

Southern, R. W. *The Making of the Middle Ages.* New Haven: Yale University Press, 1961. A deeply reflective account of the main forms of social and political organization during the eleventh and twelfth centuries along with a sympathetic evocation of the religious and intellectual sensibilities of that era.

White, Lynn, Jr. *Medieval Technology and Social Change.* Oxford: The University Press, Galaxy Books, 1966. A lively, provocative, and original work which is also the best general introduction to its subject.

INDEX

Abelard, Peter, 147
Aelfflaed, 194
Africa, 15, 18, 62, 63, 89, 90, 98, 109, 152
Agriculture, 75, 78–87, 215 n; neolithic, 75; late antique, 78–82; medieval, 83–87
Alexander the Great, 109
Alexandrian theology, 160
Allegory, 187
Amalfi, 90
Amars, 199
Ambrose, Bishop of Milan, 67, 68
America: North, 29, 76, 174; Central and South, 77, 109
Amour courtois. See Courtly love
Anagni, outrage of, 38
Ancien régime, 106–7
Andalusians, 200–201
Anglo-Irish, culture and missions, 25
Anglo-Norman state, 37
Anglo-Saxons, 13, 22, 25, 32, 79
Antichrist, 3, 70
Antwerp, 90
Aquinas, Thomas, Saint, 151, 161–64, 167, 168; on Platonic Ideas, 163; on reason and will, 163–64; on eternal and natural law, 164. *See also Summa theologica*
Aquitaine, 23
Arabia, Arabs, 17, 18, 148, 200–201
Aragon, 38
Arianism, 22, 23
Aristotle, 110, 140, 145, 146, 149, 151, 152, 155, 157–59, 161, 163, 167–68, 200; recovery of, in Middle Ages, 145–46, 160–61; condemnations of, 149. *See also Metaphysics*
Arthur, King of Britain, 186
Ash'arī, al-, 152–53, 166, 168; theology of, 153, 166
Asia, 18, 29, 109, 169
Augustine, Saint, 59, 61–65, 143, 145, 155, 160–61, 163, 168, 175–76; as architect of Western theology, 59–60; Neoplatonism of, 60; on the church, 62–

64; on free will, grace, and Original Sin, 60–61; on predestination, 61, 64; against the Pelagians, 60–62; against the Donatists, 62–65. *See also Confessions; On Christian Doctrine*
Augustinian Eremites, 67
Augustinianism, 65
Austria, 22, 23
Avars, 17, 23
Averroës (Ibn Rushd), 146, 152, 153, 161, 162, 201
Averroists, 29; "double-truth" doctrine of, 162, 201–2
Avicenna (Ibn Sina), 152, 153, 161, 201. *See also Treatise on Love*
Avignonese papacy, 39–40

Baal, cult of, 111
Babylon, religion of, 111–12
"Babylonian captivity." *See* Avignonese papacy
Balkans, 17, 23
Banking, new techniques in, 92–94
Barbarian invasions, 21–23, 29–30, 57, 115
Beauvoir, Simone de, 189, 205
Benedict, Saint, 143, 150. *See also Rule*
Beowulf, 184, 186, 188, 200
Berbers, 152
Bernard of Clairvaux, Saint, 67, 180
Bernart de Ventadorn, 197, 199, 205
Bible, 143; monotheism in, 12–14, 57–58; notion of Creation in, 57–58, 101, 167–68, 219 n; notion of office in, 52; and criticism, 167–68
Black Death, 41–42, 95
Bloch, Marc, 90
B'ois, 90
Boethius, 145
Bologna, 129; University of, 147
Boniface, Saint, 24
Boniface II, Pope, 64
Boniface VIII, Pope, 38, 41
Book of Flowers, The (Ibn Dawoud), 200–201
Bookkeeping, 93–94

223

Index

Index